AF411077

THEORY OF PSYCHOLOGY: COROLLARIES

EMILIO RIBES IÑESTA

THEORY OF PSCHOLOGY: COROLLARIES

Translated by José G. Ardila Sánchez

Co-presencias Editorial

COLLECTION: "ACADEMIC PSYCHOLOGY"
Section: Theory of Psychology
Editor:
Manuel Porcel Medina
Editorial Co-presencias

Co-presencias aims to be a critical publisher of Psychology and Philosophy of Psychology, with the commitment to build approaches to these areas with nuances of honesty and truth.

Legal Deposit: SA-664-2023
ISBN: 978-84-09-55697-7

Índice de contenido

A la memòria del meu pare i la meva mare i dels meus avis i àvies,
gràcies a ells soc el que soc.

« [...] one also forgets that developing a good theory is a complex process
that has to start modestly and that takes time.»
P. K Feyerabend, (1970, p. 68)

AUTHOR'S PREFACE

This volume is a direct consequence of the publication of *The scientific study of individual behavior: An introduction to the theory of psychology* in 2018. Much remained to be clarified, as with the result of any theoretical process, at the conclusion of that work. Many issues and topics were narrowly discussed, and others barely suggested. Hence the title of the present volume, which consists of a collection of essays that are not only a logical but also a practical corollary of the theoretical formulation. Some of these essays were published, in a span of a year and a half, as they were being written (the first five) and others (the last four) are unpublished and were written in a different order from the one presented in this volume. Each essay addresses a specific theme, which is implicit or explicit in the 2018 work. The published essays have been revised, undergoing some additions or clarifications. The first essay examines the reasons for the transition from a field theory of behavior to a field theory of psychology. The second essay discusses the concept of explanation and attempts to demonstrate that to explain, in all modes of knowledge, is to circumstantiate a relation between facts or events. The third essay analyzes the process of functional detachment from the perspective of the contacts made possible by biological and conventional reactive systems. The fourth essay grounds dispositional functions in the correspondence between nonspecific and specific activation of reactive systems and the properties of stimulus objects and events. The sixth essay explores and proposes different ways of methodologically addressing the issues raised by a field model for psychological behavior. The seventh essay makes explicit the referential nature of all human behavior and its relation to the functions of language and different modes of knowledge. The eight essay critically examines the Darwinian and neo-Darwinian evolutionary positions and their claims about psychological behavior in relation to the origin of language and social formations. The ninth and last essay posits the political nature of all interindividual behavior and its implications for psychological behavior as an ideological practice. The set of essays is not only of interest to psychologists. They may also be of interest to those engaged in the study of epistemology and philosophy of science, behavioral biology, social and economic anthropology, political theory, and the study of language.

This work is a paradoxical case for those who are fond of applying a universal psychological hermeneutic to understand people's motives. The essays contained herein are the result of a life process linked to the possibility of a science of psychology. They are presented here, despite the disappointing nature of prevailing academic life, dominated by personal vanities and meritocratic pursuits. Thus, and congruently, I can only be skeptical as to the effect these writings may have, but it should never be ruled out that they may be of interest to some pilgrim who travels the same road I have traveled.

Emilio Ribes Iñesta Xalapa, Veracruz, October 2020

AUTHOR'S PREFACE TO THE ENGLISH EDITION

The English edition of this book does not include a first essay entitled *A Theory of Behavior or a Theory of Psychology?* The rest of the book is the same that the Spanish edition, published in 2021 (*Teoría de la psicología: corolarios*). The essay not included is already published in English, in a volume edited by Diego Zilio and Kesler Carrara: *Contemporary Behaviorisms in Debate*, jointly published By Springer Nature and Paradigm also in 2021. This last volume includes also a commentary by Neves Filho and Magalhaes and a reply to them by this author. Those interested in the field formulation advanced in this volume and in a previous one in Spanish also (El estudio científico de la conducta individual: introducción a la teoría de la psicología, 2018) are encouraged to read this "missing" essay. This essay provides a general overview about the evolution of the field formulation of psychological behavior following J.R. Kantor interbehavioral proposal, espousing the fundamental categories involved in the analysis of a psychological field, the various types of functional contacts, the extension of the formulation to the study of becoming and psychological individuation, the multidisciplinary relations of psychology with ecobiological and socio-historical sciences, as well with interdisciplinary applications to education, health, housing and other relevant social areas. I hope that this volume stimulates the interest of behaviorally oriented psychologists in a field approach to psychological explanation and research.

Emilio Ribes-Iñesta

TRANSLATOR'S PREFACE

There are many reasons that *Theory of Psychology: Corollaries* poses special problems for its translator and for English language readers. Two aspects of the text are especially noteworthy and need to be commented upon here. First, one needs to be aware that, in *Theory of Psychology: Corollaries,* Ribes Iñesta frequently employs ordinary language words in uncommon ways. Words, such as *circunstancia,* which would be readily intelligible to a Spanish reader since it has a clear relation to everyday life (*no pude llegar a tiempo por distintas circunstancias* – "I couldn't arrive on time due to different circumstances"), appear here as verbs (*circunstanciar* – "circumstantiate") and as nouns (*circunstancialidad* – "circumstantiality"), thus posing a challenge even for a Spanish reader. The most visible examples are his definition of knowledge as 'to circumstantiate a relation between facts or events', and his characterization of psychological contacts in terms of their 'functional circumstantiality'. One of Ribes Iñesta's aims in *Theory of Psychology: Corollaries* is to locate psychological phenomenology in and as part of ordinary language practices, re-examining psychological words and expressions without technical jargon. This is one of the problems one encounters in translating Ribes Iñesta: there is no direct translation of ordinary language and technical scientific terms.

Second, one finds Ribes Iñesta using quite unique Spanish words that do not have direct equivalents in English. Words such as *convivencia* and *coacción* are some examples of the difficulty in finding words with similar meanings in English. As Spanish is an entirely Latin language, the sense of informality in some Latin words is lost in English, which tends to be more formal. English speakers commonly prefer Germanic words over Latinate ones (it is, for example, the difference between *coacción* and coercion). Such are some of the sort of translation problems found in this text.

Of course, there are also the usual problems that come with the project of translating Spanish to English. These problems demand special attention from the translator because there is no established way to discuss Ribes-Iñesta's work in English. Some of these decisions are made here, but they may need to be reconsidered in the future.

The present translation attempts to take into account the scholarship of Ribes Iñesta in explaining his own work in English. This translation was initiated some time ago and has undergone changes over the years as Ribes Iñesta has provided important suggestions and clarifications. It is hoped that this translation will open a productive debate about the relevance of Ribes Iñesta's work for scientific thinking writ large.

One final word, expressing my position on the translator's task. In a way, translation is the most critical form of reading of a text. The translator's task does not involve merely conveying what the original author said, partly due to the impossibility of achieving an identical application of one form of writing to another in the same circumstances. As Walter Benjamin put it, "…translation must in large measure turn its attention away from trying to communicate something, away from meaning; the original is essential to translation only insofar as it has already relieved the translator and his work of the burden and organization of what is communicated" (Benjamin, 1923/1997, p. 161).

Although the translator's task involves replacing morphologically different linguistic patterns, the translated text is far from being a faithful replica of the original. It is the result of a process of reconstruction rather than the discovery of an ideal or correct order corresponding exactly to the original text. This means the translator's task is not to establish a direct correspondence between 'original meaning' and 'translated meaning'. Therefore, the translated and original works must be articulated as different 'language games' (Wittgenstein, 1953), that is, as different cultural practices within their respective social circumstances.

José Guillermo Ardila Sánchez
Bogotá, Colombia

References

Wittgenstein, L. (1953). Philosophical investigations. Oxford: Basil Blackwell.

Benjamin, W. (1997) The Translator's Task (S. Rendall, Trans.) Traduction, Terminologie, Rédaction, 10(2), 151–165. (Original work published 1923)

ESSAY ONE: THE SUBJECT OF PSYCHOLOGICAL SCIENCE: A RELATION WITHOUT «BODY-SUBSTANCE»

Two previous writings (Ribes, 2000, 2013) have addressed the problem of the object of knowledge of psychology as a science. Two issues were emphasized in these writings. On one hand, the existence of various psychologies in terms of what they study. On the other hand, the difficulty of placing psychology in the abstracted knowledge continuum represented by the identifiable empirical sciences. Psychology is the only scientific discipline, or a proposal for a discipline, lacking consensus as to its object of knowledge. Simultaneously this has resulted in a confusing (but not blurred) delimitation with respect to its adjacent scientific disciplines.

I will re-examine this problem in three ways: first, the possibility of characterizing the 'psychological' as an object of scientific knowledge; second, the historical trajectory of the notion of the 'psychological' and its link to notions and concepts of other non-scientific modes of knowledge; third, the analysis of two complementary solutions to the problem, both questioning the 'psychological' as an object of knowledge empirically comparable to that of the other established sciences. In the latter section, we will focus on a previous formulation (Ribes, 2018), namely that the psychological constitutes only a fraction of the episodes comprised in ordinary language practices, and, in the case of the animal phylum, a fraction of the activities framed by the ecological niche.

The psychological in the world of everyday reality

The everyday reality of persons corresponds to the experiences and activities that continuously and permanently occur as a result of and in the sphere of interpersonal relations, objects, events, and the constitutive practices of social life. These practices always take place in language, which constitutes the medium enabling any social formation as a collective organization, characterized by the social and specialized division of labor and the deferred appropriation of the products of labor. Although language is commonly identified with speaking, gesturing, writing, and reading, among other occurrence modes, it constitutes something more than these conventional activities. One speaks, gestures, writes or reads, always as an indissoluble part of a social practice, even when some of these practices are apparently performed in "isolation". Gestures, verbalizations, and texts, when written or read, always occur in a proximal or distant practice between persons, where each refers something to the other, in relation to their own acts, or in relation to the circumstances, objects, persons, and events with which they have direct or indirect contact. When one speaks (gestures writes, or reads) it is always relative to something and with someone. Language does not occur in a vacuum, not even in soliloquy. Language is a collective practice preceding and sustaining all relations between people and, to that extent, it is constitutive of the various episodic forms of such practical relations.

Speaking is the most frequent form of language in social practice and together with gesturing, can be probably considered the primordial ways in which it emerged as a characteristic practice of the species, and which also appears during the socialization of human individuals in ontogeny. Ordinary language, as an everyday social practice, encompasses all the spheres in which relations between individuals occur and, to that extent, can be analyzed or segmented into different types of functional episodes, regardless of the "grammatical" forms in which the isolated expressions of its practical occurrence are classified. One segment of ordinary language practices has to do with what have been identified as 'psychological expressions' or 'mental' terms. These expressions and terms include first-person expressions, such as "I imagine that…", "I feel sad", "I think that…", "I was very excited to see you", "I haven't decided what to do yet", and the like. These types of expressions can also occur in the third person (e.g., "You look low in spirits"). Both types of expressions, those in the first and third person, are asymmetrical in origin and functionality, and their discussion is relevant to what has been called in recent times "theory of mind" (Ribes, 2004). Mental expressions and terms always occur in circumstances in which the speaker or writer is addressing another person, whether indirectly or directly. This is the meaning of referential language. Reference is not describing or denoting an object, much less a private, hidden experience. It is a relation between persons with respect to something, but said relation does not consist in describing that 'something', but in interacting with respect to it. In the case of psychological episodes, these are expressions that include terms such as 'remember', 'forget', 'reflect', 'feel', 'see', 'like', 'enjoy', 'reason', 'fear', 'hesitate', 'risk', and many others. In every psychological episode, the person constitutes and conforms to the circumstances of her relation with others expressing herself, and the expression (whether or not it is considered psychological) always takes place by combining words, gestures, and performances. Psychological episodes in ordinary language practices always constitute relevant expressive episodes, that is, something is said or shown through an expression that includes phrases, gestures, and different movements directed at others, and this expression is the nucleus of all referential practice. There is no neutral language constituted only of phonations or sequences of "aseptic" words. Words lack univocal meaning in ordinary language. Words are multivocal insofar as their sense or meaning depends on the expression of which they are part, as well as on the situation in which their practice use occurs. The meaning of any word consists in the "use" that is made of and with it, that is, in the practice in which it is employed, of the activities that are part of that practice, in relation to what and to whom it is expressed, as well as the situation and the circumstances in which it occurs. Wittgenstein (1953) stressed that the meaning of a word is always its context of 'use', and the so-called 'mental' terms are no exception. They all have different uses in ordinary language, and none of them has a univocal sense or meaning. In fact, it is nonsense to even attempt a definition of each of them separately, as the various philosophies and psychologies have done.

The expressive and communicative nature of language as a practice contrasts with the traditional Augustinian and rationalist conception of language as a system of signs that denote objects and events. In the Augustinian conception, words are signs representing objects as ideas. This representational function occurs through naming, identifying, or describing. Denoting implies that words correspond to objects and their properties and that, to that extent, language has a purely denotative or descriptive function of reality. Leaving aside the problem posed by the impossibility of an ideal language, where each word corresponds to a specific object or property, the fact that a denotative language would be redundant for others stands out. It would be a language in which one would speak of the present to others, duplicating one's own senses of sight and others. It would be a language of names and descriptions of what is present to the senses, a caricature of language since it would lack a communicative and expressive dimension. Nor do words substitute for objects and their properties in the strict sense. No one eats the word 'apple' or is transported by the word 'automobile'. The denotative conception of language assumes that spoken words are signs of things and represents them, but this is a big mistake. As words never occur in a vacuum, but in expressions, they always constitute parts of social practices between individuals. They are part of performances. Only when writing appeared did words appear as signs, but as signs corresponding to locutions, that is, as graphic transcriptions of speech, of its sounds. Words constitute signs in written language, but they are signs that correspond to spoken language and not signs that represent objects.

According to the denotative view of language, ordinary "psychological" expressions are interpreted as reports of events or entities occurring "inside" the individual, symmetrically to when one speaks about objects and events of the world, as reports of what occurs "outside" the individual. The individual is supposed to report on her conscious experiences, of which she is the only possible observer. Thus, language is posited as a simple "information" vessel to others of what is going on in a supposed "inner" world. This world does not refer only to the phenomena, activities, and events that might originate in the body itself, in the style of the Cartesian passions, but also has to do with the consciousness of the external world, which is thus reduced to a phenomenal representation in the individual's mind, in the form of sensations, impressions, percepts, or various images (the 'qualia'). In accord with this view, the individual only knows the external world through her inner world, as impressions or ideas, and passions or affections. The function of ordinary language is reduced to an information vessel between individual minds, and not as effective communication between individuals who share such language as a substantive part of their practice and social life. Therefore, for the denotative view of language, knowledge (and the constituting practices) is regulated and maintained in the "mental life" of individuals.

However, a careful examination of the occurrence of psychological expressions, and the nature of ordinary language practices allows to show how reducing the psychological to the conscious experience as mental life in an interior world is consequence of an incorrect and absurd logic. As it has been initially argued, language is consubstantial to social life as a practice between individuals and their environment (Wittgenstein, 1953). Individuality necessarily emerges from the collective. Individuals do not exist except as differentiation within a collective. Therefore, individuality can only be recognized as differentiation within the practice in a given social formation. Similarly, it is differentiation within the patterns of a species in a habitat. Individuality always constitutes a differentiation within the collective and not of its origin. Animal individuation occurs as speciation, while human individuation occurs as socialization, both individuations as patterns shared with kin. Human individuation is the result of a social process not only through language, but in language. Thus, the criteria, characteristics and identity of individuals are constituted in and by the linguistic practices of each social formation. The so-called "mental" expressions are not manifestations of an inner life prior to and independent of language, but are in fact episodes that manifest the social, practical recognition of dimensions that constitute they identity and the functional sphere of each individual. "Mental" expressions are not reports or indicators of the occurrence of psychological phenomena within individuals.

"Mental" expressions, as parts of episodes in which individuals relate to each other and to their environment, constitute psychological phenomena. The psychological does not have an entity of its own. The psychological originates and occurs only as relation between individuals in a social practice (and in animals in habitat-specific patterns, as will be discussed later). "Mental" expressions are part of the psychological phenomenon as an episode of behavior between individuals, and in no way report or inform about "private" or "internal" phenomena.

The «trick» of «mind»: A logical fallacy and a social myth

Unlike other terms referring to properties of things and beings, such as 'matter', 'life', and others, the use of the term 'mind' is relatively recent (although it has a Latin root) and comes from Anglo-Saxon philosophy. The term 'mind' was only incorporated into ordinary language in the 20th century, as a result of the progressive medicalization of social practices with respect to the "deviations" of individuals. Its use was adapted as a more socially acceptable substitute for other terms such as 'soul', 'reason', 'understanding', and 'spirit', with a religious and class tradition that made them less "neutral" as a means of explaining and characterizing the behavior of individuals in society. We will examine how the mind (and later, consciousness) was consolidated as a substantive phenomenology, susceptible to scientific study to account for the behavior of human beings, as well as its origins and difference, with respect to the behavior of animals. It is noteworthy that the term 'consciousness' was chosen to give substance to the psychological as individuality since in its Latin etymological origin, a language still used in the Renaissance as a educated language, the term meant just the opposite: shared knowledge.

Although transcendentalist thought has a long and mostly religious and political tradition, its contribution to the modern elaboration of the concept of the psychological can be found in the writings of René Descartes on knowledge. In the midst of the Renaissance, Descartes set out to demonstrate the validity of the formal method of knowledge against empiricist approaches, especially that of Bacon. However, his proposal was not limited to arguing about a method of knowledge, but also founded through its application an ontology of rationality and, concomitantly, of psychological phenomena. In the Discourse on Method, Descartes examined two interrelated issues: one, how to discern true knowledge, and second, the origins of such knowledge.

Descartes did not rule out that there was knowledge originating in sensible experience, but he did question whether such knowledge was reliable, that is, that it could be trusted. It is at this point that he equated truth with reliability as synonymous with rational faith. It is not a question of "error". Rather, it is a matter of founding that 'true' knowledge, following Augustine of Hippo (called Saint Augustine), is knowledge by revelation, and that such revelation is given independently of any attribute directly from the senses. In both cases, "self-evident" ideas, such as the idea of 'god' are revealed to the cognizant subject, either by direct divine influence or as abstractions that do not depend on sensory experience. Therefore, true knowledge is exclusive to the spirit and not to the material body, which is nourished only by the influences coming from the senses, from sensory experience. In his foundation of the method of true knowledge, abstract knowledge by revelation, Descartes also establishes the existence of two distinct substances in the human being: the material body, and rational thought as spirit. In his Discourse on Method (1998/1627), Descartes argued that:

> Because our senses sometimes deceive us, I wanted to suppose that nothing was exactly as they led us to imagine… And finally, considering the fact that all the same thoughts we have when we are awake can also come to us when we are asleep, without any of them being true, I resolved to pretend that all the things that had ever entered my mind were no more true than the illusions of my dreams. But immediately afterward I noticed that, while I wanted thus to think that everything was false, it necessarily had to be the case that I, who was thinking this, was something. And noticing that this truth—*I think, therefore I am*—was so firm and so assured that all the most extravagant suppositions of the skeptics were incapable of shaking it, I judged that I could accept it without scruple as the first principle of the philosophy I was seeking.
>
> Then, examining with attention what I was, and seeing that I could pretend that I had no body and that there was no world nor any place where I was, I could not pretend, on that account, that I did not exist at all, and that, on the contrary, from the very fact that I thought of doubting the truth of other things, it followed very evidently and very certainly that I existed; whereas, on the other hand, had I simply stopped thinking, even if all the rest of what I had ever imagined had been true, I would have had no reason to believe that I had existed. From this I knew that I was a substance the whole essence or nature of which is simply to think, and which, in order to exist, has no need of any place nor depends on any material thing. Thus this

> "I," that is to say, the soul through which I am what I am, is entirely distinct
> from the body and is even easier to know than the body, and even if there
> were no body at all, it would not cease to be all that it is.
> After this, I considered in general what is needed for a proposition to be
> true and certain, for since I had just found one of them that I knew to be
> such, I thought I ought also to know in what this certitude consists. And
> having noticed that there is nothing at all in this *I think, therefore I am* that
> assures me that I am speaking the truth, except that I see very clearly that, in
> order to think, it is necessary to exist, I judged that I could take as a general
> rule that the things we conceive very clearly and very distinctly are all true,
> but that there is merely some difficulty in properly discerning which are
> those that we distinctly conceive. (pp. 18-19)

In another passage of the same work, Descartes clarifies that the clear and distinctive things appearing as true are those that manifest devoid of sensorial features, that is, innate ideas, independent of sensory experience, and whose truth can be sustained by rational demonstration, independently of any empirical verification:

> It is, at the very least, just as certain that God, who is this perfect being, is
> or exists, as any demonstration in geometry could be (p. 21).

In these passages, Descartes established the existence of the soul, thought or mind, as a substance independent of the material body. Descartes does not use the word mind since it is a term that is incorporated in psychology from the Old English word 'gemynd', which in the 1300s was used as a term equivalent to remember and keep present, and later, in the following centuries, it was extended as equivalent to think, attend, and be aware of something. In Descartes, the soul's capacity for self-knowledge was also assumed, the truth of knowledge achieved as knowledge demonstrated rationally (and thus deduced), and the extension of the argument for the demonstration of the soul's own existence as thought to everything that is clearly and distinctly conceived, such as abstract ideas and the idea of god. Descartes established that the reflection of the spirit on itself, as a rational demonstration of its existence and of what it knows, constituted the source and criterion of all true knowledge, in principle. As a part of the rational method, the doubt about one's own existence and the revelation of one's own thought as the identity of the soul, only considered that which could be represented and demonstrated by itself, apart from the accidents captured by the sensibility. It was thus established that the soul or mind, as a spiritual substance, existed as a cognizant entity. This tradition has been maintained up to the present in the identification of the mind with the so-called cognition as a defining attribute. For this reason, the mind or its equivalents only make sense as consciousness, that is, as cognizant experience. Descartes established the separation between action and its affections as belonging to the material world and mechanical bodies, while knowledge and its actions, as rational volition, were exclusive to the mind as a spiritual substance.

In the 19th and early 20th centuries, the concept of mind gradually adapted to the interest in studying the phenomena of consciousness from an empirical and experimental perspective. In this process, psychology gradually emerged as the project of a new scientific discipline: the science of the mind as conscious experience (see the conceptual analysis of the term 'consciousness' in Ribes, 2011). Two important transformations took place in the concept of mind as conscious experience. The first consisted in breaking the isolation of the mind as a self-sufficient and independent entity of sensitive accidents. The second consisted in relating behavior to the mind as a functional system. In both cases, intentionality or purpose replaced the purely cognizant entity of the Cartesian soul.

Brentano published *Psychology from an Empirical Standpoint* in 1874. In this work, among others, Brentano founded the new phenomenology, later developed by Husserl and Merleau Ponty, among others. The empirical perspective implied in the title of this work is misleading. Unlike Wundt, Brentano did not propose an experimental discipline of conscious experience. His great contribution was to establish that all conscious experience is an experience relative to an object, but not an experience of an object as such. The object is constituted by conscious experience itself. It is an experience that, unlike Cartesian experience, does not consist of consciousness reflecting itself in an act of rational revelation. For Brentano, conscious experience is always the consciousness of an object as phenomenal experience, regardless whether or not this experience corresponds to the attributes of a real, specific object. It is a conscious experience relative to things, and thus it is a mental experience: it is always referred to an object. It is not an experience empty of empirical content, reflecting rational abstraction. Mind as consciousness is a phenomenal experience of the individual in the world. The content of the mind is intentional insofar as it is always related to some object. Intentionality is not an immanent attribution of consciousness, but is recognized from its link to an object. There is no intention without an object, for there would be no sense of intentionality in a vacuum. The content of consciousness (i.e., the object) provides the directionality that defines all psychological phenomena as intentional, but it is important to clarify that in the logic of ordinary language intention is not an "additional" performance of or in consciousness, but only the way in which the directionality of a given act is socially described (Anscombe, 1976). For Brentano, this relation to an object occurs as the first and always necessary mental experience: presentation. Thereafter, judgments and love and hate phenomena can occur.

Descartes' and Brentano's formulations share a common element: the individual is identified as an "I" in consciousness. For Descartes, it is a rational, methodical, abstracting "I" that separates itself from sensitive accidents, while for Brentano it is an "I" immersed in the phenomenal experience of objects, and to that extent an "I" whose intentionality is identified with its phenomenal experience. Despite the differences in both formulations, the psychological individual is conceived on the basis of the mind as conscious experience. It is an individual who does not act, but only experiences the world. Her experience is contemplative, not active. Language constitutes a vessel that the mind adopts as consciousness, either as thought and abstract reason, or as phenomenal experience, to report to other minds its arguments, its knowledge or its own phenomenal contents. Introspection is the method to examine the mind as consciousness, and language its descriptive or informative instrument. Language is considered a medium to denote thought ideas and demonstrations, or to describe conscious experiences. For this reason, it is incorrectly assumed that the nature of language is symbolic and that its grammar reflects the grammar of thought. From this perspective, language is an instrument conventionally used between different minds as a re-presentation of conscious experiences and of abstract ideas, criteria and rational thought demonstrations. It is a language empty of all social relation and meaning.

The Cartesian autonomous individual was revised by evolutionary thinking. The theory of evolution posed the continuity of humans as species with respect to other animal species, particularly the higher primates and, to that extent, it assumed the continuity of the mind as well. The mind ceased to be exclusive to humans, and introspection turned out to be a method not applicable to the study of the animal mind. The new approach opened the way to the systematic observation of animal behavior patterns, as well as to the first experimental studies on so-called animal intelligence and reasoning. Charles Darwin's last collaborator, John Romanes, published his books on The evolution of mind in animals and Animal intelligence in 1883 and 1884, respectively. In these works, Romanes elaborated on some of Darwin's earlier observations on the evolution of the mind, whose notes were not published until 1974. Romanes' influence was significant, especially on William McDougall, who published his book Psychology: The study of behaviour in 1912. The title of McDougall's work is suggestive, but not entirely accurate. Nevertheless, it represents a significant transition in the conception of the mind and its direct link to behavior. McDougall conceived of psychology as "the positive science of the behaviour of living things…which behave or exhibit behaviour; and, when we say that they exhibit behaviour, we mean that they seem to have an intrinsic power of self-determination, and to pursue actively or with effort their own welfare and their own ends or purposes" (pp. 19-20). Psychology was thus linked to the bodily activity of the organism. Unlike physiology, psychology was to focus on the changing, not the permanent, that is, on the activity of living beings. For McDougall, an essential part of behavior as activity had to do with consciousness. Unlike inert beings, consciousness was an inseparable component of behavior as activity of living beings. In accord with Brentano, McDougall posited that being or being conscious was with respect to an object, so that the first function of conscious activity was to know objects. This observable activity was complemented by two other functions, namely affective in terms of "feeling" the effect or attributes of the object, and connotative in terms of seeking or rejecting the object as some kind of movement. These three functions of consciousness, as general dispositions inherited by individuals of each species, constituted the structure of the mind. Thus, the mind was the functional organization of the activity of living beings, as purposeful behavior. The mind was no longer an independent entity of activity, and became part of it, an essential part of the living being, but unlike the Aristotelian soul (on which McDougall was based), the mind did not exist in the form of potency made act, but was constituted in the form of consciousness that accompanies all activity.

A new transformation in the conception of psychological phenomena occurred with behaviorism, a movement that emerged from evolutionary thinking, pragmatism, and the extension of the concept of the reflex to the study of the molar activity of higher organisms, especially human beings (Ribes

& Burgos, 2006). Although McDougall considered himself the founder of behaviorism (a purely nominal attribution due to the use of the term), it was John B. Watson who in 1931 and later years proposed behaviorism as the perspective for formulating a psychological science. Watson asserted that psychology should study the behavior of individuals, that is, what they do and say, and that consciousness was only a term of colloquial language and not an entity or a process distinct from behavior. In fact, he argued that consciousness could only be understood as linguistic habits, and it made no sense to speak of consciousness outside of language. Psychological phenomena were "externalized" with the advent of behaviorism and its development during the last three quarters of the past century, that is, they were identified with the various manifestations of the actions individuals, animals or humans. In all the versions of behaviorism (including the Pavlovian version), behavior was always related to some object, conceived as a "stimulus" and its antecedent or consequent effects. Thus, situationality and purpose were implicit or explicit dimensions of behavior. For example, Skinner incidentally commented that the study of operant behavior was the field of intentionality. However, as J. R. Kantor (1924-1926) noted, all behaviorist conceptions of psychological behavior were organocentric, regardless of the molarity or molecularity of the proposed analyses (Tolman versus Skinner). The psychological was identified with the activity of the individual. Behavior was exchange, effect, or purpose with respect to objects, but the psychological quality lay in the activity and not in the relation itself with the object. This organocentric perspective of psychological behavior had (and has) two drawbacks. The first is that it does not allow us to clearly distinguish the boundaries between biological and psychological behavior. We often fail to realize that the term behavior, at the ordinary or technical level, is not proper or exclusive to the psychological dimension of analysis. This blurring of boundaries leads to the transformation of some biological behaviors into psychological ones (heartbeat, isolated muscle action, brain electrical activity), or to the reduction of psychological phenomena to correlative or co-occurring biological activities. The second drawback is the postulation of "internal" behavior, in the form of images or implicit language, which reinstate the mind and consciousness as private psychological behavior in the form of "responses".

How to conceive the psychological dimension of scientific analysis?

Psychological phenomenology is ostensible in ordinary language practices, even though the terms 'consciousness', 'behavior', subjective experience', and 'mind' rarely appear or occur as part of them. In fact, such practices, as Ryle (1949) and Wittgenstein (1953), among others, have shown, do not correspond in any way to reports of experiences or descriptions of particular "inner" activities. The various historical conceptions of "the psychological" just reviewed (not to use the even more ambiguous term 'psychic'), share some characteristics, not necessarily all of them: 1) the identification of individuality as a psychological dimension (in the form of Self, subject, or organism); 2) the necessary relation of the individual to an object, as purpose or intentionality criterion (with the exception of Descartes); and 3) the conative disposition or manifest activity, as indispensable components to identify or observe the occurrence of psychological phenomena(with the exception of Descartes and Brentano). The psychological is centered in the individual (human or animal) in all these conceptions, and thus its phenomenology occurs in the individual, whether contemplative or in moving and performing. Locating psychological phenomenology in the individual inevitably raises the need to delimit the spatial dimensions of that location. Descartes proposed a strange paramechanical and paraoptical relation between the rational soul or spirit and the material body. The soul had no extension, but interacted with the body in an area of the body (the pineal gland), which is difficult to logically sustain. For Brentano, consciousness occurred as an initial phenomenon of paraoptical contemplation, consisting of a passive activity of 'representation' of the object, an activity based on the physiology of the nervous system, but which could not be reduced to a purely material explanation. Physiological activity supposedly corresponded to the physical properties of objects, while psychological activity, as consciousness, had to do with their interpretation. For McDougall, the mind, as the organization of consciousness, was also an activity occurring in parallel to biological activity, on which it depended, but which it directed as a purposive activity. Finally, behavior always appears in the various forms of behaviorism as the individual's bodily movement (including language and the senses as special types of response), emitted or elicited by stimuli in the external or internal environment.

A conception of the psychological not centered and/or localized in the individual will be outlined in what follows, and linked to the current perspective whereby psychological phenomenology can only be recognized in and as part of certain episodes in ordinary language practices.

An important distinction must be first drawn. The phenomena studied by the various sciences are phenomena of collective shared experience. Therefore, these phenomena are recognized, described, experienced, expressed, communicated, and transmitted in ordinary language practices. They are phenomena that are part of the collective experience itself and that as such, always constitute the situation or context in which such practice occurs. The conception these phenomena resides in the collective practice itself with respect to them or as part of them. In this sense, expressions of them historically change in correlation with the social practices under which they occur. In an initial stage (protoscience), the sciences classify such shared phenomena known to all on the basis of some common attributes to that collective experience. In this stage, knowledge of the natural history of phenomena starts, and some common characteristics are identified among them, so as to classify them and consider them similar in some sense. Generalization occurs in terms of some shared similarity. In a second stage, the sciences construct a technical language to abstract, from these classes, properties identifiable only through the analysis, the fragmentation, of concrete phenomena. In this stage, the sciences no longer approach phenomena directly, but do so indirectly through the systematic study of facts conceptualized by a theory, in the form of empirical abstractions. These facts are recognized, described, and interpreted through a technical language specific to the analytical level of the selected phenomena, and from the conceptual perspective of a theory and its specific logic. The analytical reconfiguration of the facts is based on the phenomena, but distant from their concreteness as concrete singular occurrences. While ordinary language practices (and its natural and social phenomenology) are shared by all individuals of a given social formation, the practices of scientific knowledge are restricted to a group of initiates, in the form of expertise specific to each level of analysis of ordinary phenomena.

For this reason, the meaning of expressions (and the terms included) in ordinary language practices is multivocal, that is, terms have different meanings or senses depending on the expression in which they are used and the practical context in which they occur. The meaning of terms and expressions is always episodic, circumstantial and derived from social (not individual) practice. In turn, in the technical language of sciences, the terms and some expression, while based on ordinary language, are univocal, that is, the practices associated to their "use" are precisely delimited, both in terms of the performed operations, the described or denoted properties and relations between events (technical language is indeed denotative par excellence), and the ways in which interpretations of such events can be formulated as 'scientific facts'. Thus, although the sciences attempt to understand the phenomena that are part of ordinary language collective practices, they accomplish this task by "constructing" a world of facts, processes, and relations through a technical, abstract, and analytical language that does not directly correspond to ordinary language. Several conclusions follow from this. First, there is no direct translation between ordinary language and technical scientific terms, even if the same word is sometimes used. When this is case, the technical term has only one meaning and is therefore not subject to the whims of definitional eclecticism, whether based on models, operations, or mere interpretations, as is often the case with pseudo-technical language in psychology. Second, words given the multivocality of ordinary language expressions, there are no authentic synonymies between words, not even in the different uses of the same word. Dictionaries periodically collect, with historical delay, the different circumstantial uses of the same word as part of different expressions. But also, they attempt, with little success, to establish equivalences relations of meaning between different words or expressions. This equivalence is even more questionable when it comes to translation between different languages, as experts in literature, prose or poetry can attest. Third, one cannot translate the technical terms proper to different theories in a field of scientific knowledge since such terms imply different practices and different 'facts'. This is an additional reason to question any form of theoretical eclecticism in psychology.

Considering the points presented thus far, it should be clear that psychological or "mental" phenomenology, as manifested in ordinary language practices, constitutes the "raw" matter of both the classifications of natural history and the knowledge practices specific to a scientific psychology. Likewise, it should also be evident that the concepts and facts of a scientific psychology do not have a correspond biunivocally to ordinary language terms and expressions that enable one to recognize and identify the phenomenology under analysis. Lastly, it should be obvious that given due to their multivocal nature, the terms and expressions with psychological meaning in ordinary language cannot be univocally identified as generic phenomena. Therefore, such terms cannot, prima facie, be constituted in the technical language of the scientific discipline. Their exclusion as technical language does not imply

34

the exclusion of the phenomenology of which they form part in ordinary language practices. From the phenomenological viewpoint, and there is no other possible one, we identify and recognize psychological episodes by means of expressions corresponding to the self-referred reactivity and activity of individuals in circumstance. Hence, since it is impossible to support a denotative function of the 'mental' expressions, whether in soliloquy or in self-referential expressions of practice in context, it can only be assumed that such expressions in circumstance, as insperable components of a social practice between individuals, constitute the psychological phenomena.

Some implications of the relational nature of the psychological

To the contrary of those who argue psychological terms and expressions denote entities (sometimes even called 'dispositions') or occurrences ("internal" events or activities), their episodic and circumstantial nature underscores their dispositional and relational character. Therefore, the logic underpinning the technical language and the analytical categories of a scientific approach to psychological phenomena must assume that the psychological always constitutes a relation in circumstance, but that what is related does not in itself have a psychological property. J. R. Kantor (1924-1926) proposed a field logic for examining the psychological where the individual and "the" objects (which could include other individuals) constituted a psychological segment when they established a functional contact or interaction between them. This contact was understood on the basis of different logical functions: relational, dispositional, and enabling. It is a deterministic logic analysis, in terms of the interdependence of all field-factors, which excludes the linearity of causal analysis. Field logic cancels any identification of elements or variables in terms of the internal-external distinction, characteristic of organocentric traditions. From a field logic, psychological behavior occurs as a relation between entities (the individual and the object/s) whereby this relation cannot be interpreted on the basis of the internal-external dichotomy. I will not go into detail on this formulation, as it has been described and extended previously (Ribes, 2018). My purpose is to examine the implications of this conception of what we will call psychological behavior with respect to the analytic universe of psychology, of its relation with what are considered borderline sciences (bioecology and socio-historical science), of the conception of 'individual', and of the density of the psychological in the individuals' life stream.

A first implication concerns the empirical domain of psychology as a scientific discipline. The raw material from which the psychological or 'mental' phenomenology is recognized resides in a delimited set ordinary language practices, which we recognize throughout its natural history (actually, a social history) by generic concepts with terms such as 'sensation', 'perception', 'judgment', 'reasoning', thought', 'emotion', 'feeling', imagination', 'intelligence', and many others that erroneously constitute the thematic indexes of psychology as a discipline, whether as nouns, verbs, or adjectives. As mentioned, however, scientific knowledge analytically fragments ordinary knowledge phenomena and entities and their natural history by abstracting common properties from them, regardless of their concreteness. These abstracted properties constitute the objects of scientific knowledge, and the facts to be studied as relating events. In the case of psychological phenomenology, this is reduced to the sphere of the human being and the relations of individuals with another individuals and objects under certain circumstances. The psychological universe would be exclusively human, for it is only possible to recognize its phenomenology in ordinary language practices. Although some animal species show communication patterns among their members, these patterns do not constitute conventional forms of interaction. Thus, these patterns cannot be considered linguistic interactions. However, insofar as technical scientific concepts can and must be separated from their original phenomenology, the psychological universe can be extended beyond that phenomenology. The only requirement to fulfill is that such an extension can be made in the same terms used in which psychological behavior is analyzed, that is, as functional contacts between an individual and an object. The extension of the psychological to animal behavior was historically made by analogy from the approaches of the theory of evolution, and from episodic behaviors similar to those of human beings. In analyzing Wittgenstein's 'form of life', Hanfling (2002) points to the fact that we can assume that psychological episodes can be identified in animal behavior without the need to appeal to consciousness as an internal experience or that they can talk about it. In contrast, Hanfling continues, automata could "verbalize" actions, which, however, would not be strictly related to sensory or "emotional" reactions. Wittgenstein comments, "But doesn't what you say come to this: that there is no pain, for example, without *pain-behaviour?* –It comes to this: only of a living human being and what resembles (behaves like) a living human being can one say: it has sensations; it sees; is blind; hears; is deaf; is conscious or unconscious" (1953,

36

p. 281). From a field logic, this extension of psychological behavior is based on the applicability of the category of functional contact to the study of the individual interactions of animals, insofar as the appearance of nervous tissue coincides with the reactive differentiation required in any form of psychological behavior. Including animal behavior as part of the psychological domain without any apparent phenomenology in the form of 'mental' expressions, is not the result of everyday observation (except in those domesticated, bred, or captive animals, with whom we talk and about whom we talk). The inclusion of the animal Kingdom as part of the psychological universe is the result of a process of analytical abstraction under the auspices of the technical language of scientific theory, in this case, of a field theory. The analysis of the psychological as relations in the form of contacts between individual and object allows us to go beyond the observational criteria linked to everyday experiences in concrete circumstances, of "behaving as". It allows isolating properties and dimensions in relation, shared by apparently non-comparable or qualitatively different episodes. Thus, an abstract characterization of the psychological transcends its recognition in the framework of the collective experience of ordinary language practices in two ways. First, non-linguistic animal species other than human can be included as part of the empirical domain in which psychological phenomena occur, even though psychological behavior cannot be identified with the criteria of ordinary language practices. Second, it is safe to assume the occurrence of such types of behavior in humans as part of their daily life in times prior to the rise of self-reference, possibly as the result of the rise of the first forms of State and asymmetric individual appropriation (Ribes, 2018). Self-reference as individual expression should be distinguished from self-reference as collective interaction in the context of institutional practices (Bloor, 1997). In the latter, self-reference occurs with respect to collective practice, as an institutional group (formal and informal), rather than to the individual, although the expressions are made by the different participating individuals.

A second implication has to do with delimiting the psychological from the biological and the social. That which justifies psychology as an analytic level of knowledge of the 'reality' or the 'world' of experience is the individual dimension of one of its components (the animal or the human being) and its interaction, equally, with environing objects (and not with the environment itself), whether an ecological or a sociocultural environment. To reiterate: it is a contact between the individual and particular stimulus objects (sometimes another individual). In fact, individuals always do something. talking about something with other individuals with respect to particular individuals, objects, and events in the phenomenology of ordinary language practices. It is difficult to identify in such an episode a psychological character when this is not the case. However, it is evident that individuality is a dimension that occurs only in two sets of reference systems. One, biological or bioecological systems, and two, social formations. Any individual is a living being in principle, and we usually apply this concept to the members of a given species, regardless of the problems that sometimes arise in delimiting a species. At this level, every individual is thus, and ceases to be, an indivisible organism in order to be considered as such. Thus, the psychological is an emergent of the biological, and as such the biological always participates in every psychological episode or phenomenon. The biological is consubstantial to the psychological, whereby the biological is understood not only as the organism as such, but also as the set of organisms constituting the species (otherwise the concept of individual is meaningless) and the corresponding ecological niche, including others species sharing and functionally configuring this habitat as a cross-species habitat. In the case of human beings, their dimension as individuals emerges not only from their biology but also from the set conventional practices and relations configuring a given social formation at a particular historical moment (the historical dimension also being a determinant of the bioecological relations). In the case of humans, the psychological dimension is fundamentally an emergent of the social and cultural. The individual is that who identifies herself as such socially; an individual is a person who belongs, at one time or another, to different sets of possible, but to some extent predetermined, social relations. Consequently, as entities give meaning to the individual, we can affirm that there are only two frames of reference: bioecological and socio-historical systems. There are no psychological entities or systems per se, in which the individual dimension can be identified. Moreover, given the character of the individual, it does not necessarily follow that the occurrence of psychological behavior must necessarily be assumed from his or her activity. Psychological behavior is an emergent of biological and social behaviors thus is discontinuous as an abstracted phenomenology or functional contact. Unlike biology and socio-historical science, psychology lacks entities of its own from this perspective. Individuals are differentiated biological and/or social entities. Psychology, as it is probably also the case with chemistry and linguistics (but for different reasons), would constitute a coextensive science, in this case, of bioecology and the socio-historical science, which would provide the substantive entities from which psychological behavior emerges.

38

Psychological behavior would have no place or "existence" in the absence of biological or social entities. Contrary to what is usually proposed, the psychological does not constitute an "evolutionary bridge" between the biological and social (homo sapiens as a transformation of the monkey into a social being). Actually, the psychological consists of a double intersection of the biological and the social. It is worth noting that McDougall (1912) pointed out, for reasons other than those presented here, the coextensiveness of the psychological with respect to the biological. The coextensiveness of linguistics evidently occurs with respect to the socio-historical science, while organic and inorganic chemistry is coextensive with physics (identifying chemical elements as molecules with a determined atomic weight) and with biology (compounds that are only functional in relation to metabolism).

A third implication has to do with the concept of the individual from a psychological perspective. In the conceptions of the psychological above-mentioned, the individual is the locus of psychological activity, whether as rational soul, as conscious experience, or as behavior in the form of movements and locutions. According to the organocentric tradition, the psychological individual exists by itself from birth, and its evolution or progressive development consists of an interaction between inherited factors, such as dispositions or tendencies, and what is learned from the ecological and social environment. The individual is not prior to the species or the social group (family, clan, tribe, etc.). The individual is a differentiation of the aggregation of which it is a part. One is a member of a species or of a social formation insofar as there is a functional recognition by the rest of the aggregation or group. The individual is always an outcome of the defining characteristics, relations, and functions of a group or aggregation. Therefore, the individual is so to the extent that she is recognized as such in the process of becoming, from birth to death. An individual is one who shares the internal and external functions and interaction patterns of a group or aggregation, even though sometimes she does not necessarily share the same morphological characteristics. From a psychological perspective, the individual is always first a biological and/or social individual, and her becoming a member of an aggregation or group constitutes the process of psychological individuation. Each group member is so because she shares interaction patterns and functions, but at the same time she is characteristically different from the other group members by virtue of her individuality. Therefore, individuality is differentiation within the shared, hence, the psychological dimensions of individuality are always conditional to the processes of bioecological and sociocultural individuation. From a psychological perspective, the aggregation, as species or social formation, provides the functional identity of the individual. At the social level, the individual is identified as a person, while at the ecological level, specific forms of identification must correspond to each niche and type of aggregation. Human individuation, it follows, occurs as socialization, while animal individuation occurs as speciation. Thus, the psychological always occurs as individuation in the sphere of ecological and social circumstances. Nevertheless, the processes regulating and identifying such individuation as a psychological dimension are transversal to these circumstances and to the differential outcomes among individuals. Said another way, the constituting processes of the psychological dimension of individuality are "universal", although their circumstantial occurrence results in "different" individuals. The psychological occurs in the sphere of the specific patterns of a given habitat and the practices of a given social formation. This phenomenon always occurs within the process of individuation in either of the two previous spheres. There is no psychological phenomenology if it is not in the individuation process, as identification and differentiation of each individual articulated in the relations with other individuals in specific environments. However, such individuation can be only understood, and not just observed, described and compared, on the basis of the analysis of 'universal' processes transversal to any habitat or social formation.

The fourth and final implication has to do with the 'density' of the psychological dimension in individuals' becoming always within the underlying biological and/or social dimensions. Traditional views of the psychological, whether as experience, conscious activity, or behavior as sensory-motor or linguistic activity, have assumed that the psychological occurs as a continuum from birth to death. It is the individual's stream of consciousness or activity. This assumption derives from the misidentification of every individual's performance, whether as conscious act or as movement and locution, as an occurrence of the psychological. But this misunderstanding becomes manifest when it is evident that individuals are not simply the result of the differentiation of a collective and that, consequently, they are not autonomous from that collective. Biological behavior is always continuous, from birth to death. Strictly speaking, social behavior is not continuous, although it could be considered as such, given the conventional character of all our performances, including those related to basic biological functions. In turn, psychological behavior is not continuous in the stream of individual life. How then can we distinguish the psychological dimension in the relation between two people when they talk to each other, or when they watch a soccer game, or when they enjoy a meal? Psychological episodes are always part of a social episode, without the two being in any sense 'parallel'. To put it metaphorically, every episode of psychological behavior occurs "encapsulated" in a social episode (or its equivalent in the case of animal behavior). Psychological episodes are always identified on the basis of an individual and as such constitute episodes personally or particularly configured episodes. For this reason, the analysis of social and psychological episodes is not mutually exclusive. Two psychological episodes can be analyzed in any interindividual episode under the proper conditions, each identified from each individual as a personal episode. However, no personal episodes that can be identified as episodes involving psychological behavior occur in every interpersonal or impersonal episode (Ribes, Pulido, Rangel, & Sánchez-Gatell, 2016). Psychological behavior contains an individual biographical bias in the interaction with ecological and/or social situations. Such a bias manifests as a biographical tendency to interact with present circumstances, given the particular moment in the individuation process. Such a bias and the resulting effective interaction must always constitute functional transitions in interactions within a situation or between situations. Functional transitions always consist in a process of detachment linked to the way in which the particular individual articulates, in terms of her reactive/active patterns, with the changing or modifying properties of objects (including other individuals) and events (including other individuals' performances) in a situation. Any detachment constitutes a functional reorganization of the circumstances in which one interacts. Only when this occurs can an episode of psychological behavior be identified with certainty. From this perspective, the occurrence of psychological behavior is discontinuous in individuals' life stream. This is suggested by its phenomenology in ordinary language practices, and is confirmed by a scientific analysis in terms of functional contacts. Contrary what the various philosophies of mind all organocentric psychologies framed in the autonomous individual posit, the psychological does not constitute a ubiquitous phenomenology. It is always delimited by bioecological and/or sociocultural behavior, and is relevant only in terms of the analysis of individuality as biographical differentiation of such behaviors.

Corollary

Psychology is the only empirical science (which must be distinguished from the formal sciences) lacking a body-substance entity, using Aristotelian notions. For this reason, unlike all other empirical sciences (physics, chemistry, biology, the socio-historical science, and linguistics), psychology does not have a phenomenological universe to discover distinct from its origin in ordinary language practices. There is nothing on the phenomenological horizon of the psychological that is not apparent to ordinary knowledge and experience. The possibility of contacting new phenomena, entities, or unknown vestiges does not exist for psychology, as it does for all the other sciences. What then is the meaning of psychology as an empirical science? As other sciences, psychology has a double meaning as a specific mode of knowledge. On the one hand, to systematize, on the basis of its analytical categories, the common properties of concrete phenomena that occur as singular instances, or generic at best, in the practices of direct ecological and social experience. On the other hand, to discover new ways of relating the abstracted properties of such phenomena, to understand them differently in social practice, as well as to foster new forms of practice in relation to them. Therefore, we must conclude that psychology can only discover new scientific facts, but no new phenomena.

References

Anscombe, G. E. M. (1976). Intention. Ithaca, NY: Cornell University Press

Bloor, D. (1997). Wittgenstein, rules, and institutions. London: Routledge

Brentano, F. (1973). Psychology from an empirical standpoint (English ed.). London: Routledge (Original German work published 1874)

Darwin, C. R. (1974) Metaphysics, materialism and the evolution of mind: Early writings of Charles Darwin. Chicago, Il: University of Chicago Press.

Descartes, R. (1980). Discourse on method (Spanish ed.). CDMX: Porrúa. (Original French work published 1637).

Hanfling, O. (2002). Wittgenstein and the human form of life. London: Routledge

Kantor, J. R. (1924-1926). Principles of psychology. New York: Alfred Knopf.

McDougall, W. (1912). Psychology: The study of behavior. New York: Henry Holt & Co.

Ribes, E. (2000). La psicologías y la definición de sus objectos de conocimiento. [Psychologies and the definition of their subjects of knowledge]. Revista Mexicana de Análisis de la Conducta, 26, 365-382.

Ribes, E. (2004). La psicología cognoscitiva y el conocimiento de otras mentes. [Cognitive psychology and the knowledge about other minds]. Acta Comportamentalia, 12, monographic number, 7-21.

Ribes, E. (2011). Perception and consciousness as behavior-referred concepts. In E. Ribes & J. Burgos (Eds.), Consciousness, perception, and behavior: Conceptual, theoretical, and methodological issues (pp. 191-223). New Orleans: LA: University Press of the South.

Ribes, E. (2013). Una reflexión sobre los modos generals de conocer y los objetos de conocimiento de las diversas ciencias empíricas, includyendo a la psicología. [A relfection upon the general modes of knowing and the subjects of knowledge in the different empirical sciences, incuding psychology]. Revista Mexicana de Análisis de la Conducta, 30 (2), 89-95.

Ribes, E. (2018). El estudio científico de la conducta individual: una introducción a la teoría de la psicología. [A scientific study of individual behavior: An introduction to the theory of psychology]. CDMX: El Manual Moderno.

Ribes, E. & Burgos, J. E. (2006). Raíces históricas y filosóficas del conductismo, vols. I, II, III. [Historical and philosophical roots of behaviorism]. Guadalajara/Xalapa: Universidad de Guadalajara/Universidad Veracruzana

Ribes, E., Pulido, L., Rangel, N., & Sánchez-Gatell, E. (2016). Sociopsicología: Instituciones y relaciones interindividuales [Sociopsychology: Institutions and interindividual relations]. Madrid: La Catarata.

Romanes, G. J. (1883/2016). Mental evolution in animals. Lexington, KY: Forgotten Books.

Romanes, G. J. (1884/2016). Animal intelligence. The International Scientific Series, vol. XLIV. Mami FL: Hard Press.

Ryle, G. (1949). The concept of mind. New York: Barnes & Noble.

Watson, J. B. (1913). Psychology as the behaviorist views it. Psychological Review, 20, 158-177.

Wittgenstein, L. (1953). Philosophical investigations. Oxford: Basil Blackwell.

ESSAY TWO: ON EXPLANATION AND ITS RELATION WITH THE DIFFERENT MODES OF KNOWLEDGE

The problem of 'explanation' has traditionally been discussed in the context of the problem of 'understanding' as "truth", and of the validity of scientific knowledge as the ultimate and genuine explanation of 'reality'. In this sense, explanation has been considered an epistemological problem and that of the so-called philosophy of science, and has been related to the so-called "causal thinking". In the different philosophical perspectives throughout history, causal thinking has been considered a logical-rational, symbolic process specific to science and its method (Toulmin, 1972). Even "heterodox" philosophers such as Hanson (1972) have accepted that explanation in science conforms to the formal criteria of the nomothetic-deductive method as proposed, among others, by Hempel (1970) at the time of the greatest influence of logical positivism, the dominant doctrine in epistemology and philosophy of science.

The foundations and origins of this tradition lie in the Neoplatonic doctrine of ideas, and in its incorporation by Christian patristics as a criterion for evaluating true knowledge. Plotinus and Porphyry, the immediate predecessors of Augustine of Hippo, proposed the unknowability of the One akin to the divinity and supra-ordinate to of all being. Knowledge of the true real could only be obtained from the ascension of the intuition of the intelligible by the sensible (art), to politics as moderation of the passions, to the intuition of the intelligible by the intelligible (science), and to ecstasy as reunion with the One. In Augustine of Hippo (426/2014), the latter two criteria, namely Plotinus' Nous and Soul constitute the truth knowledge criteria by revelation. These were later adopted in the Renaissance by Descartes (1637/1980), by identifying innate ideas from methodical doubt, and postulating the supremacy of the geometrical formal method and deduction as the criteria of true knowledge.

Descartes also adopted the notion of explanation as efficient cause.

In material bodies, the efficient cause consisted in the production of a movement in an inert body as an effect of the force operated on it by a moving body with which it was in contact. The Cartesian efficient cause was of a proximal nature, so that in those cases in which a cause at a distance was proposed (such as in universal gravitation), proximal causal mediations were required to cover the space between the bodies in relation. In the particular case of the human being, in addition to the mechanical causality that accounted for bodily movements (as with animals and inanimate bodies), efficient causality occurred through the volitional acts of the spirit or reason. Efficient causality as paramaterial agents moved the animal spirits through the bloodstream and nerve fibers causing voluntary movements.

Cartesian efficient causality, adopted from Renaissance science as the paradigm of causality –and the true or scientific explanation– comprised actions, as movements (or paramovements in the case of the will) and effects in terms of some kind of movement or local change in bodies. Efficient causes were constituted as mechanical or paramechanical agents of the observed movements or changes as effects. The explanation of a phenomenon on the basis of efficient causality was no more than the description of a linear time and space sequence of two actions or supposed actions, wherein the first produced the second.

Three objectives related to the concept of explanation, as a supposed form of understanding of and in scientific knowledge, are proposed in this essay: a) to debunk the argument that genuine explanation constitutes a form of causal analysis, and that reasons constitute or are equal to causes in the case of individuals' behavior, b) to analyze explanation as an explicit circumstantiation of the conditions under which phenomena and/or events occur, and c) to examine the various forms assumed by explanations (plural) in the different modes of knowledge, from ordinary, to scientific, technological, artistic, formal, religious, and ethical/juridical.

Explanation, Causes, and Reasons

Descartes' thought represented a decisive turning point in the way Western science conceived the explanation of empirical phenomena. Descartes reconciled truth by revelation as ecstasy, following Plotinus and Augustine of Hippo, with that of truth by logical or rational revelation as self-evident, self-intelligible ideas, including innate ideas (such as the idea of 'God'). Like the Augustinian idea of inner light, Descartes adopted the paraoptic notion of the spirit's reflection upon itself (Plotinus' intuition of the intellect of the intelligible), as inner perception "mechanism" of logical forms empty of sensory content. Geometry, as logic and rational method, provided the representation of any body and movement as forms in space and time. In turn, geometrical deduction allowed to go beyond the observable and account for efficient causality in terms of forces, actions, agents, and effects. Historically, the notion of efficient causality comes from Aristotle's four causes (1995, English ed.). The Aristotelian causes constituted principles, that is, origins of entities and their actualization into events related to other entities. These principles included

48

material, formal, efficient, and final causes, and they were not considered as isolated, independent principles, but the causes only made sense as a whole and always with respect to particular entities. They were not general principles about what exists, but principles of the ways of existence of particular entities. Efficient and final causes became singularized in the Renaissance as forces or motives of actions, producing or guiding them.

The concept of efficient causality, as the universal logic of all form of explanation, was based on a notion of purely contemplative, phenomenal knowledge, dismissing praxis. Divorced from the senses, practice was conceived only as action or movement and, consequently, as the phenomenon to be deductively explained and justified. To explain was to deductively demonstrate that the occurrence of a phenomenon was only an unavoidable effect given the occurrence of a necessary and immediate antecedent event or condition. However, Hume (1740), among others, questioned the explanation in terms of efficient causality, stating that it was only an inference based on the perception of regularities in successive events, and not of a necessary connection between the observed objects. Nevertheless, the logic of explanation became the logic of cause as necessity. A contact or action between the bodies was required, the moving body being the cause and the moved body the effect. In classical mechanics, the explanation of phenomena was considered to be based on the force exerted by one body on another one. Force was considered to be any agent capable of modifying the amount of motion or the shape of material bodies. However, force actually always represented action, in the form of some kind of motion of a given body, which implicitly was the agent. Not surprisingly, the main theorical problem in the history of the different domains of physics, centered on how to account for the action at a distance of one body on another (including particles). A proximal contact between the bodies as requirement promoted different formulations of force as attraction and repulsion in filled fields (ether, plasma, and others), the postulation of wave and corpuscular hypotheses of matter, as well as forms of internal movement of bodies that do not follow causal determinants and behave in a random and probabilistic manner. Hesse's (1962) study of action at a distance and the concepts of force and field in physics is illustrative in this regard.

It is clear that the logic of mechanics, and its explanation criterion or understanding by contact as actions between bodies, had a dominant influence on the development of theory in the various fields of physics. However, it is important to note that, in spite of this, physicists rarely approached their formulations with a notion of efficient causality. Philosophers were and still are the ones who have elaborated the concept of explanation in terms of efficient causality and its deductive character from general statements. Theoretical and experimental physicists rarely speak of causality, if at all, since their theories do not require it. Hanson (1972) commented that referring to causes is a practice more typical of everyday life and experience and that, if physicists occasionally talk about causes, they do so when they have to transmit their knowledge to those dealing with applications in everyday situations, such as with the various engineering disciplines. Toulmin (1960) discussed the issue of causality in a similar way:

"If one turns from the logic-books and the spare-time philosophical works of scientists, to the professional journals in which the sciences really progress, one is in for a surprise. For in the papers there printed the word 'cause' and its derivatives hardly ever appear. In the works of engineering, perhaps; in medical journals, certainly; wherever the sciences are applied to practical purposes, there one finds talk of causes and effects. But in the physical sciences themselves, the word 'cause' is as notable an absentee as the word 'true'…In the physical sciences, likewise, the regularities we find in any particular field of phenomena are represented in a way which is application-neutral…Problems of application and questions about causes arise with reference to particular contexts, but physical theories are formulated in a manner indifferent to particular contexts" (pp. 119, 122).

Following Hanson and Toulmin, it is plausible to consider that it only makes sense to speak of 'causes' when dealing with phenomena or events that occur in particular contexts, and for which it is possible to identify circumstantially related events. Law-like statements (whether in science or in jurisprudence) do not include particular events or facts. They always state general conditions of relation between events and the characteristics of these relations and their possible limits of quantitative variation (in science) or identification (in jurisprudence). "Laws" are statements of general conditions that apply when certain relations between unspecified entities and events occur. Laws do not represent or enunciate or specify causes by themselves. Therefore, laws cannot be used in causal explanatory statements that include the "why" of the occurrence of particular phenomena. For example, when a body with a certain mass falls from a certain heigh and speed, it makes no sense to attribute it to an action of the law of gravity, since saying that the body fell because of gravity adds nothing to the fact that the body actually fell. On the contrary, its fall only corroborates or confirms the fulfillment of the conditions in the law with respect to a type of relation of attraction between bodies, given certain

50

properties of the occurrence circumstances of nonspecific events or entities. These conditions thus stated cannot be the causes of themselves, and in that sense cannot explain themselves. The explanation of the fall of that particular body in causal terms can only be given in the form of an application of the law of gravity, that is, by particularizing the circumstances in which that event occurs, as an instance specified by the conditions enunciated therein.

The term 'action' is employed in physics and chemistry to describe motions and changes either in bodies, particles or molecules. The term has been used interchangeably with the terms 'act' and 'performance' in biology, psychology, and socio-historical science, which are not strictly equivalent. Action implies a physical notion of movement "caused" or even "emitted" by the body itself. In both cases, philosophers (and the biologists, psychologists, and social scientists who follow them) assume the need to formulate "causal" explanations of such actions (or acts). Causes, as direct antecedents of actions, are efficient causes. But another type of causes is also considered, namely final causes, as purposes or reasons, which are seen functionally equivalent to efficient causes. A material location is sought (usually in the brain) to substantiate this equivalence by reducing them to a special type of antecedent of actions. Hornsby's (1980) argument is a case in point, which reduces intentionality of transitive actions as bodily movements to antecedent neural events in the form of "trying to".

Reasons are erroneously assumed to be related in humans to a made-up "faculty" which is cognition, the faculty of knowing by thinking, reasoning, imagining, and remembering. Its Latin etymology comes from ratio, which is to calculate, to ponder, all acts related to commerce and agriculture and which, like many other terms, were transformed into faculties or capacities of a rational soul unique to humans. In ordinary language, acting with reason is equal to acting justly, with arguments, based on testimonies, adequately, as is to be expected, in accordance with the circumstances. To act with reason is always characteristic of doing something in a situation according to the circumstances and the consequences thereof. Therefore, reasons do not apply to actions, but to acts or performances. They occur as situational episodes and not as simple movements or changes that are the result or producer of an effect. Reasons are adduced or expressed as justifications of an act, not as its causes. To justify is to consider something acceptable or appropriate in the context of a specific or determined scenario, and reasons are always justifications shared with others. If there were no others, reasons would not be necessary, which makes it logically clear that reasons do not originate by themselves in a "rational" entity. While particular causes are usually impersonal (e.g., "I slipped because the floor was wet), reasons are interpersonal (e.g., "I was late for my appointment because I had to go to the doctor"). Reasons always justify an act or its omission, while causes always point to a circumstance responsible for the occurrence or non-occurrence of an event, including, this time, the person's movements as actions. Regardless of the distinction, appealing to causes or reasons always occurs in relation with specific, particular situations and contexts. Causes and reasons do not constitute explanatory universals, but rather marks and identification of circumstances or justifications of acts or omissions with respect to others. Moreover, reasons, unlike to causes, are always relative to the social criterion of justification. Causes are simply relevant as an explanation of the event insofar as they make sense in the situation at hand.

Some authors in the field of the so-called philosophy of mind have attempted to treat reasons and causes as synonyms, in order to equate causality in human beings with those applied to animals, plants, and inanimate entities.

Davison (1980) proposed that, in the case of humans and the social nature of their behavior, reasons and causes can be synonymous, that is, that reasons are simply "intentional" and intense causes. To this end, this author identifies intentional behavior with transitive bodily movements, that is, actions having an extrinsic effect or result, involving a something as the object of the action. In identifying intentional behavior with actions, it is argued that reasons, which account for behavior, are equivalent to causes, but causes occurring "in" or "within" the individual, similar to Hornsby's formulation. However, treating reasons as causes implies serious mistakes. As Tomasini (2014) has pointed out, this identification fails to consider Wittgenstein's (1953) arguments that the use of both terms in ordinary practices obeys different contexts and situations of explanation, One does not explain why a ball rolls down the street on the basis of reasons, nor does one explain why one person loves another on the basis of causes.

Besides the differential use of both terms as circumstances of explanation in ordinary language, another serious mistake is made by treating causes and reasons as synonyms. Reasons would be rational causes which, like efficient causes, precede intentional actions. By proposing causality criteria for human behavior synonymous to those of "natural phenomena", it is assumed that causal explanations have greater legitimacy (or adherence to "truth" criteria) than non-causal explanations. However, reasons and causes are not notions that apply with universal or "general" criteria. On the contrary, as previously argued, they are concepts that apply specifically in particular contexts.

We can conclude that Davison incorrectly identifies two specific concepts on the basis of an incorrect universal criterion. By treating causes and reasons as synonyms, he attempts to make explanations based on reasons the same as those supposedly corresponding to causal statements in the natural sciences. But this is a step in the wrong direction, for the sciences do not explain on the basis of causal statements, as philosophers have argued. Causes and reasons are simply impersonal and interpersonal ways of accounting for or explaining phenomena, entities, acts, and events in ordinary language practices, respectively.

Proposing reasons can be identified with efficient causes is not very different from the Cartesian formulation where reasons would correspond to volitions as actions of the rational spirit causing bodily movements, as intentional movements. This would amount to a resurrection of Cartesian paramechanics.

Explanation in ordinary knowledge

In the previous section, we have questioned whether causal explanations, understood as statements in terms of efficient causes, constitute forms of scientific knowledge referring to universals or general conditions. On the contrary, we have tried to show that explanations in terms of causes –and reasons–, belong to the sphere of the particular and the specific and as such have to do with ordinary language practices, or of the applications of scientific knowledge to particular and specific situations. From this perspective, scientific knowledge does not provide a better understanding of the 'world' or 'reality' than that which comes from social practice as ordinary knowledge. Both types of knowledge, which are not the only ones as we will be seen below, provide different types of explanations having different purposes and functions.

It is convenient to quote Wisdom (1991) at length in this context with respect to explanations derived from the application of laws and what he calls case-by-case explanations:

> "...many explanations explicitly or implicitly cite laws. To exhibit the relevance of the laws of physics is to show the place of [this] incident that is explained with respect to all those other incidents that fall under the same

laws. But it is misleading to suggest that in order to make an explanatory breakthrough one must state a law, or know something about a relevant law. We can present an explanation by citing laws explicitly; but we can also explain by directly venturing comparisons through a case-by-case procedure, in which no generalization is stated or resorted to. We can offer explanations in both ways. Description is placing the thing described with respect to the conceivable; explanation is placing the thing explained with respect to the actual. In each of these activities, in the end the placement must be with respect to cases; with respect to conceivable cases in description, and with respect to actual cases in explanation. A law, when we are able to state it, gives us the advantage of being a key to derive many instances, although it is abstract and lifeless. The case-by-case process gives us vividness, not scope. We can restore the law to life by mentioning the cases it covers." (p. 73)

'Explaining' can be related to three different questions regarding an event or phenomenon in any mode of knowledge, and these questions do not necessarily correspond to a general type or logic of understanding or comprehension. The attempt to understand something, when asked to explain it, may adopt one of these three questions: Why? How? Or What for? These questions are not interchangeable and the answers to them do not constitute comparable explanations. Thus, some of these questions may not make sense depending on the mode or object of knowledge. The meaning comes from what and in what circumstance is explained, and this is because explaining, no matter what mode of knowledge is involved, has to do with explicating, making explicit, evident that which is implicit in a situation, event, or phenomenon. The Latin etymology of explain is related to unfold, unravel, deploy, that is, making manifest something that is not. Explain and its roots mean the opposite of imply, which means enfold, to cover something. Therefore, to explain means to make explicit, manifest that which is implicit, that which is concealed or covered in a situation. Sometimes it is necessary to make explicit that which is not present because it has already occurred, or that which is not apparent because we do not distinguish it or observe it as part of that something. It may also be that it is not directly accessible to the senses, although it is present. Lastly, it may be that the occurring relations are not evident, although the episode or phenomenon is directly observable. In all these cases, making manifest what is not present, the non-apparent, the non-observable, or the not related is consubstantial to what we commonly understand by explaining.

54

Every explanation corresponds to a practical conventional criterion, varying according to the domain and mode of knowledge and the social aims. The criteria underpinning the various forms of explanation determine what is observed and how it is observed, since the possibility of explanation lies in the fact of observation. The outcome of observation is never 'naïve' explanation; it is not simply seeing, looking, or attending. The goal of this type of observation is noticing a non-manifest, non-apparent thing in everyday situations. In this sense, to notice is to distinguish, glimpse, appreciate, or grasp what is not evident in an undirected way. It is placing the observation with respect to a criterion, making manifest previously unperceived properties, relations, and occurrences. Said another way, explaining uncovers that which was not evident, apparent, or manifest. To explain is to remove what covers the implicit in order to make it explicit, not only for the senses, but also for their understanding. For example, the first step in the empirical sciences to understand and explain a phenomenon is to systematically observe it, not only in the circumstances in which it occurs, but also in the identification and distinction of its properties so it can be initially classified. Systematic observation is complemented with induced observation, which results exclusively from experimentation. As for what is classified and what is induced to occur, this depends on the theoretical framework that provides the explanation criteria in a given empirical domain.

The three questions relative to an explanation apply only in ordinary knowledge. Only some of these questions are relevant as indicators of understanding of a phenomenon, event, or situation in the other modes of knowledge. Austin's (1962) distinction regarding verbal expressions is useful in ordinary knowledge. Constative expressions describe, report, narrate, and recognize objects, events, properties, persons, or activities. Performative expressions constitute acts in and of themselves, for example, appointing a job position to someone, baptizing a child, or performing a self-referential activity. One of these expressions is commonly employed (but not both) to formulate explanations in the other modes of knowledge. In this sense, two types of knowing can be employed in explaining: constative and performative knowledge (Ribes, 2007). The type of knowledge employed in an explanation will depend on what is to be explained and the mode of knowledge in which that is to be explained is framed. As mentioned above, explaining in ordinary knowledge follows three types of different questions, each one of them pointing to different criteria that can be nuanced by the context of the question itself. Let us look at an illustrative example. A child asks, "what are chairs like?" and the adult says, "chairs always have four legs and a base, and they are almost always made of wood, but they can be plastic or metal". "What are they for?" continues the child, and the adult answers, "to sit on… like this", sitting on a chair as he says so. The child continues and asks why are chairs like this, to which the adult responds, "because if they weren't like this we wouldn't be able to sit, we would slip or fall", simulating what would happen if the base were not flat or didn't have four legs. Finally, the child asks "and why are they called chairs?", to which the adult replies, "because that's how they are called and not any other way. It is customary….". The question "how" is followed by a purely constative explanation, which informs about the characteristics that chairs have as objects. The question "what for" is followed by a performative explanation that shows the use given to chairs. The "why" question is followed by two different types of explanation. The first is performative, showing what would happen if the chairs were not flat and four-legged. The second is constative that simply asserts that this is the way chairs are. None of the explanations to the four questions, especially those concerning "why" can be considered causal, in the sense of establishing relations between an agent and an effect, unless one "stretches" the concept of agent to the "slope" of the seat or the arrangement of the chair legs. All the exemplified explanations, in fact, can be considered examples of reasons, of customs, of usages, or of effects.

As the example above shows, explaining is not limited to pointing out impersonal causes (the child fell because the chair legs were loose), or to giving reasons for acts (the child sat down because she was tired). In ordinary language (and knowledge) practices, explaining is tantamount to revealing the criteria and conditions that account for the occurrence of an act, an event, or how we relate to things. From this perspective, there are diverse explanation modalities and, therefore, it is meaningless to argue that there is only one form of explanation that provides certainty or that is based on "true" knowledge. The scope of an explanation depends on the domain and mode of knowledge in which it takes place. Explanations in ordinary language practices are always explanations of specific, particular events, relations, acts, or characteristics. Explanations in other modes of knowledge may be proposed to account for shared characteristics or properties, for general relations and conditions, or even for arbitrarily developed conventional rules. However, what is identified and expressed whenever an explanation is proposed is the circumstantiation of the conditions of occurrence, application, relation, or justification of events, acts, or diverse rules. To explain is to relate or link two or more entities or events in circumstance, so that the phenomenon of which they are part makes sense. This means that the explanation must be coherent and/or congruent with the criterion or context justifying the relation in circumstance, and especially with the nature of the entities and events that are explained, given the peculiarities of each mode of knowledge.

An explanation must always be pertinent to what is being explained, that is, it cannot appeal to external conditions or elements to the object of explanation. Yet, as has been mentioned repeatedly, there is no privileged form of explanation, as has been proposed from rationalist and scientific positions. The nature of what is known and thus attempted to be explained, always depends on the mode and domain of knowledge involved and its criteria as a conventional practice. Therefore, the coherence and congruence characterizing an explanation are always the result of the application of the specific criteria of the domain and mode of knowledge. Coherence and congruence are not restricted to 'one' isolated explanation, but to a system of related explanations, at the same or at different levels of inclusiveness in the corresponding domain. Any explanation of phenomena, events, relations, or given entities must share the same analytic logic as the other complementary explanations in that domain (coherence); also, such explanations cannot be contradictory, that is, they cannot imply opposite or incompatible circumstances with respect to what is being explained (congruence). To explain is to circumstantiate the conditions in which an object of knowledge takes place and, although circumstantiation implies some form of description, it is not reduced to this. Circumstantiation is always based on some criterion that transcends the mere narrative description of that which is to be explained. For this reason, it is important to consider the fact that the diversity of modes of knowledge that ramify and are sustained by ordinary language practices, as a fundamental mode of knowledge, entail different circumstantiation criteria. It is imperative not to confuse them or subordinate one to the other, as it has unfortunately been happening in philosophical practice.

Explanation and modes of knowledge

Every explanation is an interpretation of an event or entity framed by assumptions, beliefs, and unobjectionable evidence in the form of effects. Therefore, every explanation is based on a conventional criterion that guides the way in which what is to be explained is observed. Each criterion is part of a shared practice and underlies different ways of explaining an event or entity. In the different domains and modes of knowledge, each conventional criterion and its assumptions determine a specific explanatory logic. In this section we will examine how explanatory criteria vary across modes of knowledge and in some shared domains.

Elsewhere (Ribes, 2018), the various modes of knowledge and their difference with respect to the modes of knowing have been described. Both concepts were formulated in order to avoid the traditional confusion in philosophy of science between mode and method of knowledge. Science has commonly been reduced to a method, the so-called 'scientific method'. In contrast to this assumption, the proposed distinction assumes that there is a mode of scientific knowledge and not a method, but a multiplicity of methods linked to the different disciplinary domains being studied (Canguilhem, 1968; Feyerabend, 1975; Ribes, 1993, 1994). Besides scientific and ordinary knowledge (erroneously named in philosophy as 'common sense'), other modes of knowledge can be similarly identified. Ordinary knowledge is embedded in the social practices of language as a shared activity among people with respect to the world. They correspond to what Wittgenstein (1953) called a 'form of life'. All other identifiable modes of knowledge are grounded and make sense only in the general sphere of ordinary language practices. They can extend, modulate, refine, and sometimes correct ordinary knowledge, but they cannot contradict it. No product of special modes of knowledge can be counterintuitive to the ordinary mode. Such modes of knowledge consist of specialized social practices, serving specific purposes, which are adjusted, and even transformed, with the historical change of the social formations in which they occur. This means that the explanatory criteria associated with each mode of knowledge also change historically, and asymmetrically among the different modes, including the ordinary mode.

Modes of knowledge conform to institutional criteria that value the product of knowledge practices socially performed by individuals in different spheres of communal life. They historically emerge various types of episodes of individual knowledge, which we call modes of knowing – and not of knowledge. These modes of knowing have been adapted, in the course of the history of the various social formations, not uniformly or singularly, as validity criteria for the institutional modes of knowledge. Modes of knowing qua individual episodes, participate in all institutional modes of knowing. What distinguishes each of these from the others is a priority criterion regarding the validity of their products or results. Individual modes of knowing consist of episodic activities related to circumstances that can be identified in terms of: a) knowing something by verifying or confirming it in terms of its characteristics or occurrence, b) knowing as a result of obtaining a product or effect due to a systematic practice, c) knowing by revelation or sudden appearance of an unsought relation between events or entities, d) knowing by the recreation of entities or effects outside of their utility, e) knowing by demonstration that a practice, certain objects or events, only make sense in specific contexts, and f) knowing as a consequence of assessing the justification of acts in circumstance, as reasonable acts.

In turn, the formulation of conventional criteria that validate different special forms of obtaining knowledge is noteworthy in the institutional modes of knowledge. Institutional criteria constitute different ways of verifying that the result of a priority mode of knowledge is valid, that is, that it is consistent with an established criterion. Thus, each mode of knowledge correlatively establishes a "truth" criterion by establishing a validity criterion or, better said, of certainty with respect to the obtained knowledge. Consequently, different "truth" or certainty criteria can be recognized and not only the formal criteria of logic or mathematics, or those of the "truths" revealed by the various religions. In empirical knowledge it is untenable to speak of true knowledge or even of plausible knowledge. In any case, the notion of truth can be applied only to the statements of scientific theories, but not to knowledge as such, for otherwise science would not be an open, self-correcting and changing system of knowledge. The institutional modes of knowledge are, namely: a) scientific knowledge through analytical abstraction (and not by direct social experience), and whose validity criterion is the verification or confirmation of the facts under study, b) religious knowledge through interpretation of transcendent signs with respect to the ordinary practical sphere and whose validity criterion is revelation, c) technological knowledge through synthetic materialization of objects, products and effects, and whose validity criterion is the effective production of a result, d) artistic/aesthetic knowledge through the elaboration or re-elaboration of original and unique objects or events, and whose validity criterion is recreation, e) formal knowledge through definitions of abstract/conventional object systems, and whose validity criterion is demonstration, and f) ethical/juridical knowledge through circumstantial argumentation, and whose validity criterion is justification by reasons.

The previous section examined the various forms of explanation, all in specific contexts and of particular events or objects, characteristic of ordinary knowledge. In examining the other specialized modes of knowledge that emerge from and are sustained by ordinary language practices, the impossibility of postulating a privileged form of explanation, supposedly responsible for an idealized true, accurate and rational knowledge, becomes evident. We will attempt to examine and contrast the different 'explanation' forms adopts in each mode of knowledge, without going into it in depth, given the magnitude of the task. However, it is worth mentioning that the modes of knowledge do not constitute "pure" institutional practices. It has already been mentioned that in the practice in each one of them episodically participate all the individual modes of knowledge that historically gave rise, from ordinary language, to the different criteria delimiting their procedure and form of validation. Moreover, these modes of knowledge have sometimes emerged "symbiotically", like fraternal twins or triplets that separate and diverge in time and then intertwine again. This conjugation or synergy of modes of knowledge can occur between two or more modes, and their intertwining is not a mere matter linked to their internal evolution, but is largely conditioned by factors directly linked to the determinants of power institutions and ideological practices of the social formations at each historical moment. As I stated previously (Ribes, 2018), "[T]the current modes of knowledge constitute institutional specializations of hybrid modes, originally merged... these modes of knowledge have gradually been shaped as institutions throughout history (some before others), and do not constitute pure, parallel modes, which are identified as defining or delimiting a specific form of activity" (pp. 28-29).

The combined origin of certain modes of knowledge does not mean that their explanatory criteria are equivalent. On the contrary, it is possible to find similarities between different modes of knowledge. Some modes of knowledge have a common origin. Examples of these are the artistic and technological modes (tecnos in Greek), which at some point also converged with the religious mode, as part of the rituals and the construction of shrines. Architectural technique, sculpture, songs and dances, and objects elaborated as offerings converged in a single social practice, although other manifestations of these same modes of knowledge simultaneously maintained an autonomous practice. While the aim of the artistic object or event was some form of enjoyment, the technological event or object followed a utilitarian aim. While the former was always unique and singular, in contrast, the latter always tended to produce results as similar as possible and elaborated in series. A similar analysis can be made between science and technology, which have been constantly intertwined and with relatively independent histories, as shown by the development of metallurgy, agriculture, architecture, and many other technical activities that emerged before or parallel to the scientific knowledge of mechanics, chemistry, and biology. It is interesting to underscore in this relation the role of technology as auspices of progress of the experimental sciences since the 18th century. Physics, chemistry, and biology would not have made their characteristic advances without technology, which propelled the capacity for experimental research. Technologies are not a simple extrapolation of scientific findings, even if some of them are based on those findings.

The case of the formal mode of knowledge (especially, but not only, that of mathematics) linked with the technological and scientific modes is noteworthy. Geometry and arithmetic as branches of mathematics historically emerged as astronomical observation methods and its applications to agriculture (Kuhn, 1977), as well as a recording and counting system in trade-related activities in tokens, which constituted the first forms of writing (Schumandt-Besserar, 1996, 2007). In both situations, what we now call mathematics fulfilled the same functions that it continues to develop as a transdiscipline (set of methods) with respect to the sciences and other disciplines (music, for example), namely calculation and representation. In turn, Aristotle formulated the first form of formal logic, considered as an analysis of the particular with respect to the general, and thus as a method for demonstrating such relations. Logic thus represented a departure from the analysis of the categories used in language, and from its creative uses in poetics and persuasive uses in rhetoric. Logic and mathematics emerged as methods of scientific and technological disciplines, among others, but they, by themselves, are not disciplines related to events, objects and practices. They later acquired autonomy, and the method became an object of study in itself, which constituted the formal mode of knowledge. However, logic and mathematics do not deal with the world and its happenings, they are empirically empty disciplines. Their objects of knowledge are purely conventional, and deal with the formal properties of specialized languages. Mathematical and logical systems, models, and analogies do not determine the validity of scientific and technological knowledge. They only help to pose problems and questions, to systematize measurements, and to make general descriptions insofar as they dispense with the denotative terms proper to the technical languages of such modes of knowledge. However, logical and mathematical formalization are neither a requirement nor proof of scientificity or technological efficacy.

As anticipated, the nature of the explanation depends on the way of proceeding and the validity criteria of each institutional mode of knowledge. And its 'impurity' opens the possibility that on certain occasions several different forms of explanation of a situation or problem may converge. In one way or another, explaining in the different modes of knowledge consists in circumstantiating the observed relations between events, entities or properties, based on the criteria that define the general procedure in each of these modes and the validity requirement of the obtained or to be obtained knowledge. The following approximate types of explanation in the special modes of knowledge can be tentatively proposed, considering that the particular nature of explanation in the impersonal or interpersonal ordinary mode has already been examined. In the scientific mode of knowledge, explanations systematically circumstantiate the conditions that make possible and limit the relations between entities (taxonomies), events (phenomena) and properties (functional relations). The greater the inclusiveness of the circumstantiation, the greater the explanatory power of the theoretically stated relation. In the technological mode of knowledge, explanations circumstantiate the relations between the operation of standard procedures and their effects. In the formal mode of knowledge, explanations make the rules that define the studied relations and the demonstration of the different ways of following those rules. In the artistic mode of knowledge, to explain is to circumstantiate the singular characteristics of the composition and/or interpretation by recreating what exists or what is imagined. In the ethical/juridical mode of knowledge, to explain is to relate the circumstances that link the motive of the acts to the resulting, socially valued effects (Toulmin, 1950). In the religious mode of knowledge, everyday events are explained as inevitable occurrences due to transcendent circumstances that are presented as a fabricated mystery. Religious explanation is accepted by dogma and, to that extent, consists in adapting the circumstantiation of fables and singular facts to the criteria of dogma. In all modes of knowledge, including ordinary knowledge, explanations are always ways of circumstantiating the relations observed or to be observed within the frame of reference of different criteria of social validity, criteria that are different between cultures and that change in the course of history in the same social formation.

References

Augustine of Hippo (San Augustine). (426/2014). La ciudad de Dios [City of god]. México: Porrúa

Aristoteles (Aristotle). (1995). The complete works (revised trans.), Vols. II & II. Princeton, NJ: Princeton University Press

Austin, J. L. (1962). How to do things with words. Oxford: Oxford University Press

Canguilhem, G. (1968). Etudes d'historie et de philosophie des sciences, concernant les vivants et la vie. Paris: Librairie Philosophique J. Vrin.

Davidson, D. (1980). Reasons, causes, and actions. Oxford: Clarendon Press

Descartes, R. (1937/1980). Discurso del método [Discourse on method]. México: Porrúa

Feyerabend, P. (1975). Against method. Medawah, NJ: Humanities Press

Hanson, N. R. (1972). Observation and explanation: A guide to philosophy of science. London: Allen & Urwin

Hempel, C. G. (1970). Aspects of scientific explanation and other essays on the philosophy of science. New York: MacMillan-Free Press

Hesse, M. B. (1961). A study of action at a distance in the history of physics. New York: Philosophical Library Inc.

Hornsby, J. (1980). Actions. London: Routledge and Kegan Paul

Hume, D. (1740). A treatise of human nature: Being an attempt to introduce the experimental method of reasoning into moral subjects. London: John Noon

Kuhn, T. S. (1977). The essential tension: Selected studies in scientific tradition and change. Chicago: IL: University of Chicago Press.

Plotinus/Porphyry. (254-270/1985. 1992, 1998). Enéadas [Enneads]. Madrid: Gredos

Ribes, E. (1993). La práctica de la investigación científica y la noción de juego de languaje [Scientific research practice and the notion of the language game]. Acta Comportametalia, 1, 63-82.

Ribes, E. (1994). The behavioral dimensions of scientific work. Mexican Journal of Behavior Analysis, 20, 169-194.

Ribes, E. (2007). On two functional meanings of knowing. In: E. Ribes & J. E. Burgos, (Eds.), Knowledge, cognition and behavior (pp. 139-150). Guadalajara: Universidad de Guadalajara

Ribes, E. (2018). El estudio científico de la conducta individual: una introducción a la teoría de la psicología [The scientific study of individual behavior: An introduction to the theory of psychology]. CDMX: El Manual Moderno

Schumandt-Besserat, D. (1996). How writing came about. Austin, TX: University of Texas Press

Schumandt-Besserat, D. (2007). From tokens to writing: The pursuit of abstraction. Semiotics & Linguistics, 175 (3), 182-167.

Tomasini, A. (2016). Razones y causas: Wittgenstein versus Davidson [Reasons and causes: Wittgenstein versus Davidson]. Praxis Filosófica, 43, 13-36.

Toulmin, S. (1950). Reason in ethics. Cambridge: Cambridge University Press

Toulmin, S. (1960). The philosophy of science: An introduction. New York: Harper & Row

Wisdom, J. (1991). Proof and explanation: The Virginia lectures. London: The University Press of America

Wittgenstein, L. (1953). Philosophical investigations. Oxford: Basil Blackwell.

ESSAY THREE: NOTES ON THE GENESIS OF FUNCTIONAL DETACHMENT

I have recently proposed (Ribes, 2018, 2019a, 2019b) functional detachment constitutes the focal analytic process of psychological behavior. Functional detachment describes the establishment of relations between an individual and the surrounding stimulus objects based on her history of contacts, which transcend the immediate situationality of direct physiochemical relations and restrictions, whether induced or enabled by a bioecological or socio-conventional medium. Functional detachment consists in expanding, extending, and modifying the functional relations and properties characterizing the active/reactive patterns (ARPs) with respect to environing stimulus objects and events, including other conspecifics or individuals from other species. Thus, functional detachment initially occurs initially as an extension or replacement of the functions of biological behavior with respect to the properties of stimulus objects and events in the situation. It constitutes the emergence of psychological behavior from biological behavior. Later, additional functional transitions emerge from the first forms of psychological behavior, which occur as contacts by coupling contingencies.

Functional detachment as a process identifying psychological behavior always occurs as new segments of active/reactive patterns in relation to differential environing textures in the form of stimulus objects and events. Psychological behavior is always an individual's functional contact with particular environing entities, which implies changes in the segmentation of biological behavior and in the segmentation of the physiochemical, ecological, and/or sociocultural environing texture. Some of the conditions, circumstances and factors that contribute to the functional detachment and configuration of psychological behavior are outlined in this manuscript in the form of notes, which may be useful for further conceptual and experimental development.

Note 1. Detachment and biological organization

Psychological behavior is an emergent of individual biological behavior, that is, of the changes and movements occurring in the soma or body of individual living beings. However, psychological behavior does not occur in all living beings, but only in one of their 'Kingdoms', namely the animal Kingdom. The organisms of this kingdom are multicellular, have differentiated tissues, possessing sensitivity (as well as irritability), and by the capacity to show local and/or translational movements. These characteristics make animal organisms with differentiated reactive systems, not only for nutrition and reproduction, but also for defense, recognition, and establishment of a territory as a habitat. The development of multiple forms of internal and external sensitivity allows such organisms to interact in a specialized way with different kinds of physical and chemical stimulation that conjointly affect different specialized reactive systems, specifically: vision, hearing, smell, taste, touch, interoception, balance, proprioception, and various forms of mechanical, thermal, pressure or nociception and nonspecific sensitivity, colloquially called 'pain'. In contrast to organisms belonging to the other Kingdoms (prokaryotes, protists, fungi, yeast, lichens, and plants), the specialized and differentiated nature of animal reactive systems implies that the nutritional and reproductive functional processes are diversified and complex due to the reactive sensory specificity and the various forms of self-regulated locomotion that they possess. Nervous tissue is a specialized tissue that emerges with animals, first as ganglia and fibers, and later with a stranded structure. The function of nervous tissue is to interconnect and coordinate the various differentiated and specialized reactive systems of the organism. This accounts for its appearance. Nervous tissue subserves by linking all other types of specialized tissue. Unlike the organisms of the other Kingdoms, in animals, reactivity is integrated in the form of tissues and not isolated cells (including nerve tissue), and the tissues are organized in the form of coordinated functional subsystems. Therefore, animals react functionally rather than substantially to stimulating environing conditions, so that even when direct physiochemical proximal contact are involved, the reactions of animals are of a coordinated and differential character, and not "massive" or undifferentiated from the whole soma. This characteristic of the reactive structure of animals is what enables the emergence of psychological behavior as functional detachment.

Note 2. Reactive systems and functional detachment

It is plausible to suppose that psychological behavior, as a functional detachment of the organism's reactivity to the particular, momentary and unspecific properties of the environing conditions, emerges from the possibility of differentially reacting to specific properties of these conditions in time and space. Thus, psychological behavior is characteristic of the animal Kingdom where cells are organized into functionally specialized tissues, including nervous tissue. Nervous tissue appears together with the other cellular tissues in evolution, each with distinct but coordinated functions to fulfill extremely complex metabolic functions, linked to nutrition and reproduction. Therefore, it is essential to emphasize that psychological behavior does not emerge as a direct consequence of the existence of nervous tissue, but of the organization of the soma into functionally distinct tissues, including nervous tissue. As noted, the function of the nervous tissue is to functionally interconnect the differential reactivity of the set of specialized tissues, integrated as interdependent subsystems in the whole organism. Nervous tissue, whether a single ganglion or a complex encephalized nervous system, regulates and coordinates activities of the various tissues organized as functional subsystems. The activities of each subsystem have effects and are simultaneously affected by the rest of the existing subsystems. Thus, contrary to the neural homunculus model, the nervous system only contacts the activities of the organism itself, that is, with "internal stimulation". It never directly contacts the outside as an agent of the organism's activity (Ribes, 2008) since it is a tissue that by itself lacks sensibility and motility. It participates in articulating the different functions of the organism's subsystems (sensitivity, motility, respiration, nutrition, excretion, reproduction, and others), but these functions are not localized nor do they directly depend on the nervous tissue. It is an additional tissue needed for regulating and coordinating the functional differentiation of the various tissues, integrated as the organism's subsystems. Loeb's pioneering studies (1900) clearly show how nervous tissue emerges on the zoological scale as a consequence of sensorimotor differentiation and not vice versa.

Functional detachment emerges from two dimensions of reactive specificity: sensitivity and self-regulated translation (local motility and displacement). Nervous tissue, just as the tissue of the organism's other subsystems, can show functional differentiation and specialization by coordinating and articulating the activity of the organism's other reactive subsystems, which occasionally leads to erroneously assuming that determining these activities is localized in each one of the functional regions of the nervous system (actually subsystem). The various forms of sensitivity, initially consisting of specific reactive systems to specific modalities of physicochemical stimulation (photic, acoustic, gravitational, mechanical, thermal, pressure, chemical and others), and the various forms of local motricity (orienting, posture, opening/closing of cavities, and others) and locomotion (aquatic, terrestrial or aerial), constitute the necessary condition for the organism to be able to adjust to circumstantial changes in the events of its environment. Functional detachment emerges as a circumstantial adjustment to consistent changes in the stimulating conditions of the environment. The degree of functional detachment possible will depend on the differentiated sensitive proximal and distal reactivity characteristics, as well as on the local or translational motricity available to interact with environing events.

Note 3. Detachment as a spatiotemporal reactive gradient

Functional detachment involves at least three aspects of an organism's reactive interaction with stimulus objects and events. First, reactivity is differential, that is, although the organism acts unitarily, some reactive systems are functionally dominant given the characteristics of the present stimulus conditions. Reactive differentiation involves tissue specialization (not only "receptors", but entire functional systems) with respect to specific physical and chemical stimulating modalities, as occurs with the different sensory (or analyzer) and motor systems that include postural changes, local movements, and locomotion. Reactive specificity allows the organism to differentially interact with diverse environing properties, and this reactivity does not occur "en masse" and by direct proximal contact, as occurs in the prokaryotic, protist, and fungi Kingdoms. Reactive differentiation represents the possibility that different biological functions have related functional autonomy with respect to different stimulatory conditions and circumstances in the environment, and that the same objects can be interacted with at different moments with respect to the different circumstances and properties.

Second, such reactive differentiality implies that some reactive systems are not activated simultaneously in the presence of the stimulus object or event, but may be activated with a delay or non-occurrence of the corresponding reactivity/activity. The phenomenon described in terms of delayed and inhibited reactions allows the organization of interdependent reactive systems at different times as relative dominances in the coordinating and sequencing of their activity. Sechenov (1863) proposed the reflex concept to describe all bodily activity mediated by the nervous system and not exclusively identifiable with the medullary reflex arc. Sechenov proposed that one of the functions of the nervous system consisted in delaying and inhibiting automatic reactions from receptors and effectors, which allowed the emergence of psychological activity, such as memory and thought. Pávlov developed the concept of inhibition in the theory of classical conditioning as a fundamental element of the three general laws of higher nervous activity: the irradiation of excitation and inhabitation, the concentration of excitation and inhibition, and the mutual induction of both "states" from one or the other. Although Pávlov used excitation and inhibition as terms as if they corresponded to distinct or opposite states or processes, in fact he mentioned in one of his writings (Pávlov, 1932) inhibition could be only the excitation of activity incompatible with that which was in act, or be a revolving phase of a single process: "…The issue of the relations between excitation and inhibition thus far remains stubbornly insoluble. Is it a matter of one and the same process which interchanges when conditions lend themselves to it, or of a strongly welded pair animated, in certain circumstances, of a revolving movement and which lets one or the other of its components show more or less, or completely?" (footnote, pp. 384-385). Anokhin (1974), following Pávlov, proposed inhibitory excitation, the effect of which was the replacement of functional patterns.

Third, through sensitivity one responds to a part of the object properties and not to the total or complete stimulus object or condition, as occurs in nutritional cellular episodes. This role of sensitive reactivity (and the associated locomotion in some cases) was what led Aristotle in De Anima to distinguish the nutritive from the sensitive soul, whereby he established that, in the former, the external entity is incorporated by the living being, whereas, in the latter, only reactivity is actualized with respect to its form and not to its substance. Sensitivity constitutes a differential reactive organization to specific and distinct modalities of environing objects and events. Sensitivity may occur with respect to distal objects, events, or conditions, given the characteristics of each physiochemical medium of contact and the reactive organization and complexity of each type of organism. There are proximal forms of reactivity, by direct contact of the stimulus object, event, or condition with the sensitive organism. This reactivity includes mechanical, pressure, gravitational, thermal, and chemical stimulation, modalities that also operate in interoception (Ádám, 1998). These include taste, tactile, thermal, pressure, balance and pain sensitivity, among others. In distal sensitivity, stimulation specifically affects sensitive reactivity as contacts, through a medium (light, water, atmosphere), but at a distance. Given specialized sensitive tissues, chemical, light-magnetic, electromagnetic and mechanical modalities enable visual, auditory, olfactory and various acoustic-mechanical-magnetic modalities, as in fish and bats, among other organisms.

Some reactive patterns may occur including anticipatory fractional reactions to the stimulus event, when interacting distally in time and space with changes in the environment. When the organism possesses locomotion, that is, it can move itself in space in coordination with sensory reactive systems, especially the visual, which allows it to interact distally with stimulus objects and events, either by approaching or withdrawing from them. Sensitivity to distal objects and local and translational motor skills constitute another step forward in the genesis of functional detachment. On the one hand, they make it possible to establish functional contacts with objects that do not directly graze or touch the organism. On the other hand, they allow, as manipulative or orienting movements, the exposure of stimulus properties of objects, not accessible without their direct manipulation or the change of the organism's position with respect to them. Manipulation, which can take place through mechanical acts of the whole body or of localized parts such as the mouth, jaw and dentition, or limbs - including the tail, and locomotion, contribute to the formation of complex active/reactive patterns. The organism's own activity changes the environmental stimulating conditions through these patterns by producing the presence of new stimulus modalities in objects and events. Organisms alter the stimulatory texture of their environment with local and translational motricity, forming new active/reactive systems such as haptic (Jones, 2018), which involve more complex forms of functional organization, both in their differential impact and in the functional coordination they require.

In short, functional detachment is enabled through differential sensitivity to different forms of environmental stimulation, the organization of that sensitivity based on relative forms of functional dominance, the emergence of distal reactivity to stimulus objects and events in the environment, the self-regulated exposure in time and space to stimulus conditions through local and translational motricity, and change in stimulation conditions brought about by locomotion and manipulation. The regulation of the temporal and spatial distance from the conditions of stimulation is undoubtedly a significant step in making possible new forms of functional detachment in psychological behavior.

Note 4. On extra-situational temporal and spatial distancing

A different form of spatiotemporal distancing occurs when the organism responds recurrently to the stimulus conditions after a lapse of time, or when it does so in the absence of the original stimulus condition in the situation. This type of distancing is related to the different functional forms of the generically and ambiguously so-called 'memory' episodes. All the episodes thus described are not only characterized by the time lapse between two occurrences of A/R patterns with respect to a first stimulation, but also primarily by the recurrence of motor, local, or translation patterns (including those occurring when verbalizing, gesturing, or writing) included in these episodes. One speaks of 'memory' only when an A/R pattern (or a fraction thereof) that occurred previously in that situation or in another situation recurs. However, the episodes that meet this requirement comprise virtually all psychological behavior, so that it is necessary to distinguish between different types of recurrence in temporally distant circumstances in the same situation or in different situations. Although I have already examined at length the different functional meanings of 'memory' family terms (Ribes, 2018, chapters 2 and 11), I will distinguish between some types of episode based on the possible functional detachment that occurs in temporal distancing.

All episodes ordinarily encompassed under the family term 'memory' are characterized as recurrent episodes, that is, episodes that recur in some or all of their components. Actually, recurrence does not lie in the strict repetition of A/R patterns as behavior, but rather in a recurrence of episodes occurring in functionally related situations. Within the diversity of functional episodes covered by the conceptual ambiguity of the term 'memory', the following aspects are noteworthy: a) the recurrence of an interaction as a functional episode in situations separated in time, b) the fragmentary or complete recurrence of an A/R pattern in the subsequent situation, c) the reoccurring A/R pattern's characteristics and its functional segmentation with other non-conventional or conventional A/R patterns, d) the "similarity" of dispositional circumstances in the situation in which the recurrence occurs, and e) the recurrence of fragmentary or complete stimulus conditions in the subsequent situation. Obviously, depending on the dominant aspects in each episode, the functional detachment that takes place can be characterized differently, although in most cases these are contacts by coupling contingencies, and sometimes contacts by alteration, extension, or transformation contingencies.

Repeating the same A/R pattern in the same situation over time does not represent any form of detachment based on temporal distancing. The most elementary form of temporal distancing is the so-called "delayed reaction", in which an interval is imposed between the observation of the stimulus object to which one has to interact and the possibility of doing so. It is well known that this form of temporal distancing is only possible, at least initially, through the participation of postural or orienting components in the A/R patterns of animals, and of verbal components in humans. The 'memory' lies in the added participating patterns. In these cases, which illustrate functional contacts by coupling, the individual's fractional A/R patterns "cover" the temporal distance between the presentation of the stimulus object and the possibility of responding when it is no longer perceptible, so that the individual herself, through her behavior, supplements the stimulus conditions that shape present or future contingencies. The opposite of any form of recurrence of an A/R pattern in a subsequent situation, forgetting, does not constitute a case of lack of functional detachment, but simply results from the failure to register or observe the stimulus condition, or to act in the original situation. For this reason it makes sense to "remember" those episodes in which the individual actively participates in doing something, and it is only incorrectly assumed that she observed or attended to the present conditions and circumstances.

A special case is the migratory behavior characteristics of animal behavior in aggregations. Apparently, migration seems to be a recurrent manifestation of a cyclically repeated memory of the species. However, in migratory behaviors what occurs is the continuous recognition of difference changing stimulus circumstances, which differentially affect the activation of A/R patterns shared by the aggregation of individuals. These include temperature, available food, polarized light, hormonal and other changes in the organism. Distances are traveled over long periods of time, but the response is not to distant stimulus conditions in time and space, but to present conditions that vary gradually and continuously. Another type of remembering corresponds to the "projective" character of memory, as pointed out by Kantor (1924-1926). Remembering does not imply responding to events in the past, but to interact in such a way in the present that what has been acted upon serves as a recurrent vestige at a later time. In this sense, the verbal repetition of words or phrases by themselves or as a reference to actions to be performed or stimulus conditions to be recognized should be emphasized. The A/R pattern to recur partially or totally in a subsequent situation can occur in a stereotyped manner, as a narrative, or as a graphic record. At the level of human history, narration and writing constitute the condition that defines its own memory as a species. In ontogeny or individual becoming, 'memory', as recollection, always appears in relation to those circumstances in which the individual had linguistic A/R patterns at her disposal.

Remembering as a form of detachment consists in recognizing a fragment of the stimulus conditions with respect to which one acted in the original situation, while evoking consists in a linguistic interaction with respect to a fragment of a subsequent situation as if it were the fragment acted upon. In the former, the fragmentary stimulus condition is present and is recognized as a component of a functional configuration. In the latter, the fragmentary stimulus condition is introduced or presented by the individual in the situation, thereby changing its functional circumstances. There are two forms of evoking, namely directed and spontaneous. Directed evoking is a directed recollection in which the individual linguistically interacts with herself in order to recognize or make present a stimulus condition in the situation. Spontaneous evoking consists in recalling as an affective and ineffective reaction in a situation, based on an incidental stimulus component that does not functionally characterize said situation. It is "feeling" as in another time and place. This form of recollection, as evoking, should be distinguished from reminiscence or, in its most complete version, déjà vu, since in this circumstance the situation shares functional components equal but not identical to those of a previously experienced situation. Evoking comprises, in some episodes, an active alteration of the stimulus component, either by interacting with it in the situation, or by evoking it in a new situation. In the former, the name, designation, or repetition of the stimulus component is included as part of a larger referential A/R pattern, so that the verbal fragment functionally articulates with more recurrent referential patterns. This type of "amalgamated" evoking is usually called "encoding" in traditional psychology, and corresponds to many of the popular mnemonic practices. In the latter case, the reproduction of stimulus condition is graphically (drawing), or verbally (narrative) altered. As Bartlett (1932) showed, evoking is not a reproduction but a reconstruction of the original stimulus condition.

This diversity of episodes related to the term 'memory' are examples of different forms of functional detachment involving temporal and spatial distancing between two interacting situations. Most of these episodes require the participation of linguistic A/R patterns and are unique to human behavior. To be clear: None of the various meanings of "memory" are related to any storage or retrieval processes of what has been stored in the past. All psychological interactions and episodes (as those studied by the other empirical sciences) are events occurring in the present. There is no past or future event, only vestiges or prognoses. The history of psychological behavior always occurs in the present, as the initial condition of any interaction or contact.

Note 5. Detachment and linguistic A/R patterns

In principle, the conventional (and biologically arbitrary) nature of the A/R patterns involved in the different language modes –the individual's practices in society (listening, observing, reading, speaking, gesturing, and writing), allows them to detach from any property or situational component. Non-conventional A/R patterns are enabled by ecological and physiochemical contact media, while conventional patterns do not inevitably or necessarily hold a specific or unspecific correspondence with diverse stimulus conditions. The multivocal characteristic of ordinary language expressions and terms is a case in point. No term or expression in ordinary language has a single sense or meaning, but rather these are given by the practice occurring under a given context (Wittgenstein, 1953). Linguistic A/R patterns initially appear as speaking and gesturing (and their corresponding reactive modes, namely listening and observing). They are not topography-based configurations but are configured by their functional properties in the various practices, as well as by a diversified set of "internal" relations conforming the different referential practical domains. This characteristic endows A/R patterns with a wide potential for detachment throughout the individuals' life course and the historical cycles of social collectives. In fact, we collectively interact with the 'world' in which we live through the various referential practices (what Wittgenstein referred to when he spoke of language as a "second nature"). The multivocal quality of ordinary language emerges from the impossibility of a purely denotative language. Such a language would consist of an ideal language in which there would be a word or written sign for each elementary property at the existing physiochemical, ecological, or social level. It would be a micromolecular, infinite, and redundant language. For this reason, language is denotative only in very limited circumstances, wherein it is precisely restricted to the action of univocally naming or designating certain properties, entities, or events as part of a technical language. However, technical language can only be practiced in the context of the referential practices of ordinary language. Thus, the substitution of words for objects, as traditionally posited in semantic and logical theories, is rare. Words are part of practices and are not substitutes for objects or events. As components of a given referential practice, words or phrases only functionally substitute events or entities when they allow interaction with them at a distance, in time and/or space. If the practical circumstance is not given, it is incorrect to speak of signs or words as

76

substitute or substitute stimuli.

Prominent examples of the non-denotative character of linguistic practice are Bühler's (1934) deixis and Ryle's (1949) 'index' words. Index words are terms that are part of expressions relating to the situationality of the speaker, and which by themselves lack referential meaning. The reference is the person who expresses them when relating to others. As opposed to any denotative or designative interpretation, index words only make sense in context. The situation in which they take place gives them meaning as part of an expression. There are four general types of deictics or deixis: of person (I), of social status (the sir), of space (here), and of time (after). 'Index' words or compounds are obvious examples of the detachability of linguistic A/R patterns. They only make sense in the functional context of referential practices and can be "located' or "applied" in different situations. They are expressions that manifest detachment from particular persons, status, places or moments. Many of them may be part of contacts by coupling or alteration contingencies, but others may be part of comparison, extension or even transformation contingencies. As a general concluding remark, it should be emphasized that detachment in language (as a medium of contact) and through linguistic A/R patterns is configured in the form of episodes, interactions and relations with respect to conventional events and objects, but always between persons. Examples of this are what Wittgenstein (1953) illustrated as various language games as well as others such as informing, advising, arguing, persuading, warning, recommending, criticizing, and many more consisting of episodes that take place exclusively as patterns in linguistic modes.

It is important to note that there are two types of linguistic detachment characterized by the silent nature of speech, which precedes silent reading and silent writing. In the latter two, the silent character is fostered by the fact that reading and writing are performed individually and, most of the time, alone. No other listener or reader is needed apart from the individual. When the active/reactive patterns of reading and writing are acquired, these patterns can be accompanied by the corresponding speaking behavior. Once these patterns are established, it is only in special circumstances, such as in public reading of texts or in supervised writing, that what is read or written is said. There are other kinds of circumstances in which the speaker may interact silently with herself, namely in episodes in which she acts as both speaker and listener in the form of soliloquy, or as discussant with respect to conventional objects that she herself or others "produce", either by speaking or writing, in the form of colloquy (see Ribes, 2018 for extension and transformation contacts). Soliloquy and colloquy should not be confused as speaking alone, either silently or aloud, as when repeating a telephone number in a low voice, or as when speaking aloud, while alone, while going to do something or reacting to something. In all these cases, the silent nature of linguistic behavior does not represent any form of "private" activity or events, but underlines its detachable nature from any event, entity or situation. One can speak, read and write without phonation, for linguistic patterns bear no relation of necessity or inevitability to any physiochemical or biological condition. Their conventional character determines that they can occur even without constituting stimulus events for others. They constitute a universe of occurrences that do not correspond to the conditions that "explain" inorganic and organic events and entities. This is the abysmal difference between human language and the various expressive forms of animal behavior: there is no silent animal communication. It should not be surprising, therefore, that the detachability of linguistic behavior, achieved in the course of social history and individual becoming, has fostered the belief in spiritual instances residing within human beings, a belief actualized in the form of mind or cognition. Biological behavior cannot be detached in the same way as linguistic behavior. Instead of taking the form of silent behavior, it occurs, at best, as "simulated" behavior in some mammals as well as humans, as motor manifestations that do not correspond to ineffective and affective sensory and vegetative patterns.

Note 6. Final reflection

Although it does not always seem to be so for psychologists, it is clear that the abovementioned type of episodes is unique to relations between humans and human psychological contacts. Detachment in and through language, as an A/R pattern, detaches the individual from motor and stimulus objects (and thus from situationally determined sensibility), so that many of the practices and functional objects in human episodes are purely linguistic. The enabling character of language for the occurrence of psychological and social behavior is so evident that it is only necessary to imagine two extreme situations and ask ourselves whether such behaviors take place in them. The first would be one in which language does not exist and relations between individuals only take place on the basis of motor skills and sensitivity. The second would be one in which an individual is placed in a social formation whose natural language she does not know, for which there is no approximate translation, and whose customs and artifacts do not correspond to her own. In both cases, psychological behavior in a conventional medium of contact cannot occur. In the first case, only contacts proper to situational detachment can be established. In the second, it is even unlikely that such contacts can be established. The genesis of the possibility of functional detachment follows a peculiar path. It begins as a differentiated biological reaction at a distance from the properties of the stimulus objects, with the simultaneous presence of local motricity and locomotion, and concludes in circumstances in which the presence of the stimulus objects and most of the motricity is not necessary, concentrating the interactions on local conventional objects and movements, sometimes of the isolated person. Due to their conventional nature, linguistic A/R patterns differ from sensory or motor A/R patterns in one fundamental characteristic: with the exception of gesturing, one can talk and write about what is spoken and written, as well as what is perceived and done. In contrast, one cannot sensorially perceive what one perceives, nor can one move the movement. It is precisely the reflexive nature of language that endows conventional A/R patterns with an infinite possibility of circumstances and ways of functional detachment.

For these reasons, although animals and humans certainly share two types of functional contacts, coupling and alteration contingencies, it is evident that the characteristics and complexity of the conformed fields in the two types of contacts are not comparable, given the conventional nature of human A/R patterns from the first months of life, as well as the contingency relations configuring the human environment. Considering these qualitative differences between animals and humans, we can characterize the different types of functional detachment as psychological contact as follows: (a) in coupling contacts there is a detachment from the physicochemical and biological constraints of the individual's reactive patterns, as well as from the functional physicochemical properties of the stimulus objects; (b) in alteration contacts there is a detachment from the spatiotemporal constraints of the relations between stimulus objects and behavior in a given situation; c) in comparison contacts there is functional detachment from the particular objects and their absolute properties and dimensions in the situation; d) in extension contacts there is detachment from the circumstantiality of the present situation, including its dispositional dimensions; and e) in transformation contacts there is detachment from the functional characteristics of a referential practice in a given domain. Each psychological contact implies a criterion that delimits its functional circumstantiality: (a) in coupling contacts the criterion has to do with the practical conformation of behavior to environmental contingencies (whether ecological or social), (b) in alteration contacts the criterion relates to the change or modification in the occurrence or in the properties of environmental components as an effect of individual behavior, c) in comparison contacts the criterion involves judgments about differences and equivalences with respect to the functional properties of behavior and stimulus objects, d) in extension contacts, the criterion emphasizes the transfer of functional forms of participation between situations, and e) in transformation contacts, the criterion consists of the delimitation of new functional domains and the corresponding reorganization of already existing referential practices.

References

Ádám, G. (1998). Visceral perception: Understanding internal cognition. New York: Plenum Press.

Anokhin, P.K. (1974). Biology and neurophysiology of the conditioned reflex and its role in adaptive behavior. Oxford: Pergamon Press.

Aristóteles. (1978, Spanish trans.). Acerca del alma. Madrid: Gredos.

Bartlett, F.C. (1932). Remembering: A study in experimental and social psychology. Cambridge: Cambridge University Press.

Bühler, K. (1934, 1982 traducción inglesa). Theory of language: The representational function of language. Amsterdam: John Benjamins Pu- blishing Company.

Jones, L.A. (2018). Haptics. Cambridge, MA: The MIT Press.

Kantor, J.R. (1924-1926). Principles of psychology. New York: Alfred Knopff.

Loeb, J. (1900). Comparative physiology of the brain and comparative psychology. New York: G. P: Putnam´s Sons.

Pavlov, I.P. (1932, Spanish trans. 1973). Intento de interpretación fisiológica de la sintomatología de la histeria, In: Actividad nerviosa superior: obras escogidas (pp. 375-393). Barcelona: Fontanella.

Ribes, E. (2008). Brain and behavior: Misunderstandings and mis- conceptions regarding an asymmetric relationship. En J.E. Burgos & E. Ribes (Coords,), The brain-behavior Nexus: Conceptual issues (pp.101-122). Guadalajara: Universidad de Guadalajara.

Ribes, E. (2018). El estudio científico de la conducta individual: introducción a la teoría de la Psicología. CDMX: El Manual Moderno.

Ribes, E. (2019a). ¿Teoría de la conducta o teoría de la psicología? En Diego Zilio y Kester Carrara (Eds.), Behaviorismos: Reflexоes históricas e conceituais. Sao Paulo: Paradigma.

Ribes, E. (2019b). Acerca del objeto de conocimiento de la psicología. Acta Comportamentalia, 27.

Ryle, G. (1949), The concept of mind. New York: Barnes & Noble.

Sechenov, I.M. (1863, 1978 Spanish trans). Los reflejos cerebrales. Barcelona: Fontanella.

Wittgenstein, L. (1953). Philosophical investigations. Oxford: Basil Blackwell.

ESSAY FOUR: REACTIVE ACTIVATION AND DISPOSITIONAL FUNCTIONS: A MULTIDISCIPLINARY REFLECTION

(Co-author Víctor Eduardo Fuentes Barradas)

A legacy of the psychology of the faculties of the soul has been to distinguish between two separate functions, which interact in determining what the individual does or experiences: what they know how to do and what they want to do. Initially, these faculties of the soul or mind corresponded, on the one side, to knowledge (perception and judgement) and, on the other, to affection and will. Later, with the advent of evolutionary thought, instinct or drive and habit arose as equivalent axes of these two general faculties. Today, the traditional faculties of the soul or mind have been transformed into two complementary but independent types of processes: learning or cognition, and motivation and emotion. It is assumed that drive states or motives procure an "energetic" condition that increases the activity of the organism or individual, in a general form or with certain directionality, depending on the presence or absence of specific drive-stimuli, conditional stimuli, discriminative stimuli, or internal "representations". For their part, the stimulus objects or events, toward which the activity is directed, attract or repel the individual on the basis of their incentive value or their hedonic or aversive properties. In all these conceptions, a logic prevails that divides the individual's psychological behavior into two or three autonomous partitions: what they know or perceive, what they desire or want, and what they do. Operant theory does not formally establish this division. However, it emphasizes deprivation and similar operations, such as instructions (establishing operations: Michael, 1982, 1988, 1993), which determine whether the consequent events are reinforcing or aversive. In this theory, behavior that is stably emitted (or suppressed) is a direct function of the consequences to which it is exposed, so that an initial contact with the consequent stimuli, incidental or instigated, is posited. Depending on the reinforcing (positive, negative) or punitive (also positive and negative) properties, such behavior continues to occur in a certain pattern, or may decrease if it already occurs frequently. In operant theory, doing, wanting to do, and knowing how to do is a function of reinforcement, and not doing, not wanting to do, and not doing is a function of punishment or absence of reinforcement. In operant theory, the concepts of reinforcement and punishment account for all the explanatory functions, without the formulation of other concepts that incorporate the rest of the experiential operations that make the behavior-consequence relation possible. All these traditions, whether they dichotomize the behavioral processes or do not represent *theoretically* the experimental operations employed, posit that action as doing or knowing how to do, and motivation as wanting, desiring to do or following or not doing, interact as additive or multiplicative algebraic linear functions and, usually, as stable discrete segments.

In contrast to these theoretical approaches, the field logic formulated by J. R. Kantor (1924-1926) proposes a molar analysis of psychological behavior in terms of interdependent relations between setting factors, the individual's reactive systems, and stimulus properties of objects, made possible by one or more media of contact. Psychological behavior arises from the interdependent relations of these field-factors. This is conceived as a functional contact between the individual (based on their reactive systems) and an object as a segment of stimulation in the environment, based on the facilitating or interfering effects of situational and historical setting factors in the present field. Functional contact consists of a semi-stable system of interdependent contingency relations between the individual's reactive dimensions and the stimulus dimensions of objects and events in the environment (Ribes, 2018). In turn, setting factors consist of reactive biography biases, determined by the individual's interactional history, as well as by fluctuating biological states in the individual and their correspondence with fluctuating states and properties of stimulus objects and events, which make them *momentarily* functionally relevant. These stimulus objects are identified as dispositionally relevant objects (DROs). All functional contact is modulated by historical and situational setting factors that occur at the beginning and during the episode encompassed by a contingency field, respectively. Both types of setting factors facilitate or interfere with the initial and subsequent reactivity of the individual during the interactions that make up a given functional contact. Form this point of view, setting factors place the individual in *circumstance* with respect to a field of contingencies of occurrence in which a functional contact will occur.

In a field logic, the concept of setting factors replaces the traditional dichotomy between learning/knowledge and motivation/emotion, as well as the dualistic antecedents that support it in its mechanistic and vitalistic variants. This concept also discards causal attributions to motives, drives or similar 'variables', and assumes that setting factors partially modulate transitory changes in the directionality, vigor, and persistence of the individual's reactive/active patterns when interacting with stimulus objects and events. Dispositional functions are conceived as continuous, changing gradient of activation-deactivation of the individual's reactive systems with respect to stimulus objects and events in the environment. The setting factors comprising this permanent functional gradient in the psychological field influence the initiation, permanence, and termination of functional contacts. Dispositionality, to this extent, can only be analyzed in relation to the facilitation or interference of functional contacts, but never independently of them. There are no setting factors *per se*. Following this reasoning, it makes no sense to argue that there are stimulus objects or events that have "motivational" properties *per se*, or that the individual's historical experiences are indiscriminate determinants of their behavioral tendencies. Setting factors do not motivate, impel, please, displease, generate aversion, incentivize, or "energize". They are not independent of the individual's activity or the circumstances in which it occurs.

In this paper we propose a multidisciplinary reflective exercise, of a psychobiological nature, to characterize the dispositional functions that facilitate specific forms of reactivity directed to stimulus objects and events, as initial or transitional components of nonspecific patterns of *reactive activation* of the individual as a molar biological system.

The premise of this analysis is that setting factors are not events or entities but constitute relations between states and properties or functional characteristics of the individual's reactive systems and the states of the objects and conditions of the environment. At least two fluctuating or variant conditions always converge, one dependent on the biological states and interactive history of the individual and the other dependent on the general physicochemical states of the environment and the specific states and characteristics of the objects and events present. For this reason, setting factors cannot be identified with experimental operations, nor with particular objects or stimulus changes. Whereas objects and stimulus changes have dispositional properties momentarily and circumstantially in relation to the biological and historical states of the individual, experimental operations only indicate the changes that the researcher makes to propitiate, induce or restrict the dispositional conditions in the environment and in the individual. However, these operations, like the concepts describing them, do not correspond to processes taking place in the situation. Such operations or instructions are not covariant in real time and space to the changes that occur in the individual-environment relation in the form of setting factors. These changes are always observed as variations in the propensity and tendency of the individual's behavior, both in terms of its directionality and its vigor, persistence, preference and variation, as relevant molar dimensions.

In short, setting factors are not events or entities that are simultaneous or parallel to the individual's functional contacts with the stimulus objects. As factors, they are circumstances that contribute to the occurrence of an outcome and are therefore manifested in the transitions and variations that occur during functional contacts. They contribute to determining the *mo-*

mentary functional relevance of stimulus objects and events, as evidenced by the changes observed during the transition states of deprivation-satiety, orientation-habituation, startle-adaptation, and others. From the perspective of the individual's biological states, variations in general reactivity may be due to the presence of relatively prolonged states, such as those characterizing sleep-wake cycles or those traditionally called "moods" (Ryle, 1949), or to relatively momentary sates, which temporarily characterize the individual's differential reactivity-activity thresholds and the directionality of specific patterns.

Activation, Deactivation, and Changes in Dispositionality

It is important to delimit the term 'dispositionality' before proceeding further. This term only economically covers the dispositional functions of facilitation and interference of active/reactive patterns (ARPs) specific to properties of stimulus objects and events, and nonspecific to the activity thresholds of the individual's various biological reactive systems. The reactive systems of psychological behavior constitute new functional segmentations of differential interaction with specific circumstances with respect to stimulus objects and events in the environment, that is, dispositionally relevant objects (DROs). But such reactive systems always constitute primarily manifestations of the individual's biological reactive systems. All psychological reactive systems involve biological reactive systems. There are no psychological reactive systems that are foreign or morphologically and functionally independent of biological reactivity. However, the functional configuration of the reactive systems in psychological behavior cannot be reduced to that which characterizes in each case the biological reactive systems as such, that is, as a molar organization of the vital functions of the organism.

The relevance of the concept of activation (Duffy, 1962; Malmo, 1959) is emphasized in order to systematize the understanding of how biological reactivity participates in response to changes of stimulation in the environment. This participation modulates the differential activity configuration of sensory and musculoskeletal patterns with respect to object properties and stimulus events in a variety of circumstances. Activation is considered from a multidisciplinary perspective, that is, as a psychological concept integrating relevant biological knowledge, in this case, for the analysis of setting factors and functions. In proposing this concept, Malmo (1959) commented "…to include the work often referred to by the term "psychophysiology." This usage implies that the chief problems being studied are psychological ones, and it also stresses the importance of neurophysiological techniques… I believe that it will be sufficient to say that in using the term "activation" I am referring to the intensive dimension of behavior. I believe that it will be sufficient to say that in using the term "activation" I am referring to the *intensive* dimension of behavior." (p. 367, footnote). In this sense, this paper will examine the logical utility of the concept of activation to systematize the interrelation of diverse states and patterns of biological reactivity with changes in directionality and vigor of the individual's reactive/active patterns, which are part of the various functional contacts of psychological behavior. For this reason, and to emphasize the psychological nature of the concept, we will speak of *reactive activation,* and not only of activation, which is a concept proper to biology.

Reactive activation, as a psychological concept, is not restricted only to the degree of energy release (of a physical nature) linked to the metabolism of the whole organism, but includes consequent changes in the extent and intensity of the functioning of the different systems of the individual organism, as well as induced activity, not necessarily correlated with the degree of activation, as exemplified by paralysis under intense conditions of stimulation (Duffy, 1962). In contrast to a purely physiological analysis, the psychological perspective includes reactive systems as forms of reactivity historically organized in the life of the individual and, to that extent, activation not only affects the differential intensity of different biological reactive systems but is also related to differential changes in the directionality of behavior with respect to the stimulus conditions in the environment. Three distinguishable, yet articulated, systems are involved in reactive activation: a) sensory reactive systems, which constitute ineffective response systems, b) glandular response systems, which constitute affective response systems, and c) motor response systems, which constitute effective response systems (Kantor, 1924-1926; Ribes, 2018). The logic of reactive activation, as a psychological concept, is that of a dispositional category (Ryle, 1949). Dispositional categories do not refer to singular occurrences, activities or entities, but point to tendencies or propensities, identifiable only as collections of occurrences, whether simultaneous or successive, that is, as situational or historical circumstances. In turn, activation, as a physiological concept, refers to the activity of the biological system and to changes in these activities and their structures, so that its use does not obey a dispositional logic but rather that of a category of process or state. Nevertheless, knowledge of the interactions of the states of the organism, as a continuum of activation, in relation to cyclic conditions, or induced by stimulation and changes in the environment, are indispensable for understanding the differential activation of psychological reactive systems and their directionality in a dispositional continuum, not necessarily symmetrical. In the case of setting factors, as a field-laden concept, the term has a terminological and meaning coincidence with the logical category of disposition: it means 'to place in circumstance', and is in contact with many terms used in the past, such as 'mood', 'readiness', and 'preparedness', among others.

The dispositional logic of the concept of reactive activation comprises a multidimensional continuum. This continuum includes two types of activation: nonspecific and specific, as well as five 'sources' of induction: changes in the states of the organism, physio-chemical characteristics oof environmental stimulation, reactive history of the individual, functional properties of stimulus objects and events, and concurrent effects of the individual's own activity displayed as a side of their reactive/active patterns. These last five dimensions contribute significantly to giving directionality to changes in vigor and persistence of psychological behavior. The concept of activation also implies that of *deactivation*, originally employed by Solley and Murphy (1960). Deactivation constitutes the complementary intensive and extensive component of activation in a dispositional continuum. This allows to posit the permanent operation of dispositional functions in any psychological behavioral segment, in the form of differential activation-deactivation transitions with respect to stimulus objects and events and the various reactive/active patterns of the individual.

Nonspecific activation is related to exposure to changes in the intensity and type of stimulation and to abrupt changes in environing conditions. In the case of nonspecific deactivation, this is related to extreme conditions in the state of the organism (sleep, intoxication, stupor, extreme fatigue, extreme weakness, and the like), or relatively prolonged extreme environing conditions (high or low temperatures, and high or low intensities of stimulation in any modality). In these cases, four patterns can be produced in the organism: general deactivation, habituation (prolonged sustained stimulation), adaptative reactions (vascular, hormonal and muscular, including the general adaptation syndrome identified by Selye in 1950 —called stress), or extreme defensive reactions (paralysis due to startle, inactivity due to "learned helplessness", or sensitization due to decreased reaction thresholds).

Specific activation is related to conditions of short-term deprivation (of food, water, sensory stimulation), the presentation of brief and/or intense supra-threshold stimuli (distracting stimuli, stimuli new to the situation, sti-

90

muli inducing "emotional circumstances" that interrupt ongoing activity), to defense reactions in the form of withdrawal or manipulating patterns, and to orientation-approximation reactions in the form of postural, locomotion, and manipulating patterns. Specific deactivation always occurs in the form of a new, different activation.

Each type of activation, as a dispositional function, has an extended character. In the case of nonspecific activation, the extension occurs as the affectation in prolonged times of the reactive thresholds to stimulation and of organized general activity. In turn, specific activation consists of initial organized biological patterns, such as orientation and defense reactions or reflexes (Sokolov, 1963), and their functional extension in the form of reactive/active patterns participating in functional contacts, which include postural and locating reactions (specific and nonspecific), search (specific displacement), inspecting (orientation with displacement on stimulus objects), and manipulating (movement producing changes in objects). A concise review of each of these forms of extended reactive activation will follow, highlighting their dispositional relevance with respect to the vigor and persistence of the activity, as well as the reactive/active differential as directionality to functionally relevant objects in each particular situation. Obviously, this is not an updated and/or systematic review of biological activation patterns as such. Thus, we do not review the recent literature in neurophysiology, which otherwise seems rather interested in supposed correlations and localization of ordinary psychological phenomena. In fact, the analysis of biological processes as such can contribute little to the understanding of functional contacts constituting psychological behavior. The aim is to present, in an organized manner, experimental reports relevant to the analysis of reactive activation as a dispositional concept in the analysis of psychological behavior. For this reason, the processes occurring in the central nervous system, the autonomic nervous system and their patterns coordinated with the various subsystems (respiratory, cardiovascular, digestive, immune, musculoskeletal, and others) are not discussed in depth. Rather, emphasis is placed on some aspects related to sensorial quality and motricity and the determination of their thresholds. It is worth adding that in this context, the term 'analyzer', coined by Pavlov (1927) to describe each of the sensory subsystems (including the kinesthetic and, later, the interoceptive), which has a logic similar to that of the reactive system in field theory, is often used.

Nonspecific and Specific Reactive Activation Patterns

Dispositionality, to place in circumstance, is behaviorally supported by the activation of active-reactive patterns (ARPs) which, in turn, make the stimulus objects to which they are presented relevant or irrelevant. Activation participates in functional contact by altering non-directional and directional thresholds. The former are nonspecifically related to the intensity of the ARP, for instance, nonspecific or generalized orientation, nonspecific defense, adaptation, and deactivation. All are dependent on intensive properties of the situation and the state of the organism. The latter are related to directional thresholds establishing familiarity and differentiation of the situation. These are: specific orientation, which includes locating, search, inspecting, and manipulating; specific defense, which includes partial immobility, avoidance and attack, and the various specific adaptive reactions, all dependent on properties that are also specific or that characterize a dispositionally relevant object (DRO).

There are a number of factors that affect the nonspecific activation-deactivation continuum, altering the thresholds of sensory and motor reactivity, both in terms of orientation, defense and adaptive reactions. One of the most important group of factors are drugs, whose isolated or combined administration, and in differential doses, alter the sensory and motor reactivity of the organism to different degrees and levels, increasing or reducing sensitivity to exteroceptive and interoceptive stimulation, enhancing or disturbing different motor functions, and altering the various forms of sensory-motor coordination. The group of drugs that affect behavior include antipsychotics, anxiolytics, antidepressants, stimulants, hypnotics, hallucinogens (or psychotomimetics as opposed to antipsychotics), analgesics, and others such as atropine, cocaine, reserpine, and tetrahydrocannabinol (see Thompson & Schuster, 1968). The dispositional effects of these drugs are neither singular nor direct and depend, among other things, on the functional properties of the behavior under examination, the dose used, the situation in which they are administered, and their interaction with other biological factors (age, nutritional condition, other drugs administered, among others).

It should also be noted that nonspecific generalized deactivation, characteristic of anesthesia, induction of coma states, or deep sleep, does not symmetrically affect full body reactivity. Lindsley and colleagues (Lindsley, 1956, 1957, 1960; Mednick & Lindsley, 1958; Lindsley, Hobika, & Etsten, 1961;

Lindsley & Conran, 1962) employed conjugate escape procedure to assess the degree of consciousness of sleeping persons subjected to insulin coma, hypnotic trance, electroconvulsive shock, or anesthesia. Lindsley compared the escape response to a continuous auditory stimulus presented by headphones. Pressing a knob decreased the intensity and duration of the 60-decibel stimulus. The reduction or absence of response was an index of loss of consciousness (or perception of the stimulus as a sub-threshold stimulus under such conditions). The escape procedure was more sensitive than body activity as an index of loss of consciousness, and more sensitive in indicating recovery of consciousness compared to measures such as EEG, verbal report, and body activity. The precise physiological processes involved in hypnotic trance are unknown (Barber, 1969; Fromm & Nash, 1992). However, hypnosis can be used, depending on the suggestibility of individuals, to induce analgesia and anesthesia in dental and medical practice, as well as to selectively direct sensory and motor reactivity to verbal stimuli. Finally, it is important to note that, in some cases, nonspecific activation can produce specific deactivation of defense reactions, as occurs in the case of nociception (pain). It is well known from testimonies of war injuries or travel accidents, a high general activation, such as the one that characterizes violent or competitive interactions, is accompanied by a high adrenergic discharge (adrenaline and noradrenaline), a substance that, as a neurotransmitter, inhibits the activity of nociceptive receptors. Adrenergic production is reduced until the end of the excitation episode and nociceptive stimulation is reacted with pain.

Nonspecific activation participates in contact as *initial* reactivity without specific directionality to objects; it is reactive activation produced by changes of stimulation in intensity, location, cyclicity, etc. It can be seen as a gradient in which the degree of activation participates modulating intensive aspects of the contact. Nonspecific activation modulates the adience thresholds through orientation, the abience thresholds through defense, those of permanence through adaptation, and the metabolic levels related to adaptation and de-activation. In turn, specific activation participates in the contact by varying the contacted properties by regulating directionality and permanence *during* contact with specific stimulus objects in the contingency field. Exposure to haptic and conventional-dominated properties of the stimulus objects and differential reactivity changes the stimulus circumstances and affects dispositionality, so that it is not only affected by it as in the nonspecific case.

Activation-Deactivation Continuum of Nonspecific Patterns

Nonspecific patterns are functional reorganizations of the activity and analyzer systems of the organism with respect to setting factors, generally extended in time, of high intensity and chronic. Nonspecific activation is affected by the intensity, noxiousness, duration or prolongation of the condition at hand; correspondingly, the properties of the situation contact a greater or lesser degree of physiological activation of the organism, and the consequent effects on the increase or decrease of the general thresholds of reactivity. Deactivation constitutes the extreme case in which dispositional properties and physiological activation are reduced. The activation-deactivation continuum cuts across to all R/A patterns, but its effect is reflected differently in each. The following are reviewed in this regard: generalized orientation, adaptation, nonspecific defense, and deactivation.

Generalized Orientation

The generalized orientation reaction constitutes the first phase of the organism's activation pattern to: (a) novel or unexpected stimulus events (Berlyne, 1960; Lynn, 1966; Pavlov, 1927; Sokolov, 1963), (b) transitions in the signal value of a stimulus (Berlyne, 1960' Lynn, 1966; Sokolov, 1963), (c) experimental procedures of signal value change (Biriukov, 1965; Polezhaev, 1965), and (d) the onset of extinction (Biriukov, 1965; Polezhaev, 1965) during classical conditioning. Some deprivation conditions that produce nonspecific activation are: sleep deprivation (Malmo, 1959), food deprivation (Campbell & Sheffield, 1953), and water deprivation (Bélanger & Feldman, 1962). The orientation reaction is physiologically distinguished because the vascular components at the peripherical level contract while at the central level they dilate, altering the sensitivity conditions of the analyzers and blocking cortical alpha waves in the electroencephalogram (EEG). Galvanic skin resistance (GSR) and pupillary dilation are also increased (Sokolov, 1963). Increased respiratory intensity indicates activation of the respiratory center and is a measure of generalized arousal (Polezhaev, 1965). Muscle tone also increases in response to novel stimuli (Duffy, 1962). There are circumstances of arousal in which orientation is presented mixed with defense, Ukhtomsky's reaction, or pseudo-conditioning, a case in which orientation is presented in this way (Razran, 1971; Ukhtomsky, 1951).

The variables of intensity and duration of the stimuli are relatively equivalent, since their variation produces a generalized state of arousal in all the analyzers and even broadens the threshold of the orientation pattern to sub-threshold stimulus values and evocative of the defense reaction (Sokolov, 1963). In turn, stimulus repetition decreases activation, and the generalized orientation pattern disappears. The subsequent effects of repetition depend on the signal value of the stimulus, producing habituation to the absence of the signal value, or specific orientation to the signal value (Lynn, 1966; Sokolov, 1963).

Nonspecific Defense

The defense pattern occurs under conditions of intense stimulation or repeatedly presented threshold stimuli close to the upper limen (Sokolov, 1963). Noise also sensitizes defense reactions in the form of startle (Davis, 1974). The pattern components used to differentiate the nonspecific defense reaction from the generalized orientation reaction are vasoconstriction at the central and peripheral levels, measured as galvanic hand and head resistance (Sokolov, 1963). Other components are the startle and gasp response, shallow and increased frequency breathing, and pupillary constriction (Woodworth & Schlosberg, 1954). The usual startle reaction is constituted by blinking, abdominal contraction, postural change in the direction of stimulation, and neck and back movements (Duffy, 1962). Freezing (panic), cowering, crouching, fleeing, defecation, and urination responses are also common (Myer, 1971). In all cases there is an increase in muscle tone (Duffy, 1962) and it is likely that in the prolongation of the reaction there is a decrease in tone due to a decrease in activation, an effect of sympathetic-parasympathetic antagonism.

Some relevant experimental preparations are non-contingent presentation of electric shocks (Seligman, Maier, & Solomon, 1971; Overmier & Seligman, 1967), distal stimuli of high intensity (Biriukov, 1965; Myer, 1971), tasks with high or incompatible response costs (Davis, 1939, 1957; Duffy, 1962; Malmo, 1965), and traumatic escape (Solomon, Kamin, & Wynne, 1953). The parameters affecting defense reactions are stimulus intensity (Appel, 1963; Ison & Hammond, 1971), prolonged exposure to the situation (Myer, 1971), stimulus duration, as well as conditions of blocking, distraction, visuomotor conflict, and increased vigor requirement (Feré, 1903). In disrupting the organism's activity, defense and startle reactions increase both non-directional and directional thresholds, interfering with contact with new contingencies (Seligman, Maier, & Solomon, 1971). The excess vigor involved by conflict, suppression, or paralysis initially produces an increase in general sensitivity and muscular spasticity (Malmo, 1949; Prosser & Hunter, 1936). Prolonged exposure to the situation produces a general decrease in vigor, a decrease in sensitivity, and responses such as crouching or lying down (Myer, 1971). Its ultimate effect is usually a decrease in activation, and usually the defense reactions colloquially labeled as "emotional" responses.

Generalized Adaptation

In general, the analyzers and the organisms show regulatory patterns of activation to long-lasting conditions of intense stimulation or deficiencies in exchanges with the surroundings. Of note are thermoregulatory adaptation in the form of capillary contraction and dilation to sustained cold and hot conditions, respectively. Another adaptative reaction is pupillary adaptation in the form of changes in pupil diameter that adjust stimulation to conditions of increased or decreased brightness. The adjustment of visual sensitivity in the retina through the production of rhodopsin constitutes an additional adaptative reaction to light conditions and alters the thresholds of stimulus reception. The General Adaptation Syndrome (GAS), described by Selye (1950; 1976), is a generalized and nonspecific reaction of the organism to noxious environmental or organismic conditions. It occurs in individuals with severe burns, sepsis, diphtheria, intoxication, prolonged pain, anaphylactic edema, and to prolonged cold, heat, or intense "emotional" conditions. This whole set of patterns is known as general adaptation syndrome and has been vulgarized under the notion of "stress", which actually constitutes the terminal stage of the syndrome.

In contrast to the general orientation, the intensity of the adaptive reaction increases and stabilizes with repetition of the stimulus; it is maintained throughout the stimulation period and does not decrease. The effect of adaptation is specific to the analyzer and nonspecific with respect to the concomitantly occurring pattern. For example, during the vasoconstrictor reaction to cold, constriction becomes more intense and the longer the time elapses from the onset of stimulation (Sokolov, 1963). If generalized orientation is occurring as the dominant activation, the use of thermal stimuli will compete with the initial adaptative reaction. Similarly, the use of light as a conditional stimulus will initially elicit the orientation reaction and adaptation will occur upon its extinction. In the case of GAS, noxious stimulation initiates the activation of an alert pattern consisting of hypothalamic reactions related to carbohydrate metabolism (corticotropins), excessive adrenergic activation and other sympathetic components (increased heart rate, agitated breathing, etc.), followed by stabilization during the endurance phase. Prolongation leads to exhaustion of the organism culminating in death in extreme cases. The effect is generalized and its deleterious effects are: enlargement of the adrenal glands and secretion of lipid granules; impairment of the thymus, spleen and lymph nodes; and severe bleeding ulcers in the stomach and duodenum (Selye, 1950; 1976).

Sensory deprivation seems to produce dark-adaptive reactions, since the most marked post-effects are observed in brief deprivations and in the case of prolonged deprivations are manifested on the second day, after which perceptual functions normalize (Zubek, 1969). However, prolonged deprivation produces ocular and neural damages in both humans and animals (Fantz, 1965, 1967; Zubek, 1969).

Relations of the general adaptative reaction with other patterns are observed after the disappearance of the nonspecific orientation reaction, given its permanence as long as the stimulation is present. It is related to noxious conditions during the conditioning of avoidance responses, which produce the GAS when shock avoidance is contingent (Brady, 1958), and during food (Mowrer, 1960), water (Bélanger & Feldman, 1962) sensory (Fantz, 1965, 1967), and sleep deprivation (Malmo, 1949).

Nonspecific Deactivation

Notable in nonspecific deactivation are the setting (situational) factors such as continuous presentation of the stimulus condition (Berlyne, 1960), chronic repetition of a stimulus (Malmo & Wallerstein, 1955; Rankin, Abrams, Barry, Bhatnagar, Clayton, Colombo, Coppola, Geyer, Glanzman, Marsland, McSweeney, Wilson, Wu, & Thompson, 2009), decreased appetitive motivation and organismic factors such as extreme fatigue (Duffy, 1962), prolonged food deprivation (Young, 1961), extreme cold and hot temperatures (Woodworth & Schlosberg, 1954), deep sleep (Woodworth & Schlosberg, 1954), metabolic decline (Duffy, 1962), darkness (Sokolov, 1963), and alterations of activation-related systems: Glandular, hypothalamic, hippocampal, reticular formation, and others (Moruzzi & Magoun, 1949; Grastyan, 1959; Duffy, 1962). Decreased activation is characterized by attenuation of high frequency waves in the EEG, showing a decrease in cortical tone. There is interaction between homeostatic and adaptive factors with a general decrease in metabolism, increase in sensory thresholds, decrease in blood rate and pressure, respiration, body temperature, galvanic skin resistance (Woodworth & Schlosberg, 1954), and muscle tone (Duffy, 1962). Unlike nonspecific deactivation, specific deactivation always occurs as an effect of a specific activation other than the one that was operating. Strictly speaking, there is no deactivation in absolute terms in specific cases.

Activation of Specific Patterns

Duffy (1962) recognizes directionality and intensity as two fundamental dimensions of activation. Whereas directionality is an attribute of active/reactive patterns approaching or moving away from the stimulus object, intensity indicates the degree of activation with respect to the stimulus object based on its dispositional relevance. This approach coincides with that proposed for directional and non-directional thresholds. Direction is the fundamental measure in that it defines the functional contact with the dispositionally relevant stimulus object (Ribes, 2018). In turn, intensity is part of the molar dimension of vigor, usually assessed by reaction times, latency, speed or effort, but little explored as an activation factor with respect to functional contact. There is a correspondence between the intensive dimension of the pattern (vigor) and the intensive properties of the stimulus object. This is a bidirectional relation. Variation in activation alters the functional intensity of the properties of the stimulus object, just as the intensity of the properties of the stimulus object alter the reactive intensity, both in nonspecific and specific conditions.

The specific activation patterns reviewed are specific orientation and its cases: locating, search, inspecting, and manipulating. These patterns may be part of any contact, but by themselves they do not comprise any type of functional contact. The continuum of specific activation is articulated by the degree to which the pattern itself alters the conditions of stimulation in the situation. In the case of locating, the properties of the stimulus objects are not altered, but its relative position is. Search alters the contacted stimulus field and the diversity of stimulus objects by displacement. Inspecting alters the range of *possible* properties contacted by exposure, while manipulating alters the *actual* stimulus properties, through movement and local changes in the objects. In contrast, in specific defense, locomotion and manipulating are manifested as turning away or partial immobility, moving away and intense action on the object (attack). Specific adaptation is related to local changes in body stimulation or to aspects linked to specific metabolic imbalances. In the case of specific activation, deactivation constitutes an alternative and concurrent form of activation of other active/reactive patterns and not an end in a single continuum. This is because the patterns that are activated are specific and deactivation is complementary to the change in the dispositional value of the stimulus object. This means that the patterns are simultaneously activated with direction toward the DRO and deactivated toward other stimulus objects or components in the situation. The patterns, which are part of both functional contact and behavior-dependent activation, constitute an analytically fragmented continuum. The sequences occur integrated during familiarization and specific differentiation of stimulus objects (Dolin, Zborovskaya, & Zamakhovev, 1965). It is not uncommon to find sequences such as inspecting following manipulating, search following nonspecific orientation, and even deactivation or turning away following prolonged inspecting. The structuring of these sequences affects both the relevant biological activity and the articulation of relations contingent on psychological contact. In turn, these fluctuations are an effect of the variation of the dispositional value of the object, which depends on the correspondence between nonspecific and specific activation.

Specific Orientation

Locating

Unlike nonspecific orientation, specific orientation does not occur to novel stimuli, but to variation in conditional relations between events (Bridger, 1965). The ARP is specific to the analyzer relevant to the stimuli in relation, and a cumulation of arousal occurs in specific cortical areas in correspondence with the mode of stimulation of the dispositionally relevant object (Sokolov, 1965). Locating, as a specific orientation, is affected by habituation and disinhibition, the establishment of conditional relations, extinction, stimulus differentiation (i.e., discrimination), and change of signal function.

The parameters to which the greatest sensitivity is shown are stimulus intensity and duration, stimulus difference, contingency relations between stimuli, and intervals between stimuli or trials, among others. Habituation produces nonspecific activation to decrease and specific patterns relevant to contact with the repeated stimulus modality to be maintained (Lynn, 1966). Disinhibition produces the reinstatement of generalized orientation. The establishment of the conditional relation produces an abbreviation in the anticipation of the orientation response to the conditional stimulus (Lynn, 1966; Sokolov, 1963, 1965; Bykov, 1965; Anokhin, 1965, 1974), while the conditional response and postural changes and displacement to the place of delivery of the unconditional stimulus occupy the remainder of the interval. The pattern preceding specific orientation is activated with extinction (Bykov, 1965). In general terms, the locating pattern, in being part of the transition between reactive/active patterns, increases sensory thresholds that do not correspond to the dispositionally relevant object, decreases the overall arousal level, and allows for the coordinated appearence of the anticipatory pattern, as opposed to nonspecific orientation (Polezhaev, 1965).

Search

Inquisitive exploration, described by Berlyne (1960), is what is referred to here as *search*. It is the component following locating when there is displacement by locomotion in the direction of the DRO. There is no systematic information on its intensive and extensive aspects, however, it is known that there is a decrease in overall activity when the reactive pattern of search occurs. Variation in environing stimulation texture and novelty of stimulus properties or changes are the factors inducing search and subsequent familiarization with stimulus objects. Changes in novelty and complexity of stimulation has been employed to vary environmental texture. Novelty has been varied by time between trials or presentations, exposure duration, and the pre-exposure to the stimulating segment. Complexity has been varied by manipulating parameters such as texture similarity/difference, color saturation arrangement (vertical and horizontal interleaving colors or only one color), pre-exposure to environments with less texture: activity restriction, visual and lighting deprivation (Berlyne, 1960; Fantz, 1965, 1967; Jones, 1969). Other operations affecting searcg are the presence or absence of another organism or surrogate mother (Harlow, 1958), the "emotional" situation of open field (Harlow,

1958), organismic states such as hunger, thirst, and conditioned "fear" (Myers & Miller, 1954; Zimbardo & Miller, 1958). Permanent impairment of some sensory apparatuses, as blindness, results in increased exploratory or search activity, since the time required for familiarization is longer (Berlyne, 1960), with the thresholds of other analyzers decrease (Zemtsova, 1969). Correspondingly, there is a decrease in locomotion as a function of the time of present or past exposure to the particular texture segment of the environment (Dashiell, 1925; Dember, 1956; Glanzer, 1953; Montgomery, 1953), and of a uniform (less complex) texture. In turn, activity restriction produces different effects among organisms. For example, in dogs there is greater search with greater deprivation; restriction (due to the size of the experimental chamber), or motor and sensory deprivation do not produce differences in rats; the so-called "freedom" reflex in situations of constriction has been reported in cats (Berlyne, 1960; Pavlov, 1927; Thorndike, 1911). Search interacts with other types of patterns, whether of instrumental or specific activation. Search is manifested as sniffing in dogs and rats, directed towards non-apparent food (Berlyne, 1960; Thorpe, 1966), and through locomotion directed to non-apparent objects (Gibson & Pick, 2000; Köhler, 1947). Group or individual foraging food (Galef & Giraldeau, 2001; Passos & Keuroghlian, 1999; Rappaport & Brown, 2008) exemplifies the patterns occurring in circumstances of activation. When search is related to feeding, the search patterns also become affected by the number of locations where to search, the time of food availability, the quantity of food, the availability signals of the RDO (Cabrera, Duran, & Nieto, 2006), and the activity of conspecifics (Alfaro & Cabrera, 2015; Cabrera, Duran, & Nieto, 2006; Galef & Giraldeau, 2001; Passos & Keuroghlian, 1999; Rappaport & Brown, 2008). The relation between search and consumption or defense of food is well known (Alfaro & Cabrera, 2005; Thorpe, 1966). In turn, search decreases with the occurrence of adaptative or defensive patterns. Search allows the approach to dispositionally relevant objects and extends the differential properties to which the individual is exposed, facilitating the establishment of spatial contiguity relations, reducing the spatial distance between various segments of the environment and the RDO through locomotion. In turn, it establishes directional thresholds with respect to certain environing segments, for example, withdrawal or moving away (specific defense), or in search, among others.

Inspecting

Inspecting modulates the intensity of stimulus properties by increasing, decreasing, or facilitating exposure to new properties of the stimulating field. Physiological modulation occurs in the form of adaptation to these contact variations (Gibson, 1986). Visual inspection has been primarily investigated. Some of the conditions that affect visual inspection are novelty (Berlyne, 1960; Berlyne & Slater, 1957), complexity (Berlyne, 1958, 1960; Jones, 1969; Kessen, 1967), incongruence (Berlyne, 1960), variety of stimulation (Berlyne, 1960; Jones, 1969), relative stimulus intensity (Kessen, 1967), differences in saturation as contour or color (Berlyne, 1960; Fantz, 1965, 1967; Kessen, 1967), and visual deprivation (Butler, 1954; Butler, Robert, & Harlow, 1954; Jones, 1969; Zernicki, 1987; Zubek, 1969). In human newborns, inspection of bright objects occurs with initial pupillary contraction, and later with fixation and tracking. By two months of age, inspecting is coordinated with head movement (Gibson & Pick, 2000; Lipsitt, 1967; Lynn, 1966; Malcuit & Pomerleau, 2007; Papousek, 1967). This inspecting is made more complex with the introduction of haptic (Jones, 2018; Jones & Lederman, 2006; Zapporozhets, 1969), and multimodal (Gibson & Pick, 2000; Spelke, 1979, 1981, 1990) inspecting procedures. Inspecting is affected by nonspecific activation circumstances, such as sensory deprivation facilitating it (Jones, 1969; Zubek, 1969); in contradistinction, fear interrupts inspecting in monkeys (Harlow, 1958), but opposite effects can be observed as when feeding is interrupted by inspecting novel objects (Berlyne, 1960). Some parameters that decrease inspecting are RDO availability time, number of repetitions, inter-trial interval, and modal variation of the stimulus (Fantz, 1965, 1967). Inspecting alternates with manipulating in apes and monkeys in front of novel objects (Dolin et al., 1965); play, defense, feeding, and sexual behavior are organized patterns involving inspecting in lower primates (Bolotina, Rokotova, Troshikina & Nurgaleva, 1970). Additionally, the opportunity for inspecting has been employed as a reinforcer conjugate to activity in infants (Lipsitt, Pederson & Delucia, 1966; Lipsitt, 1967), and contingent to manipulating in monkeys (Berlyne, 1960; Harlow, 1950).

Manipulating

Thresholds decrease with haptic analyzer stimulation in manipulating (Milerian & Tkachencko, 1963). The decrease in threshold is radiated and inverse to the distance with respect to the stimulated point. Another reported effect is the bilateral decrease of the threshold (Milerian & Tkachencko, 1963), and the increase of tension in the opposite arm despite not being employed (Duffy, 1962; Feré, 1903). Properties such as grip strength are a function of the contingencies present: during conditioning its latency increases and decreases, and during extinction the reverse effect occurs (Ivanov-Smolenski, 1927). Grip conforms to form, size, and speed of the manipulated object (Jones, 2018; Von Hofsten & Rönnqvist, 1988). Manipulating is activated by the novelty and complexity of stimulus objects (Welker, 1956), by situations involving haptic discrimination (Harlow, 1950, 1954; Harlow, Blazek, McClearn, 1956; Zaporozhets, 1969), as well as by reach-to-grasp patterns (Gibson & Pick, 2000). Manipulating is affected by repeated presentation of the object to be manipulated (Harlow, 1950), variety of object properties (Berlyne, 1960; Berlyne & Slater, 1957), practice in manipulating varied objects and their segmentation (Neverovich, 1977; Zaporozhets, 1969), discrimination testing (Harlow, 1950; Harlow, Blazek & McClearn, 1956; Harlow & McClearn, 1954), contingent inspecting to manipulating (Harlow, 1958), contingent reinforcement to manipulating (Ivanov-Smolenski, 1927), conjugate schedules (Lipsitt, 1967), and extinction, reconditioning, generalization, delayed, external, and differential inhibition procedures (Ivanov-Smolenski, 1927). Locating and inspecting usually occur as antecedents to manipulating (Berlyne, 1960; Dolin et al., 1965). Their participation in categorization and differentiation is widely recognized (Gibson & Pick, 2000), and as a prelude to functional contacts by extension and transformation (Piaget, 1970; Ribes, 2018; Wallon, 1978). Manipulating varies the properties of objects by segmenting and changing the angles and planes of exposure of stimulus objects. In this sense, it is the pattern that enhances or diminishes to a greater degree the properties that may be dispositionally relevant in a situation.

Specific Defense

Specific defense refers to the effects noxious stimulation on specific patterns complementary to appetitive patterns related to specific orienting. The following are covered under this heading: total or partial immobility, withdrawal, and attack.

Total or partial immobility

Total or partial immobility occur as reactions to specific noxious stimulation, localizable in the field of stimulation. In the case of physically and/or functionally intense stimulation, the freezing pattern is present, in which muscle tonicity increases. This excessive activation may even interfere with the withdrawal pattern present in avoidance contingencies (Krieckhaus, Miller & Zimmerman, 1965). At other times, immobility may be partial and transient, as in hiding behaviors. A major property that modulates muscle tonicity (Duffy, 1962) and sympathetic and parasympathetic responses is the intensity of the stimulation. Other stimulus properties such as shape, size, and speed can activate the freezing pattern (Maier & Schneirla, 1964; Tinbergen, 1989), or the partial immobility pattern. This is the pattern analogous to locating, but with respect to noxious or "aversive" events. Immobility is related to withdrawal reactions during avoidance training and to the locating and inspecting of stimuli as part of the so-called "warning reflexes" (Dolin et al., 1965). The components of specific and nonspecific defense sometimes occur together: defecation and urinary excretion are generally increased, and under extended conditions body weight is lost and the general adaptation syndrome develops (Coons & Miller, 1960). An immobility pattern may interfere with or facilitate the establishment of functional contact, depending on the relation of the immobility pattern to the presentation or removal of object or contingent event. For example, organisms that freeze in predation situations tend to avoid predation, whereas freezing in avoidance situation interferes with the learning of the instrumental response.

Withdrawal

Unlike the changes related to orientation, nociception, or thermoregulation (Cohen & Obrist, 1975; Myer, 1971), changes in defense reactions are specific to stimulus events temporally antecedent (Notterman, Schoenfeld, & Bersh, 1952), or spatially contiguous (Bulgelski & Miller, 1938) to the "aversive" event, such that the defense pattern is differential to those properties. Defense patterns have autonomic and motor components associated to energy-emitting systems. Some authors (Maier & Schneirla, 1964) propose the sympathetic system as phylogenetically developed to complement the specific defense by means of the withdrawal response, as opposed to the parasympathetic system that conserves energy. Different patterns may be present in the different procedures but associated with the contingency relations involved. For example, motor thresholds associated with the acquisition of the escape response decrease as the number of trials increases (Myer, 1971). The cardiac response is maintained after extinction of the motor component of the pattern during avoidance (Werboff, Duane, & Cohen, 1964; Solomon, Kamin, & Wynne, 1953). The relation between withdrawal and activation is so close that, in the absence of *curare* locomotion, the cardiac and muscular components are maintained as part of the pattern and are even kept operating after locomotion restriction (Cohen & Obrist, 1975; DiCara & Miller, 1968; Miller & DiCara, 1967). Parameters relevant to its occurrence are stimulus intensity, the interval between noxious or "aversive" events, the interval between signals (Leaf, 1965) and signal-response, the presentation of proximal stimuli, as well as exposure to avoidance procedures prior to escape, etc. (Overmier & Seligman, 1967).

Withdrawal is analogous to search, but with respect to aversive events in which the stimulating conditions are changed by locomotion. Its establishment can be facilitated or interfered with, depending on the functional contact, by modulating the non-directional thresholds in both its motor and autonomic components. Likewise, it alters the directional relation by withdrawing the organism from the RDO, thus it occasionally interferes with the extinction process by modulating the contact relation (Mowrer, 1960).

Attack

In the attack reaction usually the presentation of a noxious or threatening (even unfamiliar) object is removed or withdrawn by a pattern that corresponds to manipulating in the orientation reaction (Miller, 1941). It occurs in conditions related to nursery care and territory defense (Lorenz, 1971), the presentation of nociceptive events, electric shocks (Azrin, Hutchinson, & Hake, 1967), strong puffs of air (Azrin, Hake, & Hutchinson, 1965), pain (Azrin, Hutchinson, & Hake, 1963; Azrin, Hutchinson, & Sallery, 1964), or the presence of organisms that are not of the same colony or species (Lorenz, 1971). In all these cases there is a decrease in the sensory thresholds and response thresholds of the components constituting the attack pattern (Lorenz, 1971). Events and presence of the dispositionally relevant object are omitted, avoided, postponed, or terminated by modifying the object by means of the operation on the object. The attack modulates the contact by withdrawing or destroying the RDO, affecting the present contingencies.

Specific Adaptation

Specific adaptation manifests itself in the form of patterns in circumstances where prolongation of a chronic condition does not produce nonspecific activation like the general adaptation syndrome, but patterns that facilitate recovery from the specific organic condition affected. As examples of specific adaptation patterns, salt appetite in adrenalectomized individuals (adrenal gland removal) and operant thermoregulation in which specific nutritional or metabolic deficiencies are compensated for will be reviewed.

Salt appetite in adrenalectomized organisms constitutes a specific adaptation to the disappearance of the hormonal mechanisms regulating saline excretion. This phenomenon also appears with salt-restricted diets (Contreras, 1977; Richter, 1936). Although the specific mechanisms are still under discussion (Krause & Sakai, 2007), there is an increase in the firing threshold of the *chorda timpany* nerve related to taste reception, which facilitates the ingestion of higher salt concentrations and a decrease in the differential threshold for lower concentration salt solutions (Bare, 1949; Richter, 1936; 1939). Its physiological components are mainly glandular (secretion of aldosterone, deoxycorticosterone, angiotensin, vasopressin and renin) related to urinary retention and excretion and to different salt concentrations, blood pressure and volemia (local blood volume). In the case of thermoregulation, the physiological pattern involves decreased blood flow, increased metabolic rate, shivering, self-friction, and increased local movements, as well as nest building in some species, all changes associated with cold compensation (Teitelbaum, 1966). Salt concentration and dietary deprivation are two relevant parameters in sodium deficit (Bare, 1949; Contreras, 1977; Young, 1961). Rats are kept without their fur at temperatures of 2°C for thermoregulation, and heat is presented by means of an infrared lamp contingent on lever press. The frequency of the operant is adjusted to maintain peripheral and hypothalamic temperature. Adjustment as adaptation is affected by the amount of time heat is presented, prior cooling, temperature acclimation, and physiological conditions that affect thermoregulatory maintenance, for example, thyroid removal, weight loss, inadequate diet, and food deprivation that prevents increased metabolic rate and body temperature maintenance (Teitelbaum,

1966; Weiss & Laties, 1961; Terrien, Perret & Aujard, 2011). Both adaptive reactions are naturally related to food and fluid intake (Richter, 1936), and their excretion and satiety (Krause & Sakai, 2007). Specific adaptive reactions bias the preference for RDOs related to nutritional-metabolic deficit, altering both non-directional (physiological) and directional (preference) thresholds. Other specific adaptations occur as preferences for flavors associated with recovery from vitamin deficiencies (Garcia, Ervin, Yorke & Koelling, 1967), riboflavin, pyridoxine, calcium, and protein (Leung & Rogers, 1986; Rozin, 1976). Similarly, specific aversions to tastes associated with toxins, radiation (Garcia & Koelling, 1966) and rodenticides are known (Barnett, 2001). Aversion is a specific adaptation to taste and cannot be established without it or with respect to other analyzers (Garcia, Ervin & Koelling, 1966). This specificity shows the adaptive relationship between taste receptors and toxic impairments of the organism.

Concluding Remarks

The analysis of nonspecific and specific activation patterns presented in the previous section takes into consideration exclusively the experimental literature for mammals, in general, and for humans in particular. However, it is possible that such analysis could be adjusted to the rest of the animal kingdom, considering the morphological-functional peculiarities of the nervous and sensory-motor systems of each of the *phyla* and their classes. However, at present, the possibility or not of its extension to the whole animal kingdom does not affect in any way its usefulness in the analysis of dispositional functions in psychological behavior.

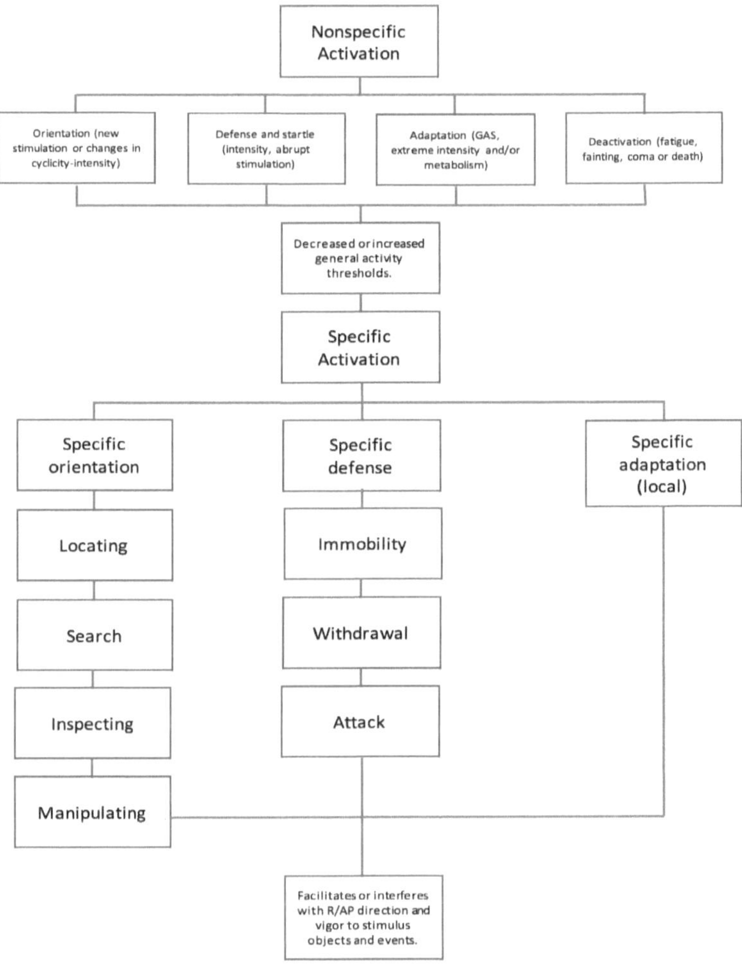

Figure 1. Different forms of reactive activation and their relations as dispositional functions.

Figure 1 shows the different forms of reactive activation and their relations as dispositional functions. On the one hand, a nonspecific activation pattern occurs as the first moment of every reactive episode of the individual. The dispositional function of nonspecific activation patterns is to alter the individual's reactive thresholds, always decreasing them in the case of orientation reactions, decreasing or increasing them in the case of defense reactions, or modulating them homeostatically in the case of adaptive reactions. Nonspecific activation patterns always occur in response to transient, abrupt, and sudden changes in the stimulating conditions in orientation and defense reactions, and to relatively long-lasting and/or chronic abrupt changes in adaptive reactions. The dispositional effect on reactivity thresholds can manifest as nonspecific locating or search in the form of sensory approach or orientation (adient behavior), as flight or panic immobility (abient behavior), or as gradual increases or decreases in stimulus exposure (homeostatic behavior). Nonspecific activation, as a somatic pattern, is not necessarily symmetrical with the intensive properties of the reactivity that occurs.

As shown in Figure 1, from the effects on reactive thresholds resulting from nonspecific activation, different forms of specific reactive activation can occur. In all cases, specific activation facilitates or interferes with reactive/active patterns directed to delimited stimulus segments, objects, and events. Such facilitating or interfering effect is manifested in changes of directionality and permanence with respect to dispositionally relevant segments of stimulation in the environment, corresponding to the individual's transient biological states and interactive history as specific reactive propensity. Specific activation affects differential reactivity to objects, and the time and variety of exposure to them is a result of the individual's own behavior. In specific activation, in mammals and humans, the visual, olfactory, and haptic modalities predominate, as well as the motor modality in the form of local postural changes or local movements (as in manipulating or reading, speech and gesticulation) or in the form of locomotion in translation or displacement. The facilitated or interfered behavior itself reciprocally affects the momentary activation states in a reciprocal way in all forms of specific reactive activation of orientation and defense, which gives rise to the transitional character of all functional contacts in psychological behavior. Forms of specific orientation include locating, search, inspecting, and manipulating, while forms of specific defense include withdrawal or non-approach, restricted mobility, and attack. Specific adaptation always involves behavior that produces specific changes in the general conditions of stimulation: gradual exposure, compensatory movements and others that regulate local changes in adaptation to heat, cold, intensity of light or sound, concentration on tastes, among many other examples.

The proposed analysis may help to delimit the meaning of some ordinary terms that are technically used in biology and psychology in an ambiguous and imprecise manner. A case in point is the difference between alertness, attention, and focus. They are commonly used to designate or appeal to covert processes that "explain" the results in situations in which there is more than one behavioral option with respect to various segments or moments of stimulation. From the perspective developed here, these terms describe conditions that consist of different states of specific activation: alertness as anticipatory locating, attention (usually called selective) as differential search, and focus as inspecting and manipulating, especially in the case of writing. Moreover, the meaning of these terms depends on the characteristics of the type of functional contact in which they participate and the contact medium that makes it possible. Ultimately, it is essential to emphasize that dispositional factors constitute correspondence functions of states of the individual and of states of the conditions and stimulation segments of the environment, which participate, facilitating or interfering, in the configuration of the contingency relations that shape functional contacts as psychological behavior. The analysis of dispositional factors cannot be carried out ignoring the biological processes that regulate sensory and motor reactivity, as well as the alteration of the states of the organism in correspondence with pertinent elements of the environment and its physicochemical conditions, in their ecological exchanges.

References

Alfaro, L. & Cabrera, R. (2015). Forrajeo en ratas: Una evaluación del recorrido de los sujetos como indicador de desgaste energético. *Conductual, 3* (2), 111-127.

Anokhin, P.K. (1965). The role of orienting-exploratory reaction. En: L. Voronin, A. Leontiev, A. Luria, E. Sokolov & O. Vinogradova (Eds.). *Orienting reflex and exploratory behavior* (pp. 3-16). Washington: American Institute of Biological Sciences.

Anokhin, P.K. (1974). *Biology and Neurophysiology of the conditioned reflex and its role in adaptative behavior.* Oxford: Pergamon Press.

Appel, J. B. (1963). Punishment and shock intensity. *Science (New York, N.Y.), 141*(3580), 528-529. https://doi.org/10.1126/science.141.3580.528-a

Azrin, N. H., Hake, D. F., & Hutchinson, R. R. (1965). Elicitation of aggression by a physical blow. *Journal of the Experimental Analysis of Behavior, 8*(1), 55-57. https://doi.org/10.1901/jeab.1965.8-55

Azrin, N. H., Hutchinson, R. R., & Hake, D. F. (1963). Induced fighting in the squirrel monkey. *Journal of the Experimental Analysis of Behavior, 6,* 620. https://doi.org/10.1901/jeab.1963.6-620

Azrin, N. H., Hutchinson, R. R., & Hake, D. F. (1967). Attack, avoidance, and escape reactions to aversive shock. *Journal of the Experimental Analysis of Behavior, 10*(2), 131-148. https://doi.org/10.1901/jeab.1967.10-131

Azrin, N. H., Hutchinson, R. R., & Sallery, R. D. (1964). Pain-aggression toward inanimate objects. *Journal of the Experimental Analysis of Behavior, 7*(3), 223-228. https://doi.org/10.1901/jeab.1964.7-223

Barber, T.X. (1969). *Hypnosis: A scientific approach.* Litton Educational Publishing.

Bare, J. K. (1949). The specific hunger for sodium chloride in normal and adrenalectomized white rats. *Journal of Comparative and Physiological Psychology, 42*(4), 242-253. https://doi.org/10.1037/h0057987

Barnett, A. (2001). *The story of rats: their impact on us and our impact on them.* Sidney: Allen & Unwin.

Bélanger, D., & Feldman, S. M. (1962). Effects of water deprivation upon heart rate and instrumental activity in the rat. *Journal of Comparative and Physiological Psychology, 55*(2), 220-225. https://doi.org/10.1037/h0042797

Berlyne, D. E. (1958). The influence of the albedo and complexity of stimuli on visual fixation in the human infant. *British Journal of Psychology, 49,* 315-318. https://doi.org/10.1111/j.2044-8295.1958.tb00669.x

Berlyne, D. E. (1960). *Conflict, arousal, and curiosity.* NY: McGraw-Hill Book Company.

Berlyne, D. E., & Slater, J. (1957). Perceptual curiosity, exploratory behavior, and maze learning. *Journal of Comparative and Physiological Psychology, 50*(3), 228-232. https://doi.org/10.1037/h0046603

Biriukov, D. A. (1965). On the nature of the orienting reaction. En: L. Voronin, A. Leontiev, A. Luria, E. Sokolov & O. Vinogradova (Eds.). *Orienting reflex and exploratory behavior* (pp. 17-24). Washington: American Institute of Biological Sciences.

Bolotina, O. P., Rokotova, N. A., Troshikina, Y. G., & Nurgaleeva, E. M. (1970). Orienting-Investigatory Activity in Lower Primates. *Soviet Psychology, 9*(1), 52-65. https://doi.org/10.2753/RPO1061-0405090152

Brady, J. V., Porter, R. W., Conrad, D. G., & Mason, J. W. (1958). Avoidance behavior and the development of gastroduodenal ulcers. *Journal of the Experimental Analysis of Behavior, 1,* 69-72. https://doi.org/10.1901/jeab.1958.1-69

Bridger, W. (1965). Los sistemas de señales en el desarrollo de las funciones cognoscitivas. *La palabra y el hombre, 34,* 169-192.

Bugelski, R., & Miller, N. E. (1938). A spatial gradient in the strength of avoidance responses. *Journal of Experimental Psychology, 23*(5), 494-505. https://doi.org/10.1037/h0058936

Butler, R. A. (1954). Incentive conditions which influence visual exploration. *Journal of Experimental Psychology, 48*(1), 19-23. https://doi.org/10.1037/h0063578

Butler, Robert , A., & Harlow, H. F. (1954). Persistence of visual exploration in monkeys. *Journal of Comparative and Physiological Psychology, 47*(3), 258-263. https://doi.org/10.1037/h0054977

Bykov, V.D. (1965). On the dynamics of the orienting-exploratory reflex reaction during the formation of positive and inhibitory conditioned reflexes and their alterations. En: L. Voronin, A. Leontiev, A. Luria, E. Sokolov & O. Vinogradova (Eds.). *Orienting reflex and exploratory behavior* (pp. 25-36). Washington: American Institute of Biological Sciences.

Cabrera, R., Durán, Á., & Nieto, J. (2006). Aprendizaje social y estrategias de forrajeo en parvadas de palomas: Efectos de la cantidad de alimento. *Revista Mexicana de Psicología*, *23*(1), 111-121.

Campbell, B. A., & Sheffield, F. D. (1953). Relation of random activity to food deprivation. *Journal of Comparative and Physiological Psychology*, *46*(5), 320-322. https://doi.org/10.1037/h0062866

Cohen, D. H., & Obrist, P. A. (1975). Interactions between behavior and the cardiovascular system. *Circulation Research*, *37*(6), 693-706. https://doi.org/10.1161/01.res.37.6.693

Contreras, R. J. (1977). Changes in gustatory nerve discharges with sodium deficiency: A single unit analysis. *Brain Research*, *121*(2), 373-378. https://doi.org/10.1016/0006-8993(77)90162-7

Coons, E. E., & Miller, N. E. (1960). Conflict versus consolidation of memory traces to explain «retrograde amnesia» produced by ECS. *Journal of Comparative and Physiological Psychology*, *53*, 524-531. https://doi.org/10.1037/h0045920

Dashiell, J. F. (1925). A quantitative demonstration of animal drive. *Journal of Comparative Psychology*, *5*(3), 205-208. https://doi.org/10.1037/h0071833

Davis, M. (1974). Sensitization of the rat startle response by noise. *Journal of Comparative and Physiological Psychology*, *87*(3), 571-581. https://doi.org/10.1037/h0036985

Davis, R. C. (1939). Patterns of muscular activity during «mental work» and their constancy. *Journal of Experimental Psychology*, *24*(5), 451-465. https://doi.org/10.1037/h0057813

Davis, R. C. (1957). Response patterns. *Trans. N. Y. Academy of Science, 19*, 731-739. 10.1111/j.2164-0947.1957.tb00564.x

Dember, W. N. (1956). Response by the rat to environmental change. *Jour-

nal of Comparative and Physiological Psychology, 49(1), 93-95. https://doi.org/10.1037/h0045411

DiCara, L. V., & Miller, N. E. (1968). Changes in heart rate instrumentally learned by curarized rats as avoidance responses. *Journal of Comparative and Physiological Psychology, 65*(1), 8-12. https://doi.org/10.1037/h0025406

DiCara, L. V., & Miller, N. E. (1969). Transfer of instrumentally learned heart-rate changes from curarized to noncurarized state: Implications for a mediational hypothesis. *Journal of Comparative and Physiological Psychology, 68*(2), 159-162. https://doi.org/10.1037/h0027510

Dolin, A. Zborovskaya, I. & Zamakhovev, S. (1965). On the role of orienting-exploratory reflex in conditioned reflex activity. En: L. Voronin, A. Leontiev, A. Luria, E. Sokolov & O. Vinogradova (Eds.). *Orienting reflex and exploratory behavior* (45-53). Washington: American Institute of Biological Sciences.

Duffy, E. (1962). *Activation and Behavior*. N.Y.: John Wiley & Sons.

Fantz, R. (1967). Visual perception and experience in early infancy: a look of the hidden side of behavior development. In: H.W. Stevenson, E.H. Hess & H.L. Rheingold (Eds.). *Early behavior: Comparative and developmental approaches* (pp. 181-224). NY: John Willey & Sons, Inc.

Fantz, R. L. (1965). Visual perception from birth as shown by pattern selectivity. *Annals of the New York Academy of Sciences, 118*(21), 793-814. https://doi.org/10.1111/j.1749-6632.1965.tb40152.x

Feré, C. (1903). *Sensación y movimiento*. Madrid: Librería de Fernando Fé.

Fromm, E., & Nash, M.R. (1992). *Contemporary hypnosis research*. New York, NY: The Guilford Press.

Galef, B. G., & Giraldeau, L. A. (2001). Social influences on foraging in vertebrates: Causal mechanisms and adaptive functions. *Animal Behaviour, 61*(1), 3-15. https://doi.org/10.1006/anbe.2000.1557

García, J. & Koelling, R. (1966). Relation of cue to consequence in avoidance learning. *Psychonomic Science, 4* (1), 123-124.

García, J., Ervin, F. & Koelling, R. (1966). Learning with prolonged delay of reinforcement. *Psychonomic Science, 5* (3), 121-122.

García, J., Ervin, F. Yorke, C. & Koelling, R. (1967). Conditioning with delayed vitamin injection. *Science, 155* (3763), 716-718.

Gibson, E. & Pick, A. (2000). *An Ecological Approach to Perceptual Learning and Development.* Oxford: Oxford University Press.

Gibson, J. (1986). *The ecological approach to visual perception.* EUA: Taylor and Francis Group.

Glanzer, M. (1953). Stimulus satiation: An explanation of spontaneous alternation and related phenomena. *Psychological Review, 60*(4), 257-268. https://doi.org/10.1037/h0062718

Grastyan, E. (1959). The hippocampus and higher nervous activity. In M. A. Brazier (Ed.). *The Central Nervous System and Behaviour* (119-205). New York: J. Macy.

Harlow, H. F. (1950). Learning and satiation of response in intrinsically motivated complex puzzle performance by monkeys. *Journal of Comparative and Physiological Psychology, 43*(4), 289-294. https://doi.org/10.1037/h0058114

Harlow, H. F. (1958). The nature of love. *American Psychologist, 13*(12), 673-685. https://doi.org/10.1037/h0047884

Harlow, H. F., & McClearn, G. E. (1954). Object discrimination learned by monkeys on the basis of manipulation motives. *Journal of Comparative and Physiological Psychology, 47*(1), 73-76. https://doi.org/10.1037/h0058241

Harlow, H. F., Blazek, N. C., & McClearn, G. E. (1956). Manipulatory motivation in the infant rhesus monkey. *Journal of Comparative and Physiological Psychology, 49*(5), 444-448. https://doi.org/10.1037/h0047817

Ison, J.R. & Hammond, G. R. (1971). Modification of the startle reflex in the rat by changes in the auditory and visual environment. *Journal of Comparative and Physiological Psychology, 75* (3), 435-452. 10.1037/h0030934

Ivanov-Smolensky, A. G. (1927). On the methods of examining the conditioned food reflexes in children and in mental disorders. *Brain: A Journal of Neurology, 50*(Part 2), 138-141. https://doi.org/10.1093/brain/50.2.138

Jones, A. (1969). Stimulus seeking behavior. In: J. Zubek (Ed.). *Sensory Deprivation: Fifteen years of research* (pp. 167-206). NY: Appleton

Century-Crofts.

Jones, L. & Lederman, S. (2006). *Human hand function*. Oxford: Oxford University Press.

Jones, L. (2018). *Haptics*. MA: The MIT Press.

Kantor, J. R. (1924). *Principles of psychology* (vol. 1). NY: Alfred A. Knopf.

Kantor, J. R. (1926). *Principles of psychology* (vol. 2). NY: Alfred A. Knopf.

Kessen, W. (1967). Sucking and looking: Two organized congenital patterns in the human newborns. In: H.W. Stevenson, E.H. Hess & H.L. Rheingold (Eds.). *Early behavior. Comparative and developmental approaches* (pp. 147-180). NY: John Willey & Sons, Inc.

Köhler, W. (1947). *Gestalt psychology. An introduction to new concepts in modern psychology*. Oxford: Liveright.

Krause, E. G., & Sakai, R. R. (2007). Richter and sodium appetite: From adrenalectomy to molecular biology. *Appetite, 49*(2), 353-367. https://doi.org/10.1016/j.appet.2007.01.015

Krieckhaus, E. E., Miller, N. E., & Zimmerman, P. (1965). Reduction of freezing behavior and improvement of shock avoidance by D-Amphetamine. *Journal of Comparative and Physiological Psychology, 60*, 36-40. https://doi.org/10.1037/h0022302

Leaf, R. C. (1965). Acquisition of Sidman avoidance responding as a function of S-S interval. *Journal of Comparative and Physiological Psychology, 59*(2), 298-300. https://doi.org/10.1037/h0021844

Lindsley, O.R. (1957). Operant behavior during sleep: A measure of depth of sleep. *Science, 126*, 1290-1292.

Lindsley, O.R., & Conran, R. (1962). Operant behavior during EST: A measure of depth of coma. *Diseases of the Nervous System, 23*, 407-409

Lindsley, O.R., Hobika, J.H., & Etsten. B.E. (1961). Operant behavior during anesthesia recovery: A Continuous and objective method. *Anesthesiology, 22*, 937-946.

Lipsitt, L. P. (1967). Learning in the human infant. En: H.W. Stevenson, E.H. Hess & H.L. Rheingold (Eds.). *Early behavior. Comparative and developmental approaches* (pp. 225-248). NY: John Willey & Sons, Inc.

Lipsitt, L. P., Pederson, L. J., & Delucia, C. A. (1966). Conjugate reinforcement of operant responding in infants. *Psychonomic Science*, *4*(1), 67-68. https://doi.org/10.3758/BF03342180

Lorenz, K. (1971). *Sobre la agresión: El pretendido mal*. México: Siglo XXI.

Lynn, R. (1966). *Attention, Arousal and the Orientation reaction*. Inglaterra: Dawson & Goodall.

Maier, N. R. F. & Schneirla, T.C. (1964). *Principles of animal psychology*. NY: Dover Publications.

Malmo, R. B. (1959). Activation: A neuropsychological dimension. *Psychological Review*, *66*(6), 367-386. https://doi.org/10.1037/h0047858

Malmo, R. B. (1965). Physiological gradients and behavior. *Psychological Bulletin*, *64*(4), 225-234. https://doi.org/10.1037/h0022288

Malmo, R. B., & Wallerstein, H. (1955). Rigidity and reactive inhibition. *The Journal of Abnormal and Social Psychology*, *50*(3), 345-348. https://doi.org/10.1037/h0041393

Mednick, M.T. Lindsley, O.R. (1958). Some clinical correlates of operant behavior. *Journal of*

Abnormal and Social Psychology, 57 (1), 13-16.

Michael, J. (1982). Distinguishing between discriminative and motivational functions of stimuli. *Journal of the Experimental Analysis of Behavior*, *37*(1), 149-155. https://doi.org/10.1901/jeab.1982.37-149

Michael, Jack. (1988). Establishing operations and the mand. *The Analysis of Verbal Behavior*, *6*(1), 3-9. https://doi.org/10.1007/BF03392824

Michael, Jack. (1993). Establishing Operations. *The Behavior Analyst*, *16*(2), 191-206. https://doi.org/10.1007/BF03392623

Milerian, E. A., & Tkachenko, V. G. (1963). The Effects of Exercise Upon the Space Threshold of Tactile Differentiation. *Soviet Psychology and Psychiatry*, *1*(4), 3-8. https://doi.org/10.2753/RPO1061-040501043

Miller, N. E. (1941). I. The frustration-aggression hypothesis. *Psychological Review*, *48*(4), 337-342. https://doi.org/10.1037/h0055861

Miller, Neal E., & Dicara, L. (1967). Instrumental learning of heart rate changes in curarized rats: Shaping, and specificity to discriminative stimulus. *Journal of Comparative and Physiological Psychology*, *63*(1), 12-19. https://doi.org/10.1037/h0024160

Montgomery, K. C. (1953). Exploratory behavior as a function of «similarity» of stimulus situation. *Journal of Comparative and Physiological Psychology*, *46*(2), 129-133. https://doi.org/10.1037/h0055101

Moruzzi, G., & Magoun, H. W. (1949). Brain stem reticular formation and activation of the EEG. *Electroencephalography and Clinical Neurophysiology*, *1*(1), 455-473. https://doi.org/10.1016/0013-4694(49)90219-9

Mowrer. O.H. (1960). *Learning theory and behavior*. NY: John Willey & Sons, Inc.

Myer, J.S. (1971). Some Effects of Noncontingent Aversive Stimulation. In: F.R. Brush (Ed.). *Aversive Conditioning and Learning* (pp. 469-536). NY: Academic Press.

Myers, A. K., & Miller, N. E. (1954). Failure to find a learned drive based on hunger; evidence for learning motivated by «exploration. *Journal of Comparative and Physiological Psychology*, *47*(6), 428-436. https://doi.org/10.1037/h0062664

Neverovich, Y. Z. (1977). The Development of Motor Acts with Objects in the Preschool Child. *Soviet Psychology*, *16*(1), 35-45. https://doi.org/10.2753/RPO1061-0405160135

Notterman, J. M., Schoenfeld, W. N., & Bersh, P. J. (1952). Conditioned heart rate response in human beings during experimental anxiety. *Journal of Comparative and Physiological Psychology*, *45*(1), 1-8. https://doi.org/10.1037/h0060870

Overmier, J. B., & Seligman, M. E. P. (1967). Effects of inescapable shock upon subsequent escape and avoidance responding. *Journal of comparative and physiological psychology*, *63*(1), 28-33. https://doi.org/10.1037/h0024166

Papousek, H. (1967). Experimental studies of appetitional behavior in human newborns infants. In: H.W. Stevenson, E.H. Hess & H.L. Rheingold (Eds.). *Early behavior. Comparative and developmental approaches* (pp. 249-278). NY: John Willey & Sons, Inc.

Passos, F. de C., & Keuroghlian, A. (1999). Foraging behavior and microhabitats used by black lion tamarins, Leontopithecus chrysopygus (Mikan) (Primates, Callitrichidae). *Revista Brasileira de Zoologia, 16*, 219-222. https://doi.org/10.1590/S0101-81751999000600022

Pavlov, I. P. (1927). *Conditioned reflexes: an investigation of the physiological activity of the cerebral cortex.* Oxford, England: Oxford Univ. Press

Piaget, J. (1970). *Genetic epistemology.* EUA: Columbia University Press.

Polezhaev, E. F. (1965). Role of the orienting reflex in the coordination of cortical activity. En: L. Voronin, A. Leontiev, A. Luria, E. Sokolov & O. Vinogradova (Eds.). *Orienting reflex and exploratory behavior* (pp. 122-140). Washington: American Institute of Biological Sciences.

Prosser, C. L., & Hunter, W. S. (1936). The extinction of startle responses and spinal reflexes in the white rat. *American Journal of Physiology, 117*, 609-618.

Rankin, C. H., Abrams, T., Barry, R. J., Bhatnagar, S., Clayton, D. F., Colombo, J., Thompson, R. F. (2009). Habituation revisited: An updated and revised description of the behavioral characteristics of habituation. *Neurobiology of Learning and Memory, 92*(2), 135-138. https://doi.org/10.1016/j.nlm.2008.09.012

Rappaport, L. G., & Brown, G. R. (2008). Social influences on foraging behavior in young nonhuman primates: Learning what, where, and how to eat. *Evolutionary Anthropology: Issues, News, and Reviews, 17*(4), 189-201. https://doi.org/10.1002/evan.20180

Razran, G. (1971). *Mind in evolution: An east-west synthesis of learned behavior and cognition.* Michigan: Houghton Mifflin.

Ribes, E. (2018). *El estudio científico de la conducta individual. Una introducción a la teoría de la psicología.* México: Manual Moderno.

Richter, C. (1939). Salt taste thresholds of normal and adrenalectomized rats. *Endocrinology, 24*, 367-371.

Richter, C. P. (1936). Increased salt appetite in adrenalectomized rats. *American Journal of Physiology-Legacy Content, 115*(1), 155-161. https://doi.org/10.1152/ajplegacy.1936.115.1.155

Ryle, G. (1949). *The concept of mind.* NY: Barnes & Noble.

Seligman, M. E., Maier, S. F. & Solomon, R.L. (1971). Unpredictable and uncontrollable aversive events. In: F.R. Brush (Ed.). *Aversive Conditioning and Learning* (pp. 347-400). NY: Academic Press.

Selye, H. (1950). Stress and the General Adaptation Syndrome. *British Medical Journal, 1*(4667), 1383-1392.

Selye, H. (1976). *Stress in health and disease.* E.U.A.: Butterworth Inc.

Sokolov, E. N. (1963). Perception and the Conditioned Reflex. Oxford: Pergamon Press.

Sokolov, E.N. (1965). The orienting reflex, its structure and mechanisms. In: L. Voronin, A. Leontiev, A. Luria, E. Sokolov & O. Vinogradova (Eds.). *Orienting reflex and exploratory behavior* (pp. 141-152). Washington: American Institute of Biological Sciences.

Solley, C.M. & Murphy, G. (1960). *Development of the perceptual world.* New York, NY: Basic Books.

Solomon, R. L., Kamin, L. J., & Wynne, L. C. (1953). Traumatic avoidance learning: The outcomes of several extinction procedures with dogs. *The Journal of Abnormal and Social Psychology, 48*(2), 291-302. https://doi.org/10.1037/h0058943

Spelke, E. S. (1979). Perceiving bimodally specified events in infancy. *Developmental Psychology, 15*(6), 626-636. https://doi.org/10.1037/0012-1649.15.6.626

Spelke, E. S. (1981). The infant's acquisition of knowledge of bimodally specified events. *Journal of Experimental Child Psychology, 31*(2), 279-299. https://doi.org/10.1016/0022-0965(81)90018-7

Spelke, E. S. (1990). Principles of object perception. *Cognitive Science, 14*(1), 29-56. https://doi.org/10.1016/0364-0213(90)90025-R

Teitelbaum, P. (1966). The use of operant methods in the assessment and control of motivational states. In: W. Honig (Ed.). *Operant behavior: areas of research and application* (pp. 565-608). NJ: Prentice-Hall, Inc.

Terrien, J., Perret, M., & Aujard, F. (2011). Behavioral thermoregulation in mammals: A review. *Frontiers in Bioscience (Landmark Edition), 16*, 1428-1444. https://doi.org/10.2741/3797

Thompson, T., & Schuster, C.R. (1968). *Behavioral pharmacology*. Englewood Cliffs, NJ: Prentice Hall.

Thorndike, E. (1911). *Animal Intelligence*. NY: Macmillan Company.

Thorpe, W. H. (1966). *Learning and instinct in animals*. Cambridge: Harvard University Press.

Tinbergen, N. (1989). *El estudio del instinto*. México: Siglo XXI.

Ukhtomsky, A. (1951). *Collected Works* (vol. 2). Leningrad: University Press.

Von Hofsten, C., & Rönnqvist, L. (1988). Preparation for grasping an object: A developmental study. *Journal of Experimental Psychology. Human Perception and Performance, 14*(4), 610-621. https://doi.org/10.1037//0096-1523.14.4.610

Wallon, H. (1978). *Del acto al pensamiento*. Buenos Aires: Editorial Psique.

Weiss, B., & Laties, V. G. (1961). Behavioral Thermoregulation. *Science, 133*(3464), 1588-1588. https://doi.org/10.1126/science.133.3464.1588

Welker, W. I. (1956). Some determinants of play and exploration in chimpanzees. *Journal of Comparative and Physiological Psychology, 49*(1), 84-89. https://doi.org/10.1037/h0044463

Werboff, J., Duane, D., & Cohen, B. D. (1964). Extinction of conditioned avoidance and heart rate responses in rats. *Journal of Psychosomatic Research, 8*, 29-33. https://doi.org/10.1016/0022-3999(64)90019-4

Woodworth, R.S. & Schlosberg, H. (1954). *Experimental Psychology*. NY: Holt, Rinehart & Winston.

Young, P. T. (1961). *Motivation and emotion: A survey of the determinants of human and animal activity*. Hoboken, NJ, US: John Wiley & Sons Inc.

Zaporozhets, A. V. (1969). Some of the psychological problems of sensory training in early childhood and the preschool period. In: M. Cole & I. Maltzman (Eds.). *A Handbook of contemporary soviet psychology* (pp. 86-120). NY: Basic Books, Inc.

Zemtsova, M. I. (1969). Characteristics of Perceptual Activity in the blind. In: M. Cole & I. Maltzman (Eds.). *A Handbook of contemporary soviet psychology* (pp. 302-325). NY: Basic Books, Inc.

Zernicki, B. (1987). Pavlovian orienting reflex. *Acta Neurobiologiae Experimentalis, 47*(5-6), 239-247.

Zimbardo, P. G., & Miller, N. E. (1958). Facilitation of exploration by hunger in rats. *Journal of Comparative and Physiological Psychology, 51*(1), 43-46. https://doi.org/10.1037/h0048820

Zubek, J. P. (1969). Sensory and Perceptual-Motor Effects. In: J. Zubek (Ed.). *Sensory Deprivation: Fifteen years of research* (207-253). NY: Appleton Century-Crofts.

ESSAY FIVE: METHDOLOGICAL CHALLENGES FOR A FIELD THEORY OF PSYCHOLOGICAL BEHAVIOR

Traditionally, the teaching and divulgation of science artificially separates logic and concepts from the theories, methods, procedures, and measurement criteria used. In the case of psychology and social science, "methodology" courses are customary, as a corpus independent of the theory or theories that make up the discipline(s). This tradition is partly due to the influence of logicism as a theory of the science and its method (Feyerabend, 1970; Toulmin, 1972). The scientific method is spoken of as a universal method shared by all empirical sciences. However, there is no such universal scientific method. There is a scientific mode of knowledge coexisting with other modes of knowledge (ordinary, technological, artistic, ethical-juridical, religious, and formal), each with distinct institutional purposes in society. Each mode of knowledge, including the scientific one, implies but does not make explicit any particular method. Modes constitute only criteria of presentation and acceptance, but not of knowledge generation (Ribes, 2013, 2018). Methods, at least in the sciences, but also in other modes of knowledge, are specific to the domains in which knowledge is generated, and these methods change historically with the internal criteria of each domain of knowledge, gradually modulating the characteristics of each mode. Another reason for the separation of theory and method has to do with the absence of a logic of consensual theoretical and conceptual analysis in these disciplines, so that to theoretical eclecticism is added, as can be expected, a methodological eclecticism that assumes certain universal criteria of validation and quantification of empirical knowledge. However, no method makes sense disarticulated from the concepts and criteria that identify the facts and significant properties of the phenomena and events that make up a knowledge domain. The great transformations in the history of science have always consisted of changes in theory and research methodology (including the representation and measurement of facts and relations). At times, theory may precede methodology, as in Newton's gravitational mechanics, and, at other times, the instrumental components of the methodology foster the theoretical change, as in the case of microscopy and the development of experimental and evolutionary microbiology.

The methodology of science encompasses different aspects: the fundamental one is related to the formulation of appropriate and pertinent questions considering the way in which the conditions and properties of the phenomena under study are conceived. Another aspect has to do with the design or elaboration of experimental preparations or observation procedures that allow the analysis of the occurrence "in vivo" of the conditions and properties of the phenomena under study. A third aspect has to do with measurements as relevant data for the theory and, partially, with the aspects of instrumentation to be used in the observation and recording of the facts and properties that are relevant from the theory that frames research. In the latter aspect, technology and science have historically been intertwined, with independent but mutually influential courses. Lastly, the problem of the representation of the operations and phenomena recorded and observed is highlighted. In the latter problem, two important moments can be highlighted. One, the explanation of what has been studied, which we have already addressed in a previous work. Second, the incorporation of mathematics as a transdisciplinary instrument to systematize the quantitative analysis of the observed facts in the form of data and, when convenient, the symbolic representation of the relations found, usually in the form of equations or geometrical descriptions of some kind. The methodological problems of a field theory will be examined according to these four aspects just mentioned.

Object of knowledge and research questions

A theory constitutes a coherent system of definitions concerning how to interact with a set of phenomena, objects, and events. A theory establishes the criteria for identifying its object of knowledge, and the relations between properties characterizing it, among other things. In this process, general categories are elaborated and specified, which constitute the logic of analysis of the theory. The general categories define "spaces" of different relations and properties whose confluence allows us to understand and explain the phenomena examined. Each category delimits the functional nature of the different concepts elaborated and/or used as the technical language of the theory, on the understanding that these concepts constitute the fundamental instrument of knowledge, given that the other aspects comprising the methodological "matrix" of a theory derive from or depend on them. Previously (Ribes, 2004; Ribes, Moreno, & Padilla, 1996) we have described a model of scientific practice in psychology (which has to be adapted to each particular discipline) that identifies four different types of categories (taxonomic, operational, measurement, and representation) and which are related to the criteria of analysis that we will follow in a general way. This model, in addition to other factors, assumes a dependence of the rest of the categories on the taxonomic categories, which identify the objects of knowledge of the discipline. The

126

empirical world abstracted by a scientific theory is initially classified into taxonomic categories: the states of matter and particles of the atom in physics, the elements in the periodic table of chemistry, the kingdoms of life and their divisions in bioecology, and the types of social formation in the socio-historical sciences. In psychology there is a multiplicity of taxonomies, the most frequent as adjectives of the "mental" terms of ordinary language establishing differentiations (working memory, visual memory, musical perception, spatial perception, etc.), operational classifications linked to conditioning methodology (Pavlovian, operant, instrumental, and associative), or the concepts established by psychometric construct validity of some ordinary language terms, referring to performance in problem solving, instructional recognition, or assessments of behavioral "abnormality". Kuhn (1977) keenly perceived the close linkage between the categories of theory and the research they frame and foster. One of his definitions of paradigm was that of the exemplar. An exemplar constitutes the referent of what a problem is to be investigated, the type of questions that can be formulated and the method(s) by which the problem (or theoretical puzzle) can be solved. The theory, in the form of methodological exemplar, delimits and restricts the way of seeing the phenomena as problems to be investigated, the questions that make sense and, consequently, the ways in which they can be answered. Obviously, the ways have to do with the relevant experimental procedures and arrangements to study a phenomenon.

The revised version of the field theory of psychological behavior (Ribes, 2018) retained the same general logical categories of the previous formulation (Ribes & López, 1985), but modified the taxonomic concepts and the processes concepts implied therein. In the first place, the interaction between individual (previously 'organism') and stimulus object formulated by Kantor (1924-26) as stimulus-response function was replaced by the category of functional contact. Five types of functional contacts were maintained, but with a different characterization. Each general type of functional contact represents a type of psychological field as an organization of interdependent contingency relations between occurrences linked to stimulus objects and events and occurrences linked to the individual's behavior based on the various ongoing active/reactive patterns. The concept of stimulus-response function suggests (although not necessarily) a momentary, molecular interaction between the individual and the stimulus object, while the contact implies a synchronous molar episode encompassing several diachronic, successive and/or concurrent interactions, so that its duration (and the changes occurring as the defining process of the contact) is not brief, nor can each of the punctual interactions be counted as independent contacts. They are always different moments of the same contact. Functional contacts by coupling and by alteration contingencies are seen as semi-stable processes that can synchronically coexist in the same field and that are reversible in principle. These two contacts are assumed to most prevalent contacts in psychological behavior. Functional contacts by extension and by transformation contingencies are not reversible and constitute single-episode processes, which upon conclusion they "become" part of new contacts by coupling, alteration, and comparison. The latter type of contact shares the reversibility of contacts by coupling and alteration contingencies and the mono-episodic character of contacts by extension and transformation contingencies.

The concept of adjustment was retained only as a description of the outcome in terms of the new segmentations in the behavior-environment continuum, although it was diluted in the different forms of functional detachment characterizing each contact, thus eliminating the temptation (always latent) of establishing a predetermined relational criterion based on some type of achievement. Regardless of the achievements, effects or outcome in a functional contact, the process always consists in some form of functional detachment, varying among individuals and in circumstances or moments for the same individual. In fact, functional contacts only can be identified in the different moments of the process of functional detachment with respect to the initial conditions represented by occurrence-contingencies. Once the detachment has stabilized as functional contingencies, psychological behavior concludes. The new stable condition is equivalent to a new circumstance of occurrence-contingencies, unless new transitions occur under the auspices of changes in the relations or properties of stimulus objects and events and/or in the course of the individual's active/reactive patterns. Thus, the so-called steady states of operant behavior, at least under certain conditions of temporal and spatial consistency, could not be considered in a strict sense psychological behavior. From a theoretical view, the fundamental interest is to formulate relevant questions about the process of functional detachment in each of the contact types, the conditions and parameters that determine transitions within and between contacts, and ways of describing as precisely as possible the characteristics and properties of objects and events as stimulus segments, as well as those of the individual's active/reactive patterns. Depending on what questions are asked in this regard, the course of experimental research will take different directions, some probably not very fruitful. The use of the technical concepts of the theory does not guarantee the formulation of appropriate and pertinent questions and, at times, one may revert to questions linked to previous or different theories, but disguised in the garb of the terminology of a field logic, a phenomenon that occurs frequently in the history of sciences (Ribes, 1986).

Another important change in the theory was the incorporation of historical dispositional factors as characteristics of nonspecific and specific reactive activation of set of active/reactive patterns with respect to the characteristics, properties and changes in the stimulus objects and events, as we have previously examined in an essay in this work. Leaving aside nonspecific changes in the environment related to temperature, visibility, noise, and similar situational aspects, dispositional functions are not independent of the transitions occurring in the detachment process, so that successive and/or concurrent dispositionally differential episodes can occur in the same field. As we have mentioned in another work, dispositional functions are not unrelated to changes in the different molar dimensions of behavior, including their directionality. These functions can also differentially affect in a specific way those dimensions more sensitive to changes in behavioral intensity, such as some modalities of vigor like speed and effort, and of persistence as duration and density of recurrence or repetition of components of some patterns. Therefore, incorporating the possible dispositional transitions as part of the detachment process and developing a comprehensive descriptive system of these functions and their transitions as components of functional detachment is a priority.

Although we will examine in detail this issue later, the fact that animal research may have little relevance for the analysis of human psychological behavior should be highlighted. Obviously, the main reason is the conventional-linguistic nature of human behavior. Thus, theoretical concepts must establish this difference and make it explicit in the research questions and, consequently, in planning of experiments, measures to be considered and the interpretation of results. In the case of animal behavior, the set of reactive systems is biological in nature, and is constituted by sensory and motor modes, so that its active/reactive patterns are always regulated by the physiochemical and ecological properties of the stimulus objects and environing events. The case of human beings is different since although all their psychological behavior is based and originates from biological behavior, they additionally have biologically arbitrary reactive systems, whose composition and functionality are conventionally determined by socially relevant criteria. When behavior occurs in a conventional medium of contact, we also ought to consider the conventional reactive systems, the conventional stimulus objects, the mixed composition of reactive systems based on sensorimotor and linguistic modes, the mixed composition of objects (graphemes and physicochemical modalities) and stimulus objects (locutions, gestures, and physicochemical modalities), as well as the processes of functional integration of both (reactive systems and stimulus objects/events) and their various forms of interaction in functional contacts. It is fundamentally important to note that in a molar field model environmental texture and the activity/reactivity of the individual are not identified from isolated objects, properties or "stimuli" ("pure" events) nor as specific, discrete responses. Stimulus objects and events, as well as the active/reactive patterns in psychological behavior always constitute segments whose composition varies based on the ongoing processes of functional detachment. According to the ongoing functional contacts, the interactions between the composition of both segments, active/reactive patterns and environmental texture, are configured based on correlational, dependency, interchangeability, correspondence, and pertinence criteria (Ribes, 2018). Hence the importance of identifying in each type of functional competence and each particular field the formation of the active/reactive patterns and of stimulus objects and events.

Lastly, we will examine in this section the convenience of having a notational system for the different concepts and processes occurring in a psychological field. There are antecedents in operant conditioning theory of different notation systems, all of them formulated for the description of procedures, an interest proper to an operational approach (Findley, 1962; Mechner, 1959; Snapper, Knapp, & Kushner, 1970). In the case of field theory, a notation system would be useful as a descriptive tool for the types of contingency relations, the composition of active/reactive patterns (including discrete components with specific functional properties) and stimulus objects and events, changes in dispositional functions, the course of spatiotemporal transitions of functional contact, and the possible episodic characterization of different moments in the process of functional detachment. Some examples can be mentioned for each type of functional contact, as tentative classificatory categories of exemplary episodes of the different types of functional contact, but they should by no means be considered a formal proposal at this stage. In contacts by coupling contingencies, we can identify episodes of spatiotemporal coincidence, proximity/distancing permanence, correspondence/complementation, repetition/reproduction, tracking, choice/alternation, sequencing/coordination, and recognition. In contacts by alteration contingencies, we could note episodes of temporal modification, spatial modification, spatiotemporal modification, manipulation as spatial composition or decomposition, interrupting and unblocking, calibration or dosing of stimulus event magnitudes, and production of stimulus events. In contacts by comparison contingencies, we could identify episodes of transposition, similarity, grouping, proportions, functional translocation, and interposition or interlocation. In contacts by extension contingencies, we can identify three general types of episodes of actualization of non-present contingencies in the situation: retroactive extension, concurrent extension, and proactive extension. Lastly, in contacts by transformation contingencies, we could identify three general types of episodes: intradomain reorganization, interdomain reorganization, and transdomain reorganization.

The quest for experimental arrangements

In the history of the sciences, when significant theoretical changes take place, they do not necessarily occur simultaneously with changes in the methods and procedures employed until that point. This is not different in the case of psychology. The development of interbehavioral formulations has been closely linked historically to pragmatism (Dewey, 1896) and to different versions of behaviorism (Watson, 1924; Skinner, 1938), both conceptually and experimentally. Kantor's (1924-1926) proposal constituted a radical logical and perhaps only a partial conceptual break with these traditions. However, it did not offer a new methodological strategy to study psychological phenomena in terms of procedures, experimental arrangements, and data analysis strategies. Therefore, it is not surprising that the starting point of experimental and observational research came from the tradition represented by the free operant methodology and classical and operant conditioning procedures.

Skinner's (1956) great contribution to psychology is undoubtedly linked to the free operant method. However, the fundamental contribution is not linked to the operant conditioning procedure itself (Fester, 1953), but to his emphasis on recording the occurrence of behavior in real time, for prologued periods in relation to the employed experimental variables. Skinner's free operant offered the possibility of conducting sustained studies in a single individual, in which changes in the values of the employed variables or in changes of variables could be evaluated. Discrete trails were replaced by the free movement of the rat (initially) in the experimental situation, providing temporal continuity to the interactions of the individual with the conditions examined. A not inconsiderable additional advantage was the possibility of eliminating average measurements from different individuals as if they were representative of the behavior of a single individual. Skinner freed the temporal dimension of the occurrence of behavior, but did not do the same in with the spatial dimension. His interest in the persistence of discrete occurrences resulted in the reduction of the spatial feature of behavior to a limited area of the already small experimental chamber. In his view, the frequency of a specific, discrete, repetitive response constituted an index of the probability of behavior. As described, in detail, by Skinner (1966), the design of the experimental chamber had the purpose of fostering the occurrence of this response over any other form of behavior. He considered, without much foundation, that the properties of that response, rather its electromechanical effects (the closing of a microswitch by lever pressing or key pecking), were the defining property representative of all the behavior in the situation, insofar as it was the event producing the delivery of water or food (the reinforcer; Skinner, 1935). Everything else that occurred in addition to the predetermined operant response was "nonresponse" or "no responding". Nevertheless, the interest on the study of the temporal continuum of the operant response was determinant for the "discovery" of the cumulative record as a way to measure the response patterns with the other forms of unrecorded behavior, that is, the nonresponses. The cumulative record, which distributed the responses over the actual intervals in which they occurred was precisely a representation of the response rate, that is, of the different local response densities over the recording period. In addition, cumulative record, as a measure of response and no response patterns in real time, allowed analyzing the transitions in behavior and, to that extent, evaluating the processes of change on a continuous basis (Ferster & Skinner, 1957). Rate is not the same as frequency of response, as usually described by so-called experimental behavior analysts. Frequency is just the number of responses per time unit, which is what they regularly report. Rate represents speed and rhythm or acceleration (as the slope of the cumulative curve) of the lever-pressing response relative to the other behaviors in the experimental situation. In replacing the cumulative record with the reporting of total frequency per session or period, the direct measure of temporal organization of the operant response pattern was lost (Skinner, 1976). The use of curve fitting and regression analysis has even eliminated the temporal dimension as an analytic criterion, not to mention that such representations are based solely on samples of total behavior. The

132

analysis of nonresponses as classes of inter-response times suffers from the same problem: they are represented as frequencies regardless of the particular times at which they occur.

Schoenfeld repeatedly pointed out the continuous nature of behavior in time and space, and the need to directly examine its dimensional properties. The reflex tradition had led to the conception of the response as a discrete single occurrence that did not allow the context of that occurrence to be assessed, making it difficult the interpret the various effects of the same variable on behavior. Schoenfeld & Farmer (1970) demonstrated that through the direct reinforcement of "non-responses", equivalent in duration to the operant response, the occurrence of the latter could be systematically affected. From the fact that operant responses do not occur "alone" or in isolation in the experimental arrangement, other authors have examined the same problem by considering the components preceding the operant response, including inter-response times (Henton & Iversen, 1978; Mechner, 1994). As I have previously stated (Ribes, 1996), Schoenfeld lamented that at that time there were no instruments to continuously record behavior in space, nor was there any form of analog mathematics that could represent such an uninterrupted flow. The publication of some studies showing important effects on operant behavior as a result of changes in the spatial arrangement of operanda and dispensers in the experimental chamber (Cabrer, Dazar, & Ribes, 1975), led us to design an experimental situation that would enhance the spatial properties of the contingencies involved in operant conditioning. The characteristics of the standard operant conditioning chamber imposed operational restrictions on the type of problems that could be studied. To put it metaphorically, "Skinner's box" determined what questions made sense to ask and, in advance, anticipated the type of results that should or could be found.

The main purpose was to continuously measure the behavior of the rat (in our case) in an enlarged space that facilitated displacement and in which multiple operanda, dispensers, and sources of visual and auditory stimulation could be installed to increase the complexity of the experimental environment. The lack of digitized visual technology hindered for many years that availability of an experimental arrangement that would free the special constraints of the standard operant conditioning chamber. A first effort in this direction was reported using an enlarged area of approximately one square meter, with food and water dispensers placed on opposite side walls (Ribes & Chávez, 1988). In this study, the behavior of two rats was filmed, and a code system was established to observe and classify the different behavior types occupying the total film time. A second effort consisted in using a standard operant conditioning chamber, but with two working panels, such that each panel had two operanda and a food or water dispenser. This modification to the standard chamber partially removed the traditional spatial restrictions at least for the stimulus objects. Two photocells were attached to each water dispenser and levers, one in the center and two on the sides. The series of photocells allowed to record the displacement and/or permanence of the rat in five zones of the chamber as well as head entries in the water dispenser (Ribes & Torres, 2000; Ribes, Torres, Correa, & Montes, 2006). Lastly, at the annual convention of the Association for Behavior Analysis in Chicago in 1999, I met Dan Sussman, who was Schoenfeld's former graduate student and at that time working for Coulburn Instruments. It was not difficult to explain to him the type of experimental chamber we required, so that within a year we had the coveted experimental arrangement with us at the University of Guadalajara: an approximately one square meter chamber with modular walls, so that operanda, dispensers, and stimulus sources could be inserted at different locations on each of the walls, with an elevated digital camera located in the central part that continuously recorded the rat's position, and which could be subdivided into 0.2 second cuts. The experimental chamber was commercially patented by the company, without any acknowledgement of our contribution (Coulburn Instruments, E14-05 model). The original digital camera has since been replaced by Ethovision devices, without changing the system's main operations. The first study using this preparation (Ribes, Palacios, & Hernandez, 2020), published 17 years after it was conducted, allowed describing the rat's behavior based on multiple molar measures (Ribes, 2007). This was the first study to examine behavior in terms of directionality, variation, preference, vigor, and persistence. In this and other study (Ribes & Tamayo, 2021), non-contingent water delivery were employed, typical of contacts by coupling contingencies. In later studies, alteration contingencies with additional spatial variations have been introduced. In the first study of this kind (Ribes & Tamayo, 2020), levers and water dispensers were presented on each of the four walls of the experimental chamber. Water delivery was implemented in some conditions independently of the rat's behavior, while in other it was presented according to a traditional fixed-interval (FI) schedule. These presentations were simultaneous and independent at each dispenser, establishing strict or sequential concurrence (not operational) in a given order (as if they were "pure" multiple schedules). In another study (Ribes & Tamayo, 2021), two experiments were conducted where a radial maze was superposed on the displacement chamber, replicating the same conditions as in the previous study. In one of the experiments, four arms of an eight-arm radial maze led to levers and dispensers. In the other, the arms of the maze were not closed, so that the rat could move around the periphery and "dead" zones of the camera as well. Both experiments constitute an attempt to integrate studies of operant and instrumental conditioning empirically and operationally, as variations in the restrictions imposed on the temporal and spatial continua of the field contingencies.

Experimental preparations (including observational systems) for human behavior have also been explored. In this case, the spatial dimension adopts different characteristics from those of displacement and locomotion. Motor skills such as displacement and coordination have an important role in forming the active/reactive patterns of psychological behavior only in the early stages of becoming. Later, these aspects are part of stereotyped biological and social behaviors with no clear psychological function. Human geography in everyday life is strictly conventional, even in explorers, it is a geography of maps, directions, preestablished routes, operational routines, travel restrictions, and so on. In an early period (Ribes, Ibáñez, & Hernández-Pozo, 1986), we explored the use of the interactive computational matching-to-sample procedure as a common arrangement for relating animal and human behavior. Second-order matching-to-sample was preferred under the erroneous assumption that it favored what were then considered selector interactions. In addition, the number of comparison stimuli were increased to four thus avoiding artifacts due to chance or position bias effects, and sample and textual comparison stimuli were occasionally used, as well as names correlated with the geometric stimuli ordinarily used. The functional level of the interaction was evaluated based on three types of transference tests (intrasituational, extrasituational, and transituational). In considering the linguistic nature of the interactions of the human participants in the studies, an alternative strictly textual-written response system was developed (Ribes, Moreno, & Martínez, 1998). Instead of selecting the comparison stimulus with the mouse, the participant had to fill in a paragraph with blanks by choosing options from a bank of 27 texts. These texts allowed describing the characteristics, properties or relations of the second-order stimuli, the sample stimulus and the selected comparison stimulus. Thus, a matching response analogous to the participant saying what she "saw" and "attended to" while selecting the comparison stimulus was obtained. The texts exhausted all descriptive possibilities based on criteria of stimulus naming, listing its properties, and the relations related to the other stimuli. The use of a system of incomplete texts, as well as that of explicit conventional stimulus properties (Ribes, Hernández-Pozo, Sánchez, Gutiérrez, & González, 1987), can afford methodological advantages for assessing the functions of mixed (conventional–non-conventional) components in the stimulus and the active/reactive segments.

A significant part of the virtual experimental procedures where different response options are required are always based on the old paradigms of associating pairs and matching to sample. For this reason, many of the new experimental arrangements have a family resemblance with those paradigms, even though there are great differences between them and functional aspects are evaluated that have little to do with their original purposes. Recently (Ribes, León, & Andrade, 2020) we have presented an experimental arrangement to study stimulus transposition, which constitutes part of a yet to be completed set of distinct procedures for examining different forms of contacts by comparison contingencies. Contacts by comparison require conjugate active/reactive patterns by permutation of the properties of stimulus segments that can participate in relational contingencies based on their absolute values on one or more continua. This experimental arrangement accounts for the ordinal permutation of stimulus values, the choice between different values, modalities and continua, the ranges of variation of stimulus values, as well as the directionality, variation, and persistence of the response patterns in the situation. The new arrangements allow assessing moment-to-moment transitions in the active/reactive conjugate patterns actualized and, to that extent, determining the moment in which the comparison process concludes as functional detachment. Additional experimental arrangements are in the process of design and testing to examine other types of functional contacts by comparison, which will likely be adaptable to the analysis of the other forms of theoretically identified functional contacts. Dimensional or modal stimulus continua, and continua based on practical (non-formal) referential criteria in purely conventional circumstances, are considered in all these experimental arrangements. The new arrangements account for the analysis of relational contingencies of relative properties of the stimulus segments, of equivalential properties of similarity, of proportional properties between stimulus segments, of properties of relative grouping, and of properties of functional dislocation of the properties of the stimulus objects. Noteworthy in all these arrangements is the possibility of continuously and directly assessing the defining functional dimension of contacts by comparison: the occurrence of search and inspecting patterns (Berlyne, 1960).

Other experimental arrangements to be tested are part of two doctoral research projects of Fabio Medeiros and Víctor Fuentes Barragán, which will most likely be reported starting 2021. These arrangements are related to some of the old problems of perception. From the current perspective, they are considered from two complementary levels. One level corresponds to spatial contingencies configuring the texture of stimulus objects always as figure-background or object-context relations. Although the participants interact with the stimulus conditions in real time, the configurations are static and non-changing, so that they constitute samples of atemporal space in a strict sense, without changes in the position of their elements or changes in their constituent elements. A second level analyzes individuals behaving differentially under unstructured stimulus environments, with poorly differentiated texture and without superimposed contingencies. The individual differentiates and configures the environmental texture through its operation in the stimulus conditions, based on the establishment of perimeters, volumes, creases, and distinct areas. This type of behavior is called prolative behavior and is fundamental in the first months of life when the infant recognizes, discriminates, and manipulates objects and their stimulus properties, coordinating visual, auditory, and haptic sensitivity, and orientation, search, inspecting, and manipulating motor patterns. Once the functional texture of the environment has been individually differentiated, the prelative behavioral patterns that dispositionally determine the differential preferences for the different segments and stimulus properties of the environment emerge.

In regard to observational methodology, a multidimensional observational system of mother-infant dyadic interactions was reported some years ago (Ribes & Quintana, 2002). Such a scale highlights the episodic nature of the infant's behavior always with respect to another person, which was the mother in this "abstract" case. These episodes occur in different situations where one must consider the particular functional properties comprised in the mediated interaction with stimulus objects and events, the dynamic (dispositional) properties of the segments involved. It is also relevant to examine the progressive integration of sensorimotor and linguistic modes in the infant's active/reactive patterns, as well as the identification of the type of functional contacts that develop and establish.

We now turn to the issue pertaining the actual "design" of experimental studies. Behavioral research traditionally emphasizes steady states, commonly predetermined based on some specific interest (e.g., "matching", "temporal" discrimination, etc.) or response percentages indicating some achievement criterion tantamount to the "acquisition" of the behavior under study. In fact, the number of experimental sessions is commonly based on individual approaching or meeting preset stability or achievement criteria. High response frequencies, percentages of obtained reinforcers, percentages of correct/incorrect, appropriate/inappropriate responses, are usually the data sought and evaluated in the "normal" planning of experimental studies. From our field theory, the fundamental empirical interest is identifying, classifying, tracking, and representing the transitions between states of the field. The psychological processes participating during functional detachment always consist of transitions between states. The states correspond to occurrence-contingencies, which do not represent psychological behavior, but its antecedent or its outcome. This task must be developed considering a single individual in continuous time and space, and criteria to identify changes as transitions between states, their episodic properties, and their functional trajectory. It may be instructive to examine previous efforts, albeit from a different perspective (Norman, 1966; Weiss, 1970).

Measurement and representativeness of the records as «data» of the theory

One of the central problems of any theory is to determine which feature of the records resulting from the experimental arrangement constitute relevant facts, that is, what part of the records are "data". Response frequency was considered as the basic measure of behavior in the operant tradition, thus incurring in a threefold error. First, as we have recently examined, frequency and rate of response were equated. However, frequency is the number of events per unit time, while rate describes local proportions or densities of a frequency and its changes. Unfortunately, frequency was ultimately imposed over response rate, and an index of pace and speed of operant response and pattern formation with non-responses was lost. Second, frequency was assumed to be identifiable with probability, and that the latter was an objective index of the "strength" of an operant. In this case, the probability of an event is assumed to be higher when its relative frequency compared to other events is greater, so that if, for example, pressing a lever has a high frequency in one period, its probability of occurrence will be greater in the future. However, this is not the case since whether a given behavior occurs at a given time it not only a function of its absolute frequency (and the estimated relative frequency), but depends on the set of circumstances under which it occurs at both times and/or situations. Skinner himself assumed this in his analysis of verbal behavior, whereby he restricted the probability of a verbal operant to the circumstances of the situation and not to the number of times said operant had been emitted (Skinner, 1957). Finally, a third misunderstanding is that frequency, the number of occurrences of an event, is not a measure of the properties, characteristics, or functions of said event. It is simply a count in time. The number and frequency of entities or occurrences is a statistical measure, but not a dimensional one. Said another way, it does not describe, denote, or point to the characteristics of the event or entity under study. Thus, frequency cannot be considered a basic measure of behavior. However, studies have been conducted to differentiate some dimensional properties of operant responses. Some of the properties that have been studied are duration and strength of the response (Notterman & Mintz, 1965), the positional displacement of the response (Herrick, 1964), and the most obvious case of differentiation during the shaping the lever pressing response, as a modification of the geography and topography of the behavior.

As we have argued, psychological behavior constitutes a functional detachment of biological and social behavior (in the latter case, linguistic behavior). In the case of biological behavior, we can measure its spatiotemporal dimensions, relating to changes of position in space or to local changes in the same position, that is, translational or coordinated movements in the same position, such as orienting, manipulating, among others. In the case of conventional behavior, a diverse, segmented and discontinuous set of gestures, phonations, and articulated local movements is superimposed to the biological behavior continuum, which adds other dimensions to its measurability.

Previously (Ribes, 2007), the molar dimensions to behavioral measurement were described within the framework of a field theory. The relevance of considering molar measures from the spatiotemporal continuum in which the functional contacts constituting psychological behavior occur was underscored. As previously discussed, given their origin in the logical paradigm of the reflex (Ribes, 1999; Ribes & López, 1985), the theoretical and methodological tradition of behaviorist approaches has favored the analysis of psychological behavior as "learned" or "acquired" behavior based on macromolecular criteria. Schoenfeld and Farmer (1970) highlighted the paradox represented by the fact that the experimental sciences first developed molar concepts and theories and, in a second historical stage, molecular analytic levels were formulated, while in psychology the opposite has occurred, whereby continuous episodes in space and time have been fragmented into psychological or behavioral atoms. Operant theory recovered the temporal continuum, at least methodologically, but space was reduced to a restricted location of behavioral occurrence as discrete, determined, and continuous "responses", which explains the emphasis on frequency as measurement criterion. In accord with this view, environing objects that constitute more or less constant conditions and can be identified as states, were reduced to their local changes as "stimuli". As "responses" do not occur in a vacuum, neither do "stimuli", so that stimuli per se can only correspond to discrete events having a finite duration with identifiable beginning and end. Therefore, is incorrect and confusing to identify stimuli with the objects in which the changes that produce them occur. This confusion leads to identify as stimuli prolonged changes in the condition of an object (for example, the color in a lightbulb), when the actual stimulus consists only of the event of change of properties in the light emitted by the lightbulb (transition from one color to another).

The molar measures of behavior that we have proposed are directionality, variation, vigor, persistence, and preference. Achievement measures are complementary since they have to do with behavioral outcomes and are not dimensions of behavior. It is important note that, as with any theoretical proposal, these molar measures are tentative and can be modified or expanded, depending on their usefulness and consistency in the analysis of the processes of functional detachment. All molar measures of behavior (initially biological) are identified in one way or another from movements or physiochemical changes in and of the organism, that is, from the biology of the individual as a whole. As with any movement or event, its identification and description must be made in continuous spatiotemporal coordinates, in terms of changes in the position of the reactive systems of the organism with respect to themselves, or changes in the position of the whole organism with respect to other entities in the environment. Local or translational movements, as changes in space, constitute the temporal dimension of behavior. Insofar as psychological behavior is always described in terms of functional contacts with stimulus objects and events, directionality is the fundamental measure.

Directionality consists of orienting, approaching, or withdrawing from individual behavior with respect to stimulus objects or segments in the environment. Directionality is the adient-abient dimension of behavior (Maier & Schneirla, 1965). Directionality involves what in ordinary language is described as the intentionality or purpose of the behavior. Directionality can be measured in two general ways. First, by having the individual fixed

140

in the same geography (two-dimensional space), that is, without changing place while moving in a three-dimensional space (in "height" or volume) as local changes in her own body. Second, by considering its displacement in three-dimensional space, during which there may be local directionality changes when the translation is interrupted or stopped. Directionality is always measured as movements relative to one stimulus object or segment with respect to another stimulus object or segment. We have employed different directionality measures with respect to animal behavior in our studies. Below we will examine the measures in the case of human behavior, both in its "biological" dimension as movements, or its conventional dimension as "pure" or "mixed" linguistic patterns. In the case of animal behavior, using the experimental chamber described in the previous section (which we have informally named "Schoenfeld's box"), the first directionality measure used as reference point consists of the analogical routes of rats' displacement in the experimental chamber. Routes are segmented based on a temporal criterion and/or the repeated presentation of a stimulus event (e.g., water or food delivery). This procedure allows to assess the way in which the routes change throughout the session, between sessions, and between experimental phases or conditions. The presentation of the total analog routes in a session is called "spider webs", showing changes in their "density" in different portions of space, their repetitiveness or recurrence, their pattern or structure, as well as their degree of variation over the course of the experimental conditions. Trajectories represent a variation of analog routes as vectors, that is, lineal abstractions of the route. Trajectories underscore the origin and destination of the behavior, but eliminate all transient aspects occurring in real time; they are a route idealization. A third measure of directionality is identifying whether in the cycle in which the route is segmented, the path was completed or truncated, that is, it did not reach some of the possible stimulus objects in the experimental arrangement. A fourth variant consists of identifying complete routes as functional or non-functional, considering whether or not they end at the location of the dispositionally relevant object or event. Finally, a fifth directionality measure is proximity or distance of the rat's position to the corresponding location at the time the dispositionally relevant object and/ or event is presented or occurs. These are not the only possible measures of directionality and their development depends on the experimental conditions under which the individual's behavior is analyzed. All other measures are based on directionality and, fundamentally, on the analog route as a real-time record of the rat's movement.

Variation is a dimension related to two important variables. On the one hand, it has to do with the reactive diversity of the individual based on her specific and unspecific history with respect to the situation in which she interacts. On the other hand, it illustrates the stimulus diversity of different environing segments and, therefore, the changes in directionality that can occur in different dispositional conditions, environmental texture, and complexity in the type of occurrence-contingencies in the situation. We have employed three specific variation measures in our experimental studies. First, the maximum distance of the analog route from the ideal straight-line trajectory: the greater the distance, the greater the variation in the possible route. Second, the change in angularity during the route. Third, the number of non-repeated cells traversed by the rat during its displacement in each session. The experimental space is divided into 64 cells for recording displacement. The more non-repeated cells visited, the more variation in the route, while the smaller number of repeatedly traversed cells, the more the stereotypy. Other possible measures of variation may be the number of repeated analog routes seen as a densification of the routes: the higher the densification of a route, the lower the variation. Other specific measures of variation can be established depending on the complexity of the ongoing occurrence-contingencies, including sequences of route segments, and so on.

For vigor we have employed specific measures of speed and acceleration. One of them is the speed of displacement in each route consisting of traveled distance (i.e., number of cells in cm) and the required time. A more sensitive measure is the net or effective speed, which includes only running speed itself, discounting the time of stays or visits equal to or greater than 3 seconds in any cell of the route. Total travel distance per session, or in periods of the session, is an index of vigor as effort. Average or differential acceleration are two complementary options. Average acceleration is calculated by averaging the changes in speed over a route or portions or the entire the session. Differential acceleration is calculated in two ways. One, by comparing the average acceleration of the first five session cycles of the session with the last five cycles. Second, by examining the differences in acceleration in the first five cycles with respect to the last five cycles of a session. Other optional vigor measures are related to measuring the physiochemical effects on or by the individual. One of the latter measures is the physical force (as work) exerted, recorded in ergs or newtons according to the device on which the force is exerted or applied. Duration (or amplitude) of a fraction of the pattern participating in activating a device is another complementary measure. Finally, the heat pro-

142

duced by the movement of the individual can be used as measure of vigor of behavior via the use of infrared sensors that can continuously track the energetic changes that occur. Other measures may be proposed, depending on the instruments available and their relevance to the phenomenon under study.

There are multiple persistence measures. In operant conditioning, they are represented by the repetitive frequency of a discrete response on a preestablished operandum (key, lever, or chain). Interval schedules actually constitute continuous schedules of reinforcement (CRF) where only one response is required for the delivery of the "reinforcer", but with a non-functional, "dead" time interval after each delivery, prescribed as the value of the schedule. Therefore, the reinforcer intermittency is not a property of the schedule, but a characteristic of the organism's performance that emits non-required responses. Response frequency is a measure of persistence of behavior under these schedules, higher for fixed than variable values, but depending on the absolute value of the interval. The same may be said about pause and differential schedules of reinforcement of inter-response times. In turn, the functional nature of response frequency is different in ratio schedules since a certain number of responses is established for the reinforcer to be presented. Response frequency is not only an index of persistence, but also of vigor, as shown by the characteristic break-and-run patterns and higher response frequencies. "Extinction" is simply a measure of persistence of behavior in all intermittent schedules of reinforcement. In the molar analysis of behavior, the persistence dimension can be studied using different measures. These include: recurrence of non-required patterns, sampling of dispensers without water or food, staying in the area adjacent to the dispenser after consumption, repetition of non-functional routes, visiting and sampling non-functional dispensers, and re-entry to the area adjacent to the dispenser after having consumed and exited it.

Preference has to do with the density of the absolute and relative distribution of behavior in space. Specific measures include the total time spent in each of the cells or different areas of the experimental space (including visits and stays), the total number of stays longer than 3 seconds in each cell or area of the experimental space, the relative densities of occupancy of different locations of the experimental space (time/space ratio), the special location of the beginning of the sequence of a new route, the initial direction to a location of the experimental space, and the relative number of samples and consumptions in each dispenser (with the same or different type of consumption).

Concerning the human behavioral dimensions of a biological nature, the same measures abovementioned can be used, adapted to the specific experimental arrangements. For example, in a traditional second-order matching-to-sample arrangement, directionality can be measured by tracking the route of the mouse as it travels through the various stimulus segments, variation by sequence changes in the route, vigor as the net speed the route is traveled, persistence as repetition of the route segments prior to choosing and repeated choosing of an incorrect comparison stimulus on corrective trials, and preference for the stimulus segments through which the route is initiated and due to position biases in choosing the comparison stimulus. This example is obviously that of a simple arrangement, not designed to assess the diversity of molar dimensions that occur in different functional contacts in human tasks.

Field theory does not assume that the various dimensions and that their specific measures must covary in one way or another in the different functional contacts. Insofar as these measures constitute continuous indices of the transitions occurring during the establishment of the function-contingencies in the different contacts, their values will depend on the different possible interdependencies between the present occurrence-contingencies, including the individual's behavior, and on the changes in the dispositional functions during these transitions. The studies conducted thus far do not suggest a necessary correlation between the different measures, so that preference may not correlate with functional routes, and speed may remain significantly unchanged when there are changes in routes or persistence. The different contingency fields require specific functional interpretations of the ways in which different molar measures are related, including differences between two or more specific measures of a dimension. Linear relations or correlations between measures should not be assumed given the inherent complexity of the functional transitions taking place in the occurrence-contingencies articulated by the individual's own behavior (and its "mensurable" dimensions). Composite or 'consolidated' measures can be offered. These would consist of inclusive measures of more than one molar dimension, and could reflect with a high degree of sensitivity the contingent circumstances under which the behavior occurs. A traditional example in operant conditioning is that reported by Notterman and Mintz (1965) using effort as measure. Effort was conceived as the integer in time of the physical force exerted upon the lever, that is, physical work and duration were consolidated in ergs. In the case of molar measures, Hugo Palacios' (2016) doctoral dissertation proposed a consolidated measure called "temporal waves". This measure divides in radians the experimental space of a

144

"Schoenfeld's box" with two water dispensers on diagonally opposite walls. In Palacios' dissertation, each dispenser delivered a drop of water available for 3 seconds based on 40-s and 120-s fixed-time schedules on each dispenser, respectively. The temporal waves, delimited by each of the radians, represent and calculate the net running speed that the rat had to deploy at different points in the chamber, based on the time elapsed from the last delivery of each of the fixed-time schedules, in order to consumer the water in the limited available time. Speed was higher or lower depending on the distance from the dispenser, and always in the form of a straight trajectory. In this project, this measure could describe the contingency relation between direction of the dispenser, time availability of the water, remaining time for water presentation, and effective net speed to be able to consume it. Different temporal waves could be calculated and recorded in a single between water delivery interval.

In concluding, it is important to address the problem of linguistic behavioral measures, regardless of their occurrence as part of different types of biological dimensions of behavior. The biological dimensions are restricted and limited in many episodes to active/reactive patterns of local orienting movements or involving affective responses (Ribes, 2018). These are episodes generally constituted by purely linguistic active/reactive patterns: gesturing, speaking, reading, observing, listening, and writing. These episodes may include non-conventional objects (albeit possessing conventional functions), conventional objects, or "mixed" objects. It is unnecessary and pointless to attempt a classification of the types of conventional objects, since they are all graphic-textual and are always automatically articulated with and in referential practices, as physicochemical (non-conventional) objects are articulated by the sensorimotor reactivity of the individual. Traditionally, linguistic behavior has been identified and measured based on formal, a posteriori categories of dead language (Kantor, 1963). Such categories have characterized "psycholinguistic" research by recording inventories of grammatical forms as criteria of "development" or "competence". Four measure dimensions of linguistic behavior as set of referential practices can be tentatively identified for the purpose of searching for functional criteria: a performative dimension wherein behavior consists exclusively of saying, gesturing/indicating, or writing something (always to someone) as a directed act; a constative dimension wherein reacting occurs with respect to a non-conventional object or event or to the linguistic behavior of another with respect to objects, events, or actions; a reflexive dimension (proper of contacts by transformation contingencies) wherein linguistic behavior consists in speaking (or speaking to oneself), or writing about the functional dependency relations of the set of referential patterns of a domain, that is, about the way in which one referentially interacts in a given functional domain; and dislocation as a fourth dimension wherein the temporal and spatial axes of situational contingencies. The exploratory use of these categories of molar measures of linguistic behavior will allow to assess their utility or their sudden obsolesce.

Field representation and functional contacts

Phenomena always occur in time, space, and in a certain number. It is impossible to imagine something if it is not at a certain time, in a certain place, and in a certain quantity. This is true even for imaginary, fictitious phenomena or objects: there are heavens or hells and immemorial times or times to come. However, time and space are not actual entities, that is, independent of our language and with immanent "existence" in "natural" reality. Time and space are categories, logical dimensions, on the basis of which we relate to natural reality, to ourselves, and to the conventional objects we elaborate. Among such conventional objects are the concepts of time and space themselves, which are applied in very different ways, according to the referential practices in which we participate with respect to phenomena and things as phenomena and things in a given place and time. Time and space are imposed categories in and by our practices, so that their changes reflect the changes in our referential practices. Although time and space are assumed to be absolute properties of things and phenomena in reality, this is only an artifact of language. Time and space are only conventions relative to different practical referential domains. They are part of the grammar of very different language games, borrowing Wittgenstein's (1953) use of this term, with respect to our collective life with things and persons.

In a previous writing (Ribes, 1992), time and space were analyzed as psychological dimensions. In this text it was proposed that although time and space are based on physical metrics for social practical purposes (e.g., position of the stars, compasses, different types of clocks, unit measures of length, height, volume, among others), in each of the "realities" segmented by the scientific mode of knowledge, time and space are manifested with different functional criteria. For example, new units and conceptual frameworks are created to categorize time and space in astrophysics, as well as in bioecology, and the socio-historical science. In the essay just mentioned, the relative functional dominance of the temporal and spatial dimensions in the configuration of psychological contacts (then-called stimulus-response functions) was highlighted. At present, such an analysis is still acceptable. However, it not sufficient to address the problem of the spatiotemporal representation of psychological contacts as abstract empirical relations.

In psychology, time and space have always been conceived as independent dimensions. In fact, space is superficially mentioned as a situation or context of temporal phenomenology. This is to be expected since mind and/or behavior always have a fixed locus, whether in the subject as consciousness, the brain as a privileged organ, or the body as a moving system. The temporal dimension is conceived as identifiable events in relation to discrete durations or intervals between occurrences. The subjects of temporal perception, temporal discrimination, and temporal judgements are treated as if time was a discrete variable with respect to which an individual can differentially respond. As previously mentioned, in the free operant method, where the individual lacks movement restrictions in principle, there is in fact a restriction and elimination of the spatial dimensions of behavior and environmental variables by reducing the possibilities of interaction (the operandum, the source of stimulation and dispenser or the thinker or equivalent) to a limited and fixed segment of the experimental chamber (or any other extension of the method).

The t-T system (Schoenfeld & Cole, 1972) was an attempt to organize the schedules of reinforcement as stimulus schedules, recovering the discrete rules of stimulus presentation as changes of varying extension and relative to a single response in a continuous time dimension. This system was constructed as an operational methodology with three main goals: (a) to generate all types of performance of the different rules of scheduling reinforcement (interval, ratio, their combinations, and later, "stimulus control" and "aversive" stimulation) through variations in a single temporal continuum; (b) minimize "contamination" in the occurrence of the reinforcer and/or stimuli as a result of the first or "n" response on the part of the organism, so that the independent variable would not be determined by the dependent variable; and (c) to relativize time as a dimension in terms of stimuli availability regardless of the absolute value of elapsed time, using the tested T and tau parameters as ratios in continuous repetitive cycles in which there was limited availability for the occurrence of the stimulus. However, despite recognizing the continuity of behavior as a flow in space, due to the limitations of the time, the definition and recording of specific responses at a fixed point was maintained, and the view of "non-responses" as temporally (not spatially) defined units. Later

147

we will propose a revised t-T system as a starting point for a framework of operational representation of interdependent contingency relations in a field. Before doing so, an analysis of the interdependent nature of time and space dimensions and thus of the properties of objects and events and their relative measures is warranted.

We have already mentioned an old practice of considering that time and space are equivalent to absolute entities that been always and forever been there, and that our life represents the changes occurring in these infinite, objective, and absolute continuous entities. Minkowski (1907-1908/2012), who provided the mathematical formalization of Einstein's theory of relativity, proposed the spacetime concept according to which physical phenomena are the same in all inertial reference frames, because each inertial observer has its own space and time. As Petkov (2012) pointed out "that fact implies that the Universe is an absolute four-dimensional world in which space and time are inseparably amalgamated; only in such a world one can talk about many spaces and many times" (p. 32). This quote is important for several reasons. First, although time and space are seemingly separately recorded, time and space are inseparable from each other, not only in terms of the occurring phenomena, but also in reference to the observers of those phenomena. There will be as many descriptive frames of phenomena in space and time as positions and moments of their observation. Time-moment and space-place always occur from the now and here (the present) of who says or writes it, or with respect to another of whom it is said or written. Not only do the terms and expressions of ordinary language make sense based on the situationality of its practice, but the same criterion applies to the categories and logic framing scientific practice. The phenomena observed are always phenomena framed in the logic of a theory. Theory of relative and the spacetime category posit that phenomena are always relative to a specific spacetime referent. They are not phenomena occurring in separate absolute time and space. The latter corresponds only to the way in which phenomena occur in the sphere of ordinary language practices, and make sense as a social practice at the time and place. However, it also accounts for the fact that in different social formations, and thus forms of life, an apparently identical phenomenon is "understood" and shared in different ways.

In the case of physics, the special theory of relativity applied to the description of speed and distance as measures of time and space, changed the way we talk about these properties. They ceased to be absolute measures of absolute time and space and became measures relative to the observer's own distance and motion (speed). This conclusion highlights that there is no absolute, fixed world, which is gradually known, but that knowledge of the world is conditional on the circumstances of what is observed and of the observer. This is not a postmodern "relativism", but a specific relativity between what is known and the circumstances and mode in which it is known. Bridgman (1927), Nobel laurate in Physics, distorted in his proposal of the operational analysis of scientific concepts by the "operationalism" derived from the logical positivism that took root in psychology with Stevens and Bergman (Ribes, 2003), stressed that Einstein's great contribution had nothing to do with direct empirical findings, but with a new way of speaking and perceiving such findings theoretically. Bridgman argued that "…In general, we mean by any concept nothing more than a set of operations; the concept is synonymous with the corresponding set of operations" (p. 5). He goes on to clarify that "… For of course the true meaning of a term is to be found by observing what a man does with it, not by what he says about it" (p. 7). He gives as an example Einstein's concept of simultaneity: "…Einstein [now] subjected the concept of simultaneity to a critique, which consisted essentially in showing that the operations which enable two events to be described as simultaneous involve measurements on the two events made by an observer, so that "simultaneity" is, therefore, not an absolute property of the two events and nothing else, but most also involve the relation of the events to the observer…Of course Einstein actually went much further than this, and found precisely how the operations for judging simultaneity change when the observer moves, and obtained quantitative expressions for the effect of the motion of the observer on the relative time of two events" (pp. 8-9). Feyerabend (1970) argued a similar criterion in examining Galileo's contribution to the concept of motion in relation to the Copernican theory of the planetary system. Galileo modified the concept of motion as absolute motion on the motionless (geostatic) planet (Earth), to a concept of geodynamic motion in terms of a motion relative to the circular inertia of the planet's motion.

A flat space without accidents in the form of local changes or changes between places is a space without time, so that time is incorporated when there is any change in space. In a psychological field, these changes can be changes within a single position in the form of a local change: an orienting movement, inspecting or manipulating on the part of the individual without moving from the same point or place, or a modification in a fixed object in space, such as the delivery of food or water at a dispenser, a local displacement of a fixed lever, pedal or chain, or the switching on of a lightbulb, or the presentation of a sound in a device on a wall. Changes between locations correspond to changes of position in the three Euclidian coordinates, which may be associated with local "simultaneous" changes. These translational changes correspond to the locomotion of the individual, or to movements in space with change of location of the stimulus objects, such as a light moving along the walls, or even the presentation of water, food, or "successive" stimulus changes at different 'fixed' points in the environment. 'Simultaneous', 'fixed' and 'successive' are used in quotation marks because such changes can be determined as operations from the experimenter as observer, or from the contact that may or may not be established by the individual as observer. The spatial relation between an individual(s) and the stimulus object(s) is also relative between these entities. In discussing the configuration of a system, Maxwell (1877/1925) established that in order to know this configuration it is necessary to know the positions of any point of the system with respect to any other point at that instant, that is, the relative positions of its elements, one with respect to the other. In the case of a psychological field this means that the individual's local and translational changes (and that of the stimulus objects when they occur in one or both forms) continuously modify the relative positions of one or the other, so that the configuration of the field, initially seen as a "static" field, is continuously modified by dynamically altering its limits.

The spacetime concept provides a field theory with a logical framework for the representation of functional contacts as processes of functional detachment. Spacetime emphasizes: 1) the inseparability of time and space and the need for measures that account for both integrated dimensions; 2) the reciprocal interdependence of changes in the behavior of the organism relative to changes in the stimulus objects; 3) the possibility of identifying distinct slices (so as not to use the word worlds) of phenomena in spacetime dimensions relative to the position and momentum of the observer of the phenomenon, in our case the researcher or the individual participating the field relations; 4) to account for the synchrony of functional contact (and its circumstantiality) as a spacetime cut based on different molar criteria and segmentation of the field elements; and 5) to identify the psychological phenomenon or behavior in terms of the functional boundaries of the field, represented as a dynamic (not static) geometry of invariant boundaries, reflecting the transitions comprised in the functional detachment and fluctuations in dispositional factors.

From the perspective of a spacetime logical framework, two objectives can be pursued. First, to develop an operational methodology that allows an integrated spacetime representation of those experimental operations of variable presentation and registration that are usually not explicit and occur separately with respect to the spatial and temporal dimensions. Second, to represent descriptively the phenomena occurring in spacetime as functions integrated on axes that clearly specify the parameters of relativity of these functions. Of course the approaches we will make are tentative and could be considered exploratory questions rather than specific proposals.

The operational logic of the t-T system can inspire a starting point for the representation of contingencies in a spacetime-based field. Such a system represented a temporal continuum, segmented into repetitive cycles of the same length, where brief stimulus changes or subcycles of so-called 'time outs' (TO) –periods where no stimulus contingency operated, could occur. The individual's behavior was recorded as changes relative to each cycle, which began as a 'zero' time and restarted without interruption at the programmed length. The time continuum of each cycle and between cycles can be sub-divided for analytical purposes into a digitized continuum of smaller units (seconds, tenths, or hundredths of a second). The absolute time specified as the value of each cycle and the total number of cycles of an experimental session is relativized by dividing each cycle into at least two functional periods (the type and number of divisions in a field analysis would have to do with theoretical-experimental purposes). The cycle is usually divided into two subcycles, namely a discriminative t in which a dispositionally relevant stimulus (water, food, electric shock) is presented non-contingent or contingent to a predetermined response on the part of the individual, and a t delta subcycle in which such stimuli are not presented, or if they are presented it is with a lower probability, frequency, or density than in the discriminative subcycle. The proportion of the discriminative time interval with respect to the total time of the cycle (the quotient of discriminative t over discriminative time plus delta time) yields an index called T tested. This index describes the proportion of absolute or relative "functional" time (when stimuli are also presented in t delta) within the total time of the cycle. T tested constitutes a relative functional time with respect to the intra-cycle or the inter-cycle time continuum. Schoenfeld and colleagues identified T tested with the probability that a response, if it occurred in the discriminative time subcycle, would be followed by the stimulus. Of course, the response was not predetermined in the no contingency and the probability of either response being followed by the stimulus that was 0.5 for the predetermined response (lever pressing) or a nonresponse (any behavior other than lever pressing).

The spatial continuum was not considered in such a system and the analysis was kept in terms of frequencies and rates of a predetermined response. However, each cell in the Schoenfeld's box always coincides with a moment of an individual's movement, as well as the stimulus presentations. From this perspective, the route is actually a spacetime continuum whereby there are two criteria to identify time: first, as continuous time corresponding to the positional or postural changes represented by the individual's movement; second, as discrete time represented by the presentation of discrete stimulus events, with a beginning and an end, that is, with a determinable duration. The issue now arises as to the operations that jointly include the functional properties of stimulus events and behavior segments in spacetime, that is, specifying the durations, locations, and intervals of joint occurrences of stimulus events and the individual's behavior, or as asymmetrical individual/object length segments as synchronic units, although diachronically they don't necessarily show point-to-point correspondences. This requires the formulation of a conjunctive S/T notation system under contingency (K) and non-contingency (NK) circumstances, so that time is not represented independently of the space in which stimulus changes occur nor the local or translational movement of the individual. Directionality, vigor, variation, preference, and persistence are measures that can be seen as parametric dimensions of spacetime relativity at different slices of the continuum of transitions in the ongoing functional contacts. It should be noted that the goal is not correlating molar measures of behavior with occurrences in space. It would not make sense to include a S system parallel to T system since space and time are not independent dimensions. It would be redundant to propose a discriminative S (space) and a S delta (space) since the discriminative time can only be associated with the discriminative space. An integrated representation of the measures of spacetime change that includes both dimensions in the stimulus objects as well as in the individual is required. It is important to point out that the operational representation of spacetime cannot be equivalent to the functional representation as a description of the phenomena studied. The former describes the operations of presentation and recording of variables in the experimental arrangement. The latter is a description of the relations found.

In operational representation of spacetime, a first aspect to examine is the continuity-discontinuity of the extension of the dimensions involved. A change can be defined in the stimulus object that is not symmetrical with the change criterion in the individual. This asymmetry can be established in two ways: one, in the localization or location of the change in the stimulus object and in the individual, so that, for example, an individual's displacement and/

152

or manipulation pattern occurs at point A while the functional change in a stimulus object occurs at point B or NOT A. A discontinuity in spatial extension would then exist with respect to the temporal extension continuum. This implies that the functional contact does not obey a strict simultaneity, but an extended connectivity. The proportionality of T/object (EB) is therefore always dependent on the extensive properties of the individual's displacement from EA to EB, whether or not it is a situation where the changes in the stimulus object are contingent or non-contingent on the individual's behavior. Some of the different possible combinations are: 1) a local change in an object, but with discrete or extended duration, such as water delivery in a dispenser, where water availability is restricted to brief periods or is permanently available until it is consumed; 2) the changes in the stimulus objects are spatially extended, that is, the object is mobile and displaced, but also the functional availability of the change is intermittent or continuous, which implies a double change in the stimulus object; 3) the individual's reactive pattern is local, but varies in temporal extension, depending or not on the extensional properties of the stimulus object in spacetime; and 4) the individual's reactive pattern may or may not be functional depending on variations in its extension. Other spacetime relations between stimulus objects and individual behavior may also be possible. In any case, a descriptive system of operations prescribing or specifying these relations as occurrence-contingencies in the experimental arrangement is required. Here we have mentioned only one fixed or moving stimulus object, but more than one may occur (e.g., concurrent, successive, and sequential contingencies), which results in a web of overlapping, juxtaposed, separate or interlaced space-time relations, from the perspective of the individual's behavior in the experimental situation. These complex contingencies can establish different relative symmetrical/asymmetrical relations in time of segmentations of the spacetime continuum in the form of before, at the same time as, after, far from, over, near, parallel to, and many others. Stimulus segments consisting of two or more stimulus objects (e.g., lights or sounds preceding or following water or food delivery) must be considered, as well as the differentially limited availability of both behaviorally contingent and non-contingent presentation of dispositional stimulus conditions in time and space.

A second type of presentations have to do with describing the observed functions, that is, functional detachment as a transitional process. This type of representations are those that progressively constitute the structure of the theory in terms of empirical generalizations. Representations of empirical generalizations based on the systematic assessment of conditions, variables, and parameters allows describing in detail the processes related to a great diversity of particular findings. These representations can take two forms, namely graphic and abstract formal types (i.e., mathematical equations). The latter should be the final step in the formulation empirical generalizations (so-called laws), and should be the result of a development reflecting the nature of the relations experimentally found. They should not be used during early stages, as a heuristic device, to guide research in the absence of well-grounded experimental observations supported by the logic of theory. Mathematical representations should constitute abstract descriptions and not models of the studied phenomena. For these reasons, we can only aspire to empirical generalizations of the first type in the current stage of the theory (and of any theory in the ambiguous discipline of psychology), that is, graphical representations that go beyond mere casuistic description of the parameters and dimensions of occurrence of the phenomenon under study. At present, any proposal is provisional and exploratory with the goal of partially assessing the merits of different types of representation. Graphical representations can cover the contingency fields as a spacetime domain with relative distance dimensions between stimulus objects, between changes in these objects, and between these changes and their position and the individual's relative spacetime distances from them. This representation would be a gradient of relative spatiotemporal functionality of the individual's behavior with respect to changes in stimulus objects and their momentary dispositional properties. The gradient functionality would include availability, opportunity, simultaneity, options, anticipation, inertia, and recurrence of contacts as proximity or withdrawal relations. Spatiotemporal distances, such as the previously mentioned "temporal waves" always constitute relative and asymmetrical distances, which determine changes in the dimensions of individual behavior, its directionality, its variation, its speed, its permanence, and the recurrence of activity segments, whether as travels, visits, inspections, among others. The individual and the stimulus objects always have relative positions with respect to each other as a result of the very dynamics that the individual's movement imprints on the present and possible relations between all the field elements. An oversimplified example may illustrate the complexity and relativity of the successive and concurrent field contingencies. If the rat is 60 centimeters from the water dispenser, but water remains available only 2 seconds, the relative distance as spacetime will be greater than if the rat is 1 meter away from another dispenser where water is available 5 seconds. In representing a spacetime domain, the hypothesized

154

relative functions can be compared (based on previous data or operational calculations) with respect to the relative functions that have occurred. The discrepancy between both types of functions should allow adjusting the theoretical criteria to the relativity relations systematically identified.

A special problem about which little can be said at this point is that of the graphical representation of relative functions in conventional spacetime of practical referential domains. Its solution is left for another time.

References

Berlyne, D.E. (1960). Conflict, arousal, and curiosity. NY: McGraw Hill.

Bridgman, P.W. (1927). The logic of modern physics. NY: The MacMillan Co.

Cabrer, F., Daza, B.C., & Ribes, E. (1975). Teoría de la Conducta: ¿nuevos conceptos o nuevos parámetros? Revista Mexicana de Análisis de la Conducta, 1, 191- 212.

Dewey, J. (1896). The reflex arc in psychology. Psychological Review, 3, 357-370.

Ferster, C.B. (1953). The use of the free operant in the analysis of behavior. Psychological Bulletin, 50, 263-274.

Ferster, C.B., & Skinner, B.F. (1957). Schedules of reinforcement. NY: Appleton Century Crofts.

Feyerabend, P.K. (1970). Against method. In M. Radner & S. Winokur (Eds), Analyses of theories and methods in physics and psychology (pp. 17-130). Minnessota studies in philosophy of science, vol. 4. Minneapolis: University of Minnessota Press.

Findley, J.D. (1962). An experimental outline for building and exploring multi-operant behavior repertoires. Journal of the Experimental Analysis of Behavior, 5, 113-166.

Henton, W.W., & Iversen, I.H. (1978). Classical conditioning and operant conditioning: A response pattern analysis. NY: Springer Verlag.

Herrick, R.M. (1964). The successive differentiation of a lever dis- placement response. Journal of the Experimental Analysis of Behavior, 7, 211-215.Kantor, J.R. (1924-26). Principles of psychology. NY: Alfred Knopf.

Kantor, J.R. (1936). An objective psychology ofgrammar. Granville: Ohio: Principia Press.

Kuhn, T.S. (1977). The essential tension: Selected studies in scientific tradition and change. Chicago: The Chicago University Press.

Maier, N.R.F., & Schneirla, T.C. (1965). Principles of animal psychology. NY: Dover Press.

Maxwell, J.C. (1877/1925). Matter and motion. London: The Sheldon Press.

Mechner, F. (1959). A notation system for the description of behavioral procedures. Journal of the Experimental Analysis of Behavior, 2, 133-150.

Mechner, F. (1994). The revealed operant: A way to study the characteristics of individual occurrences of operant responses. Cambridge, MA: Cambridge Center for Behavioral Studies.

Minkowski, H. (1907-1908/2012). Space and time: Minkowski's papers on relativity. Montreal, QUE: Minkowski Instituye Press.

Norman, MF. (1966). An approach to free-responding on schedules that prescribe reinforcement probability as a function of interresponse time. Journal of Mathematical Psychology, 3, 235-268.

Notterman, J.M., & Mintz, D.E. (1965). Dynamics of response. NY: John Wiley.

Palacios, H. (2016), Medidas molares y análisis no lineal de los datos [molar measurements and non-linear data analysis]. [Unpublished doctoral dissertation] Universidad Veracruzana, Xalapa, México.

Petkov, V. (2012). Introduction. In H. Monlowski, Space and time: Minkoski's papers on relativity (pp. 1-37). Montreal, QUE: Minkoski Institute Press.

Ribes, E. (1986). Historia de la Psicología ¿para qué? [History of Psychology, what for?] Revista Mexicana de Análisis de la Conducta, volumen monográfico, 12, 443-466.

Ribes, E. (1992). Sobre el tiempo y el espacio psicológicos. [On psychological space and time] Acta Comportamentalia, 0, 71-84.

Ribes, E. (1996). Obituarium: William N. Schoenfeld (1915-1996). Revista Mexicana de Análisis de la Conducta, 22, 93-112.

Ribes, E. (1999). Teoría del condicionamiento y lenguaje: un análisis histórico y conceptual. CDMX: Taurus.

Ribes, E. (2003). What is defined in operational definitions? The case of operant psychology. Behavior and Philosophy, 31, 11-126.

Ribes, E. (2004). Concepts and theories: relation to scientific categories. In K.A. Lattlal & P.N. Chase, (Eds.), Behavior theory and philosophy (pp. 147-164). NY: Kluver Academic/Plenum Publishers.

Ribes, E. (2007). Estados y límites del campo, medios de contacto y análisis molar del comportamiento: reflexiones teóricas. [Field states and boundaries, contact media and molar analysis of behavior: Theoretical reflections] Acta Comportamentalia, 15, 229-259.

Ribes, E. (2013). Una reflexión sobre los modos generales de conocer y los objetos de conocimiento de las diversas ciencias empíricas, incluyendo a la psicología. [A reflection on the general modes of knowing and the objects of knowledge of the various empirical sciences, including psychology] Revista Mexicana de Psicología, 30, 89-95.

Ribes, E. (2018). El estudio científico de la conducta individual: una introducción a la teoría de la psicología. [The scientific study of individual behavior: An introduction to the theory of psychology] CDMX: El Manual Moderno.

Ribes, E., & Chávez, R. (1988). Efectos de la comida no contingente en la conducta libre de la rata blanca: consideraciones sobre el análisis del segmento de respuesta. [Effects of noncontingent food on free behavior in the white rat: Considerations on response segment analysis] Revista Mexicana de Análisis de la Conducta, 14, 247-255.

Ribes, E. & López, F. (1985). Teoría de la Conducta: un análisis de campo y paramétrico. [Behavioral theory: A field and parametric analysis]. México: Trillas.

Ribes-Iñesta, E. & Torres, C. (2000). The spatial distribution of be havior under varying frequencies of temporally scheduled water delivery. Journal of the Experimental Analysis of Behavior, 73, 195-209.

Ribes, E., & Quintana, C. (2002). Mother-child linguistic interactions and behavioral development: A multidimensional observational system. The Behavior Analyst Today, 3, 442-454.

Ribes, E., & Tamayo, J. (2020). Evaluación experimental de diferen- tes contingencias temporales y espaciales en un ambiente experimental ampliado con cuatro dispensadores de agua. Revista Mexicana de Análisis de la conducta, 45.

Ribes, E., & Tamayo, J. (2020). Análisis del efecto de dos condiciones de restricción especial en la distribución espaciotemporal de la conducta de la rata. Acta Comportamentalia.

Ribes Iñesta, E., & Tamayo, J. (2021). Efectos de dos condiciones de restricción espacial en la distribución espaciotemporal de la conducta de la rata. Acta Comportamentalia: Revista Latina De Análisis Del Comportamiento, 29(2). Retrieved from https://www.revistas.unam.mx/index.php/acom/article/view/79611

Ribes, E., Ibáñez, C., & Hernández-Pozo, R. (1986). Hacia una Psicología Comparativa: algunas consideraciones conceptuales y metodológicas. Revista Latinoamericana de Psicología, 18, 263-276.

Ribes, E., Moreno, R., & Padilla, M.A. (1996). Un análisis funcional de la práctica científica: extensiones de un modelo psicológico. Acta Comportamentalia, 4,205-235.

Ribes, E., Moreno, D., & Martínez, C. (1998). Second-order discrimination in humans: the roles of explicit instructions and constructed verbal responding. Behavioural Processes, 42, 1-18.

Ribes-Iñesta, E., Torres, C., Correa, L., &Montes, E. (2006). Effects of concurrent random time schedules on the spatial distribution of behavior in rats. Behavioural Processes. 73, 41-48.

Ribes, E., León, A., & Andrade, D. (2020). Comparison patterns: An experimental study of transposition in children. Behavioural Processes, 171, 104-024.

Ribes-Iñesta, E., Palacios Pérez, H.B. & Hernández Eslava, V. (2020). Continuous measuring of temporal and spatial changes in rats' behavior under water temporal schedules. Psychological Record, 70, 267-278.

Ribes, E., Hernández-Pozo, R., Sánchez, A., Gutiérrez, F. y González, E. (1987). Substitutional mediation in matching to sample with words: comparison between children and adults. Revista Mexicana de Análisis de la Conducta, 13, 337-362.

Schoenfeld, W.N., & Farmer, J. (1970). Reinforcement schedules and the "behavior stream". In W.N. Schoenfeld (Ed.): The theory of reinforcement schedules (pp. 215-245). NY: Appleton Century Crofts.

Schoenfeld, W.N., & Cole, B.K. (1972). Stimulus schedules: The t-T systems. NY: Harper & Row.

Skinner, B.F. (1935). The generic nature of the concepts of stimulus and response. Journal of General Psychology, 12,40-65

Skinner. B.F. (1938). The behavior of organisms. NY: Appleton Century Crofts.

Skinner, B.F. (1956). A case history in scientific method. American Psychologist, 11, 221-233.

Skinner, B.F. (1957). Verbal Behavior. NY: Appleton Century Crofts. Skinner, B.F. (1966). The phylogeny and ontogeny of behavior. Science, 153, 1205-1213.

Skinner, B.F. (1976). Farewell, My LOVELY! Journal of the Experimental Analysis of Behavior, 25, 218.

Snapper, A.G., Knapp, J.Z., & Kushner, HG.K. (1970). Mathematical description of schedules of reinforcement. In W.N. Schoenfeld (Ed.), The theory of reinforcement schedules (pp. 247-275). NY: Appleton Century Crofts.

Toulmin, S. (1972). Human understanding: The collective use and evolution of concepts. Princeton, NJ: Princeton University Press.

Watson, J.B. (1924). Behaviorism. NY: W.W.Norton & Co.

Weiss, B. (1970). The fine structure of operant behavior during transition states. In W.N. Schoenfeld (Ed.), The theory of reinforcement schedules (pp. 277-311). NY: Appleton Century Crofts.

Wittgenstein, L. (1953). Philosophical investigations. Oxford: Basil & Blackwell.

ESSAY SIX: EVOLUTION OF PSYCHOLOGICAL BEHAVIOR? REFLECTIONS FOR A COMPARATIVE PSYCHOLOGY

There are multiple sides related to the topic or problem (whichever is preferred) of the evolution of psychological behavior and, in turn, of psychological behavior in evolution, and comprises several relatively independent, though interconnected issues. Three themes can be identified. One is the historical impact of the theory of evolution on the emergence of experimental animal psychology. Another is the one related, first, to the origin of life and, later, to the evolution of life and the formulation of the theory of evolution of species, including humans. A third concerns the logical and conceptual relevance of positing that psychological behavior evolves as a covariation inherent to the biological evolution of the species and that, to that extent, it constitutes a bridge between biological evolution and the emergence and supposed evolution of social life. This calls into question the meaning of a comparative psychology and its scope of analysis. Each of these themes or sections will be examined separately, in order to be in a position to propose a conclusion on the object of the general question posed and the possibility of a comparative theory of psychological behavior.

Theory of Evolution and the Rise of Experimental Animal Psychology

The publication of the theory of evolution by Darwin (1871, 1872, 1974) and Wallace (1871), following the previous contributions of Lamarck (1809) and Spencer (1855), initially proposed the possibility of mental life in animals and its evolutionary continuity to human beings. Several problems emerged at that time for the nascent psychology, which later converged in the formation of the study of individual animal behavior. The first problem, derived directly from Darwin's writings, was related to the continuity-discontinuity of mental life in animals and humans. A second problem, closely related to the concept of natural selection (the struggle for life, for survival, in fact, and, later, for reproductive success), was directed to the study of so-called animal intelligence. It was argued, implicitly or explicitly, that individual adaptation to the environment was essential in the process of natural selection of a species as a population. It is not difficult to infer that the underlying assumption was that in the struggle for life, there was a natural selection of those individuals who were the fittest, the most intelligent. Animal intelligence was soon related to the learning of new forms of adaptive behavior, which led to the study of habit and its conceptual incorporation with the theory of conditional reflexes formulated separately by Pavlov and Bekhterev. The so-called learning theories that dominated experimental interest for more than fifty years in the past century, were born out from this approach (Hilgard & Bower, 1973). A third problem appeared in terms of the relation between phylogeny and ontogeny in the form of the nature-nurture, instinct-learning dichotomies, a discussion that re-emerged during the half of the past century with the irruption of ethology, not only in the field of animal psychology, but also in the interpretation of the evolutionary origins of human behavior and its role as a source of social conflicts. The historiography of these problems will not be covered as Boakes (1984) has described them in detail. Nor we will examine the first round of comparative psychologies that emerged in this context, since their analysis will be included in the final section of this writing.

The Evolution of Mental Life

Darwin posed very early on the problem of whether the "mind" had also evolved and whether it had done so, fundamentally, under the principle of natural selection. He wrote about these problems initially in his M and N notebooks, On Metaphysics, Mind and Materialism (1974). The mental life of animals included not only the identification of identifiable forms of intelligence and reasoning in adaptive behavior, but also that some form of consciousness could be attributed to them. It is important to recall that the "psychology" of the nineteenth century is the psychology of the contents of consciousness and that, from on the work of Brentano (1874) onwards, consciousness as a psychological phenomenon was identified with the consciousness of an object. The object, as a phenomenon of consciousnesses, endowed the psychological with meaning or intentionality. Conscious experience could not exist if it was not the experience of an object. It is precisely on the basis of evolutionary thought that the existence of psychological phenomena in animals was proposed, despite their lack of language and, consequently, of the expressive and communicative criteria that are consubstantial to their identification. It should not be forgotten, however, that the term 'consciousness' is a term of ordinary language and that it is applied in different ways and with various meanings. As we have examined elsewhere (Ribes, 2011), an individual is said to be conscious: (a) when reacting to the presence of an object or event or to a change, (b) when something (an object, a property, an event, a person, a fact) is said to be perceived, (c) when perceiving occurs as reflexive behavior, which is accompanied by reasons or descriptions that justify what is perceived, what is done, and the manner in which it takes place, and (d) when objects are present, events, behaviors and circumstances that are not in the situation and, therefore, cannot be perceived in the strict sense, a presence that only takes place as linguistic behavior in the form of retrospection or prospection, and which is confused on a myriad of occasions with the use of terms such as 'remembering', 'thinking', 'calculating', 'planning' and 'imagining'. It is in the first two senses of the term 'consciousness' that mental life in animals was originally conceived.

Darwin never explicitly pronounced himself on the very nature of mental phenomena. From the perspective of evolutionary theory, mental phenomena were intermingled with instincts and were ultimately a function of the nervous system. Emotional expressions, communication patterns, memory, habit acquisition, and animal intelligence or reasoning, among others, were supposed to contribute to the adaptation of individuals to their environment thus also being subject to a process of natural selection. It was Romanes (1883) who explicitly addressed the problem of mental evolution in animals. Romanes identified mental life with the daily conscious experience of the human individual: with her sensations, her feelings, the association of ideas, memory as recollections, and the perception of objects, among others. He assumed, like Descartes, that this individual conscious experience is undeniable for the subject, and therefore corresponds to a type of phenomena, at least, different from those of the body as a physical and biological entity. Biological phenomena, even those of a nervous nature, are not conscious and, to that extent, are distinguished from mental phenomena, which, being based on nervous tissue for their existence and occurrence, are conscious for the very subject who experiences them.

Romanes established a necessary relation between neural and mental phenomena, but he did not advance an explanation as to the type of interaction they hold. Consequently, certainty about mental life comes from the self-consciousness of its phenomena, always associated to the subject's own activities in relation to objects and events. The objective method based on the observation of the choice activities of others does not allow, however, to ensure the occurrence of mental phenomena insofar as there is no access to their conscious experience. In the case of animals, introspection is not an option due to the impossibility of obtaining verbal reports. Hence, Romanes proposed the ejective method for the study of the mental life in animals, which consisted in assuming via analogy that the intentional activities of animals are accompanied by mental phenomena similar to our own. Romanes correctly established that "mental" life required nervous tissue to coordinate differential reactions to environmental excitation. Reflexes constituted complex forms of nervous functioning, but they were not part of mental life *stricto sensu* since they did not operate in the sphere of consciousness. Romanes correctly asserted that it was impossible to distinguish in a nervous process in itself whether or not it was accompanied by a mental element. He assumed that the first level of consciousness occurs in the coelenterates, to which he attributed sensations and thus progressively identified increasing levels of neural complexity (from the ganglia to the encephalon) in the different phyla of the animal kingdom: echinoderms, annelids, mollusks, arthropods, and the different classes of vertebrates. Romanes assumed that from the annelids one could identify forms of animal intelligence and, consequently, of establishment of new habits by some mechanism of association of ideas, memory and reasoning. One of the origins of instinct was intelligent behavior, when it decayed through disuse or automation, which gave instinct the characteristic of being conscious, insofar as it provided it with intentionality.

The theory of evolution, whose main objective was to account for the origin of humans as the culmination of the animal scale, and in particular of the hominid primates, was truncated and lost meaning if it could not include language as a product of evolution. Consciousness, as proposed by Romanes, could be inferred by analogy between the activities of humans and those of animals, starting from the premise that consciousness, as a phenomenon of mental life, occurred whenever a choice could be made, that is, that the individual's behavior could occur in two ways or with respect to two objects or conditions. Instincts were not a manifestation of consciousness given their stereotypy and unidirectionality, as was also the case with reflex behavior. In *The descent of man, and selection in relation to sex,* Darwin (1871) attempted to establish the evolutionary continuity of language between animals and humans, appealing to communication and the imitation of birdsong. Following this line of reasoning, other authors increased the possible sources, always on the basis of phonemes and onomatopoeic expressions derived from reactions to pain or surprise (Mowrer, 1960), the imitation of sounds of different animals and of nature (wind, waves, blows of objects, and others), as well as through the progressive vocal accompaniment of hand and foot gestures (Tomassello, 2003). But to the difficulty of explaining how natural selection could have progressively transformed the capacities of vocal articulation and inscription, several questionings were added by Alfred Russell Wallace (1871).

166

Wallace formulated the principle of natural selection to explain the evolution of species simultaneously and independently of Darwin, while in Malaysia and Borneo. However, he questioned whether "natural selection" (in Wallace's own quotation marks) had anything to do with the most important characteristics of the human body and its practical abilities, including language. These questions emphasized that the lack of variation in the human body for thousands of years, the size of the cranial cavity, the lack of fur, the articulatory refinement of human vocalization, the loss of prehensility of the toes, the fine motor coordination and opposition of the thumbs in the hands, the moral sense, and language as a way of anticipating what is going to happen and of abstracting, among other characteristics, could not be explained by "natural selection", although natural selection (without quotation marks) could have contributed to the transformations of the body when it was still in the process of becoming homo. Wallace attributed these characteristics of human beings (in all races, even if some were still "primitive"), to the sympathetic, mutualistic nature of collective life, where everyone looked out for others, including the sick, children, the old, and the weak. Labor was divided and food was divided among all. Everyone was protected, sheltered and cared for, so that natural selection had no way to operate. Natural selection operates on animals because they survive as individuals, and the incapable or weak die when conditions change, food or water is lacking, or predators increase. In the case of human beings, society neutralizes and cancels the action of natural selection.

Nevertheless, Darwinian thinking on natural selection has persisted, both in the field of linguistics and psychology. A case in point is that of Tomassello (1999) who, despite rejecting the idea of a universal grammar of language, maintains an evolutionary thesis in which knowledge capacities are the result of a biological process in the species. I quote him at length because his argument leaves no room for interpretation. He states that "Human cognition is a specific, in the literal meaning of the word, form of primate cognition. Human beings share the majority of their cognitive skills and knowledge with other primates—including both the sensory-motor world of objects in their spatial, temporal, categorical, and quantitative relations and the social world of behaving conspecifics in their vertical (dominance) and horizontal (affiliative) relationships. And all primate species use their skills and knowledge to formulate creative and insightful strategies when problems arise in either the physical or the social domain... In the current hypothesis human beings do indeed possess a species-unique cognitive adaptation, and it is in many ways an especially powerful cognitive adaptation because it changes in fundamental ways the process of cognitive evolution… This adaptation arose at some particular point in human evolution, perhaps fairly recently, presumably because of some genetic and natural selection events. This adaptation consists in the ability and tendency of individuals to identify with conspecifics in ways that enable them to understand those conspecifics as intentional agents like the self, possessing their own intentions and attention, and eventually to understand them as mental agents like the self, possessing their own desires and beliefs. This new mode of understanding other persons radically changed the nature of all types of social interactions…" (pp. 202-203).

The origin of language was no exception to Darwinian thinking. Chomsky (1957), following the framework of the Cartesian argument of innate ideas, whose grammar manifests itself in language as an epiphenomenon, based himself on the Darwinian hypothesis of natural selection to postulate the existence of a universal grammar of language, structured in the very organization of the brain. Natural languages turned out to be only a circumstantial variation of the operation of the innate system, computational in nature which, on the basis of a universal syntax, generated linguistic variations adapted to particular circumstances. From this perspective, it could be said that the different natural languages constitute a phenotypical expression of a universal genotypical grammar. Obviously, no one has been able to identify the shared brain structures that have evolved to form the universal linguistic device proposed by Chomsky, let alone identify genomic correspondences with the structure of the nervous system.

Daniel Everett (2017), a linguist who lived for nearly 30 years with the Pirahá, a sedentary tribe of hunters, fishermen, and gatherers in the Amazon River basin, questioned the thesis of language evolution as an operating system of brain structure. From his study of all forms of sound production by humans and the three general forms of "grammar" identifiable in all existing or recorded languages, Everett concluded that language is an invention of Homo erectus living in society. Language is a cultural product that allows the sharing of knowledge between individuals and does not emerge from animal communication as part of an evolutionary process. Everett concluded that "More than 60,000 generations ago, Homo erectus introduced language into the world. Not merely another form of animal communication, language is an advanced form of cultural expression, based on abilities unique to human cognition…" (p. 291). It is not the mind that creates language (Pinker, 1994), but culture and collective social practice.

Animal Intelligence, Natural Selection, and the Concept of Habit

The theory of evolution formulated by Darwin was based on three explanatory or determining principles: natural selection of the fittest in the struggle for life or survival, inheritance of acquired characters, and sexual reproduction. These principles were based on inferences from naturalistic observations or even from living with domesticated animals. We will examine this approach in a later section. For the purposes of the present section it is sufficient to highlight the role of natural selection and the inheritance of acquired traits in shaping the experimental study of animal behavior in the late nineteenth century. Although the study of animal intelligence partially intersected the problem of mental life in non-humans, it had a precise delimitation insofar as the subject of analysis was not the presence or absence of "conscience", but rather the capacity to solve problems linked to survival: obtaining food or water, escape or avoidance of noxious stimuli, and similar aspects. In other words, animal intelligence had to do with adaptive efficiency and the establishment of habits, a concept used in this context by Darwin himself. Herbert Spencer posited the psychological nature of habits, prior to Darwin's writings. He described three general principles characterizing mental phenomena in his Principles of Psychology (1855), which were and remain cornerstones in the later shaping of the so-called learning theories: contiguity as a condition of association, pleasure-displeasure determining the direction of behavior (somehow a mental representation of the operation of natural selection), and exercise as repeated use (the definitive feature of all habit).

Romanes wrote the first book on the subject, entitled Animal Intelligence (1884), distinguishing intelligence from instinct, which was reflex behavior that had incorporated elements of consciousness. In contrast, he said that "Reason or intelligence is the faculty involved in the intentional adaptation of means to ends. It therefore involves conscious knowledge of the relation between the means employed and the ends attained and can be exercised in adapting to new circumstances equal to the experience of the individual and those of the species" (p. 41). However, aside from some observational studies, it is plausible to establish the beginning of experimental research on animal intelligence with the work of Edward L. Thorndike (1898, 1911) and its almost immediate transformation into the study of learning as a habit or conditional reflex. From this form of study of learning, the problem of the "acquisition" of new behaviors through experience in and with the environment was approached. Influenced by Llyod Morgan's (1890) non-experimental observations of accidental learning by trial and error as he described it, Thorndike designed several "trick" boxes for cats and dogs to systematically study how animals learned to get out of the box to obtain food. Eventually Thorndike also employed chicks and a monkey as experimental subjects, but they did not offer the grooming advantages of cats and dogs. The various wooden trick boxes were designed to record the time required for the animal to operate a mechanism that allowed it to open the door and get out of the box or cage. Sometimes the device was on the door itself, sometimes on the opposite wall, and the use of cat and dogs was to establish cross-species comparisons, which ultimately proved implausible. Habit establishment was measured by the change in the escape latency from the trick box to consuming a bit of fish or meat on a plate placed outside. Thorndike observed that in the first trial animals made many fortuitous movements until they accidentally operated the door-opening mechanism. In subsequent trials, the time required to exit decreased, until after 4 or 6 sessions, the animals exited the box immediately. The downward record of response latencies constituted the first "learning curve". Thorndike also found that the habit was not lost, as it was "retained" until 78 days after it had been acquired without additional training. Following Morgan's canon of always appealing to simple processes whenever possible, this led him to question Morgan himself, who explained trial-and-error learning based on the association of ideas, confirming that these habits did not require an additional memory process.

Thorndike formulated the law of effect, a principle that continues to support an important part of the theoretical and experimental developments in animal psychology and its extensions to human behavior. The law of effect stated that the strength of a connection between what the individual did, and the situation increased if it was followed by a satisfying state of affairs and, conversely, if it was followed by an annoying or disturbing state of affairs, the connection weakened. The connection referred to neuronal conductivity, without specifying a particular physiological mechanism. The satisfying or disturbing state of affairs was identified in terms of the individual not avoiding it or even maintaining or producing it, while a disturbing state of affairs tended to be prevented or avoided. In the first version of the law of effect, the symmetry of the effects of rewards and punishments was assumed. In doing so, Thorndike integrated two of the Spencerian principles of psychological phenomena: association by contiguity and the search for pleasure and avoidance of displeasure. He eliminated Morgan's association of ideas and thus established an empirical principle for the systematic study of animal behavior and habit acquisition. He extended his studies to verbal habits in human individuals, whose explanation he complemented with the law of exercise, only relevant to situations of learning by repetition, thus incorporating Spencer's third principle.

Simultaneously with Thorndike, the theories of conditioning were independently developed in the Soviet Union by Pavlov (1927) and Bekhterev (1913), based on the concept of the reflex. Although both were evolutionists, their formulations and procedures were not directly linked to adaption as result of natural selection. However, the concept of conditional reflex and the first processes identified in its establishment and elimination (inhibition, extinction, delay, generalization, induction, and others), were adopted by those who followed the study of animal behavior based on trial-and-error learning initiated by Thorndike. The concept of adaptation, pertaining to the fittest, was central to all learning theories up to the present day, either explicitly or in a concealed form. The three fundamental strands that stood out in the last century, with Watson (1914) as irradiating core, were the so-called conditioning or instrumental learning studies using trick boxes and different types of mazes (Guthrie, 1935; Hull, 1943; Tolman, 1943), research using the free-operant method (Skinner, 1938), and lastly, from the ill-named cognitive revolution (actually, an involution) (Neisser, 1967), studies on animal cognition (Mackintosh, 1994). The conceptual trajectory of each strand is distinct and impure, as it were, since they draw from common sources to support different theoretical approaches. We will only examine the first two strands, linked to each other by the concept of reinforcement, related to the adaptive nature of behavior. The cognitive strand is nothing more than a revival of interest in the mental life of animals, based on mental representations, and their possible evolutionary relation with human psychology. Using computational logic, animals, especially birds and mammals, are attributed perceptual processes, decision-making, memory, recognition of natural categories, imagination, and many others, with the association of representations being one of the privileged mechanisms.

Clark L. Hull, who amassed, for and against, the discussion and research on learning for almost four decades of the last century, should be highlighted in the case of instrumental conditioning theories. This is neither the place nor time to examine Hull's theory, but it is relevant to point out that his concepts responded to an attempt to clarify how habits were closely related to adaptation and, consequently, to survival. Three concepts are central in this regard: drive, force of habit, and reinforcement. For Hull, habits were stimulus-response connections or associations that required two conditions to be established. The first condition was a contiguity relation between stimulus and response following the principles of classical conditioning (actually, they were usually successive sets of exteroceptive, proprioceptive, and reinforcing stimuli, as well as approach or withdrawal and consummatory responses). The second condition was that such association was followed by reinforcement, that is, that one of the stimulus components, the ensuing one, reduced a drive state or stimuli associated with the drive state (which were also part of the stimulus component of the habit). Habits were established by classical conditioning whenever the reduction of a drive state occurred, which defined the function of reinforcement. Thus, every habit was initially established for an adaptive purpose, to satisfy a biological need or to avoid physical harm. The drive reduction relative to the magnitude and frequency of reinforcement should always be greater than the reactive (and conditioned) inhibition, which operated as a parallel drive state induced by the activity, and whose relief was provided by rest. The diversification of habits with autonomy from direct drive reduction occurred through the establishment of secondary reinforcers by association with the occurrence of primary reinforcers. Hull's general approach, beyond its internal logical adequacy and its ultimate severe questioning by his own disciples on empirical grounds, supported its validity in principle on the assumptions of natural selection as a struggle for life and the perpetuation of the species. It was an attempt to provide the Darwinian evolutionary thesis with experimental support in the individual behavior of organisms.

The operant theory proposed by B. F. Skinner is another approach to the acquisition and maintenance of behavior, in order not to use the terms habit and learning, especially avoided in this formulation. The path followed by Skinner comprises two moments, without an explicit internal connection. At first (Skinner, 1938), the 'scientific program' was based on the theory of reflex. It is useful to recall that Watson (1916) emphasized the conditional reflex as the analytical unit of the new behaviorist perspective, and that the habit constituted an integrated chain of conditional reflexes. In the first epoch of operant theory, neither natural selection nor adaptation is mentioned as a substantive dimension of the behavior of organisms (Ribes, 2018a). Skinner "emptied" the concept of reflex of its neural content, and highlighted its functional nature related with the covariations or correlations between changes in stimulus and changes in response. He distinguished two types of reflexes based on the temporal relation between stimulus and response. The first type of reflex, the respondent, corresponded to the type of relations studied in classical conditioning, in which the presence of a stimulus change provoked a response from the organism. In the second type of reflexes, the behavior was "emitted" without a prior identifiable stimulus (Skinner suggested that it could be an internal stimulus linked to the drive, although he used the term as equivalent to a state of deprivation). However, a relation could be established so that an identifiable response fraction produced the stimulus presentation. Thus, the respondent reflex comprised a relation between an antecedent stimulus and a provoked or evoked response, and the operant reflex a relation between an effective response on the environment that produced the occurrence of a subsequent stimulus. Skinner later abandoned the term, but not the concept, of reflex and argued that all individual behavior could be divided into these two general types, and that most behavior occurring in natural situations, including human behavior, was operant in nature. Operant behavior, by producing a subsequent stimulus change, was in turn affected by it. This stimulus effect, a consequence of the operant behavior itself, is what he called reinforcement, and two types of reinforcement (and, consequently, two types of reinforcers) were identified. Positive reinforcement was the addition of a stimulus as consequence of the response, and the effect was to increase its frequency (or future probability). Negative reinforcement consisted of the subtraction of a stimulus as a consequence of the response, and the effect was also to increase the frequency of the response. Positive and negative punishment phenomena (not very systematized) always consisted of the effect of reducing the frequency of the response when it produced a stimulus or when it withdrew it (again, addition and subtraction). Usually, the presentation of negative reinforcers, as a consequence of the response, had the effect of positive punishment (even when the functional relation was different) and the elimination or withdrawal of positive reinforcers had the effect of negative punishment. In sum, operant theory proposed that the acquisition and maintenance of behavior was the result of its stimulus consequences, that its, of its effects on the environment.

Without an obvious logical connection to the modified theory of the reflex underpinning the concept of operant conditioning, Skinner (1966, 1981) introduced the concept of selection to account for the importance of contingencies of reinforcement (production-effectiveness) in shaping new behaviors. In the 1966 paper, *The phylogeny and ontogeny of behavior*, he drew a parallel between natural selection in phylogeny and the selective role of reinforcement on operant behaviors that were acquired, maintained, or eliminated in the individual in its relation with the environment. He assumed that both types of contingencies may be relevant to the understanding of behavior, but that their operation represents different times. Phylogenetic contingencies may have been initially configured as ontogenetic contingencies common to all members of a species in a given environment and subsequently appear as "inherited effects" in the same environment. Both types of contingencies shared characteristics, such as "purpose" or "adaptation", although the processes responsible for the establishment of these contingencies are not the same. In this regard, he mentions that "…Both kinds of contingencies change the organism so that it adjusts to its environment in the sense of behaving in it more effectively. With respect to phylogenic contingencies, this is what is meant by natural selection. With respect to ontogeny, it is what is meant by operant conditioning. Successful responses are selected in both cases, and the result is adaptation" (pp. 1211-1212). In Selection by consequences (1981), Skinner definitively adopted the principle of natural selection and formulated it in three variants, as an explanatory principle of the living world. He states:

"Selection by consequences is a causal mode found only in living things, or in machines made by living things. It was first recognized in natural selection, but it also accounts for the shaping and maintenance of the behavior of the individual and the evolution of cultures. In all three of these fields, it replaces explanations based on the causal modes of classical mechanics" (p. 501). Selection by consequences becomes an explanatory and integrative concept of the process of change in the biological, psychological, and social worlds.

Selection by consequences represents Skinner's adoption of the neoliberal dogma "scientifically" sustained in the new evolutionary synthesis. Based on the genetic theory of natural selection (Fisher, 1930), this dogma sustains the importance of the competitiveness of individuals, one with respect to the other, as a criterion for the survival and improvement of the species (and society). The fittest survive (and excel in their environments) and perpetuate themselves through sexual reproduction to the detriment of the less fit, so that natural selection acts through the collective replication of the genes of the fit individuals. We will examine the peculiarities and inconsistency of this doctrine in a later section. It is sufficient for the moment to underline that selection by consequences assumes an individual who tends to maximize or optimize the "positive" effects of their behavior in proportion to the effort or cost of doing so. Therefore, individual behavior is regulated by a principle of maximization or optimization of consequences (and complementarily by minimizing loss, damage or inconvenience). Various mathematical models have emerged from this doctrine, some of them well known, such as the so-called "Prisoner's Dilemma", which attempt to give it a rigorous appearance through its formalization. However, what this doctrine assumes is a rational individual, who behaves through decisions based on the calculation of the costs and benefits of each option compared to the others. The doctrine has been extended to the field of society, arguing that economies are regulated by the subjective decisions of individuals and that the free market, to that extent, behaves on the basis of rational criteria and self-regulation. Zoology, animal and human psychology (including operant psychology, for example, the law of effect), and economics abound in models and hypotheses derived from or supported by the principle of natural selection as explicit or implicit rational choice of consequences. Ecological and behavioral processes are examined as microeconomic relations, which evolutionarily precede the free market economy (blatant circularity), while returning to the rational Cartesian individual who decides before acting, and whose decisions determine the equally rational regulation of the social economy and its articulations as a collective composition of the actions of individuals as a whole. Jeremy Bentham (1789) and John Stuart Mill (1848) never imagined that their utilitarian ideas of the role of the individual in society and the economy would have such an impact on modern science and life after the evolutionary theories of Darwin and his followers, associated with the emergence of marginalism in economic thought.

Heredity Versus Environment: Instinctive Behavior

The theory of evolution left a double legacy to psychology, linked to the importance of heredity as a transmission mechanism of the characters shaped throughout the phylogeny of each species. One of the legacies was the rise and consolidation of eugenics, of which Francis Galton (1869, 1889), Darwin's cousin, was the founder. Galton proposed the existence of races, as subspecies of Homo Sapiens, among which there were differences as an effect of the natural selection of the corresponding ancestors, and the existence of superior and inferior races and individuals, being the Caucasian European the superior race and within this race, the educated and wealthy individuals with greater capacities. In establishing eugenics, Galton recovered the mathematical concept of correlation and formulated that of linear regression, standard deviation, and bivariate distribution. He used the latter concept to formulate his thesis regarding the stability of human populations and the relations in statistical means and their variations through the generations (ancestral inheritance). Galton formulated the existence of biotypes and anthropotypes, carrying out experiments similar to those of Mendel, although with different conclusions that were later integrated by Ronald Fisher. He founded psychometry and differential psychology by measuring reaction times and sensory discriminations, as well as creating the questionnaire technique. He intervened in forensic medicine by establishing a typology of criminals through the analysis of fingerprints, an adaptation of phrenology to physical characteristics. Lastly, he established the difference between nature/nurture, to account for the inheritance of capacities in human begins as innate characteristics. The other legacy had to do with the identification of instincts as behaviors phylogenetically inherited from one generation to another by the members of the different animal species, including humans. This aspect will be examined in more detail.

Contrary to popular assumption, the biological concept of heredity is of relatively recent use in biology and medicine. Heredity was first used in the first half of the nineteenth century in French medicine to account for the origin of insanity and chronic diseases. Later, heridity was naturalized as an explanatory concept in biology, psychology, and the social science with the formulation of the theory of natural selection and the preeminence of instinct as a phylogenetic result of natural selection. Mendel's findings contributed to its consolidation. However, the concept and the term heredity itself is a biological reification of a metaphor originating in Roman civil law. The word inherit comes from Latin, and is the action of attaching, donating, or bequeathing something, primarily to relatives or descendants. Therefore, what was inherited was that which was donated by the original possessor. The noun inheritance resulted from the reification of hereditary, as an entity or causal agent of what was donated or bequeathed. Inheritance became the cause of what was "acquired" as a result of the transmission of what was possessed by an individual to a descendant (López Beltrán, 2004). A legal concept was transferred from a social practice between lineages to the transmission of biological and behavioral characteristics between biological "lineages" by kinship. Mendel's rediscovery of what we now call population genetics (distribution of characteristics by crossing varieties of the same species) consolidated the use of the term heredity in a new subdiscipline, genetics (Dubb & Dobshansky, 1946; Fisher, 1930). The concepts of heredity, and that of race and genetically determined individual differences, marked social practices, based on a false "scientific" support. These concepts determined, and continue do so, social conceptions that justify individual, social, and national poverty, based on inherited differences, emphasizing that rich nations and the wealthy classes are so because they are "endowed" with capacities and traits that distinguish them from the poor nations and dispossessed classes. In the case of psychology, the need to debunk the arguments that IQ, social class (meritocratic promotion), and racial affiliation are correlated and hereditarily determined is still recent (Jensen, 1973; Herrnstein, 1973; Kamin, 1974; Schoenfeld, 197; Gould, 1981).

The deterministic assumption of heredity, as genetic transmission, is based on the fact that the phenotype, that is, the manifest characteristics of an individual, as physical and behavioral traits, are manifestations or expressions of its genome, that is, of the structure of nucleotide amino acids in the chromosomes. However, the concept of phenotype, applied to certain physical characteristics of the soma, is only an inference based on population statistics, and not the result of the identification of genes that directly and univocally determine these characteristics. In fact, modern genetics cannot locate, in the genes as such, any of the organs or functions of the soma. What is known is that alterations in the organization of the amino acids that make up the genes can produce enzymatic and metabolic dysfunctions at different levels in cells and tissues, but nothing more. To suppose that the genome contains the map of somatic heredity, and even of the reactive functions of the organism, is a fiction, equivalent to that of memory as a store of psychological life. Neither "memory" is a storage of the experiences of ontogeny, nor is the genome a storage of the experiences in phylogeny. The genome is not an organ. It is the organization of chromosomes in the nucleus of ALL cells of the organism. Chromosomes contain the nucleotides, DNA and RNA, which generate proteins, usually enzymes, hormones, and elements of the immune system. Reproduction is the replication of the individual, starting from its functional cellular structure. The same process occurs in the growth of the individual, from the embryonic stage of gestation, when it is the case, as well as during the growth period (when it is also the case). Reproduction is modified when the aging process takes place. One "inherits" to the extent that, from one individual or pair of individuals, others necessarily emerge with the same characteristics. In simple organisms, reproduction as replication of the individual into new individuals occurs by bipartition or some form of mitosis, while in more differentiated organisms it occurs by meiosis, where the total chromosomes are not reproduced, but only part for each reproducing individual. However, in higher organisms, such as vertebrates, cell reproduction within each organism, such as growth and replacement, still occurs by mitosis. The chromosomes of the cell nucleus are replicated in the new cell. Every cell (including neurons), in every type of tissue and in every organ and system, continuously reproduces its characteristics as a unit of life. During the embryonic period, starting from the zygote, new cells are reproduced which, based on their spatial arrangement, develop into specialized cells (and specific stem cells). In this context, it becomes clear how absurd it would be to speak of an internal "inheritance" between cells, tissues, and organs, isomorphic to the "inheritance" of an individual as the reproduction of two shared individuals.

The concept of instinct preceded the rise of genetic theory and the postulation of heredity as a functional entity in biology. In speaking of inherited characters or traits, emphasis was placed on the apparent innate nature of the reactions of organisms, especially when these reactions were shared by all or a large part of the same species in a given habitat. Both Darwin and Romanes identified instincts as adaptive behavior and not simply reflexes and, even when they appeared to be innate in nature, accepted that a species in different habitats sometimes displayed different patterns of behavior. They assumed that instinctive behaviors, in addition to including reflexes (which were invariant) also involved forms of adaptive, intelligent behavior that had "lapsed", that is, had become automated given habitat invariance. Thus, part of the origin of instincts lay in automated habits and, sometimes, in characters acquired by experience, in Lamarck's sense of continuous use and disuse, and shared by successive generations in the same environment. Darwin in his last period speculated on a mechanism of pangenesis, through gemmules, attached to the gametes, which would be sexually "transmitted" to support the reproduction of individually acquired characters. At this point it is pertinent to point out that it was Francis Galton who discredited this proposal by performing blood transfusions between rabbits of different colors and finding no differences in their offspring. It was with Galton's rediscovery of Mendel that a dichotomy of the origins of behavior was posed and, consequently, the contrast between instinct and habit, the former inherited as innate, the latter as learned by the action of environmental agents. Galton formulated the nature-nurture opposition to explain individual differences in human beings.

The nature-nurture dichotomy became a false problem, unsolvable like any false problem, in which "heredity" was contrasted with the influence of experience in the environment as the origin of the behavior of organisms, especially vertebrates. This problem has permeated research on animal behavior since the beginning of the last century, and remains in many contemporary approaches. In the case of human behavior, the problem remains open in differential psychology, in developmental psychology and in the field of psychiatry and psychopathology. The development of ethology, as the study of the behavior of species, within the framework of zoology, strengthened the counterposition of the influence of heredity with respect to the environment on instinctive behavior (Tinbergen, 1951; Lorenz, 1965; Thorpe, 1966). It is not our purpose here to review the state of the art in ethology with respect to the study of animal behavior from the perspective of conditioning and learning theories. Empirical research does not yield answers to false problems or ill-posed problems. On the contrary, it sometimes contributes to increasing confusion. To that extent, the good or bad sense of the arguments underlying the innate-acquired or nature-nurture counterpositions will be examined.

The first attempts to systematize a comparative psychology among different phyla and zoological classes addressed the question of distinguishing whether certain types of instinctive behaviors were innate or learned. Watson's (1914) analysis in his *"An introduction to comparative psychology"* is noteworthy. He described instincts as reflexes that unfold serially and as such are innate forms of behavior, that is, they are congenital reactive forms, with which one is born. The concatenation of reflexes is determined by stimulus conditions that are presented in a given order. Observations on the various forms of instinctive behavior showed that they were not necessarily adaptive; they could be totally vacuous or neutral, or even detrimental to adaptation. He accepted that instincts are phylogenetic modes of responses, whereas habits are acquired during ontogeny, in the course of the life of individuals. But habits also are formed from reflexes, so there is no incompatibility between the two types of behavior. Therefore, "pure" instincts can only be observed in their first occurrence, since they are subsequently interwoven with conditional reflexes that form habits, as occurs in the song of birds exposed to the song of another species, or the refinement of the component acts of an instinct through repetition or exercise.

Kuo (1967) proposed an epigenetic approach, questioning the very validity and meaning of the distinction between innate and learned or acquired. The epigenetic approach views the development of behavior as a continuous dynamic process of energetic exchange between the developing individual and its internal and external environment, during the prenatal and postnatal period until death. Each dynamic exchange changes the mutually affecting properties of the behavioral patterns of the organism and the stimulation patterns of the environment. In this continuous conception of becoming, the innate-acquired distinction loses all meaning. Each moment of the process is an antecedent of the next, from the very moment of fertilization of the zygote in the species in which this occurs. This view, shared by other distinguished developmental scholars such as Lehrman (1962) and Schneirla (1956), questions the usefulness of emphasizing the inheritance of behavior as an effect of natural selection in phylogeny (an otherwise entirely inferred process), or, in contrast, the acquisition of behavioral patterns as an effect of experience from birth onward. Neither of these two views is independently empirically verifiable and makes no logical sense when considering the development of behavior as a dynamic continuum of interaction between organism and environment.

In concluding this section, it is important to point out the lack of a key distinction in the approach to the problem. There is a conceptual confusion resulting from a false terminological identity. The innate-learned distinction is applied to the term 'behavior' or other equivalent terms, such as acts, action patterns, or sequence of movements, but these terms do not distinguish two different levels of qualitative functionality: bioecological functions and psychological functions. In confusing the two conceptual levels by the use of one term, namely 'behavior', one loses sight of the fact that all psychological behavior involves biological behavior, but not the reverse (Ribes, 2018). Psychological behavior represents the establishment of functional contacts from the detachment of functions proper to biological behavior. To discuss whether psychological behavior is innate or learned is meaningless. All the active/reactive patterns included in psychological behavior are based on the biological reactivity of the individual, which is the reactivity of a body or soma replicated from the progenitors, in a regressive process difficult to determine, in which somatic characteristics vary due to the very nature of sexual reproduction, at least in vertebrates. In turn, functional contacts, as bidirectional relations between the individual and objects, other individuals, or environing events cannot be characterized from the perspective of the logic of the concept of learning. Relations between entities are neither learned nor unlearned, nor does it make sense to examine them in this way. Thus, discussions about the innate or learned nature of psychological behavior, its hereditary character, its phylogenetic roots, and its genetic determinants, are conceptual knots that can never be solved empirically by observation or experimentation.

Evolution and Natural Selection: A Questionable Doctrine

Different problems underlying the Darwinian formulation of evolution and the origin of species, including the concept of evolution itself, will be examined and questioned in this section. We will point out a diversity of aspects that lead to the raising of questions rather than to proposing alternatives or solutions to the problems pointed out. It would be absurd and unfair to deny the scientific concerns underlying the formulation of Darwinian theory, partly inspired and influenced by the ideas of Jean Baptiste Lamarck and Erasmus Darwin. However, it would also be inappropriate to ignore the social motivations and historical circumstances that led to its formulation and acceptance. The ideas of evolution took place in nineteenth century Victorian England, a rising empire that spanned the five continents, and in which the two great industrial revolutions occured in a short period of time. The British Empire gave rise to the rise of the new industrial capitalism and the reordering of productive forces in the world, as well as the rise of today's social classes, including the working class and the so-called middle class. The new working class, the urban industrial proletariat, and the definitive economic subordination of the countryside to the city emerged irreversibly. Moreover, the process of transformation of mercantile capitalism into industrial capitalism was necessarily sustained by the international division of labor sketched out by British imperial expansion.

Two collateral, but no less important, aspects of this process of social transformation in England are worth noting: first, the justification of the existence of two major classes of individuals in the social formation, those who achieve success and have access to education and all kinds of satisfactions, and those others, less skilled or disabled, who have to subsist on the labor provided by the proprietary class; second, the justification of empire based on the existence of superior and inferior races, and colonization as a means of providing a better life for inferior cultures and incorporating them into the advantages of Western civilization. Darwin took the idea of natural selection, as a replacement for divine design, from T. R. Malthus (1798) in his Essay on the principle of population. In that paper, Malthus stated that population was increasing at a greater rate (geometric) than food production (arithmetic), so that famines and demographic catastrophes would occur within a century. To prevent this, he proposed measures to reduce the reproduction among the wretched and vicious, who, by virtue of being the weakest segment of society, would in any case perish. Darwin recognized Malthus' influence in formulating the principle of natural selection, in which the wretched and less gifted are replaced by the fittest to adjust to the demands of the natural environment. The social-economic dimension was transformed into a biological-economic dimension. In society, the dominant classes establish the criteria of subsistence for the different segments of the population, criteria explicit in economic, political, and legal relations. The capable, educated and morally virtuous individuals are those who reach the highest levels of satisfaction and recognition on their own merits. The vicious, the weak, and the ignorant are those who inevitably occupy the lowest social status and are prone to disease and misfortune.

This regulating principle of English society, representative of the liberal ideology prevailing in the new stage of transformation of economic and political life, was adapted to the new formulation of the origin and evolution of the species, so that both would correspond in their assumptions and aims: nature selects the fittest and strongest, and the weakest and unfittest become extinct. Only those who live longer reproduce and evolve, while individuals and populations of species that are unfit for the requirements of nature will inevitably disappear, leaving their place to other individuals and species. The "selective pressure" of the environment presupposes demands on individuals and populations that are not self-evident. In fact, it constitutes a transplantation of social criteria to nature, and turns it into a system that requires a permanent effort to adjust to an invisible demand, so to speak. Natural life is limited to the struggle for survival and the perpetuation of the species, in a scenario where apparently everyone competes for the same thing, conspecifics and nonspecifics. Hence the invention of a "selfish" gene to justify natural selection at a genetic level (Dawkins, 1976). It is a sordid representation of nature, in which it is difficult at best to account for the evolution of plants, let alone the other kingdoms, prokaryotes, Protoctista, and fungi.

On the contrary, Kropotkin (1902) proposed mutual aid as a fundamental evolutionary principle, emphasizing that gregarious animals are those that show a better adaptation to all the conditions of natural life in contrast to those that live individually. Recently, supporters of the new synthesis have additionally proposed the existence of an "altruistic" gene, a fiction that balances the "selfish" gene (Dawkins, 1976), either as a refined form of selfishness (Wilson, 2006), or as the natural basis of morality (De Waal, 1996). The extinction of species, and not in isolation or in relation to each other, does not seem to have occurred as a result of daily environmental "pressure" in the form of a struggle for life of individuals against each other, in which the strong survive and the weak perish. Rather, before the appearance of Homo Sapiens, the great extinctions seem to be due to natural disasters, cataclysms, meteorites, deluges and floods, glaciations, formation of new continents and others, in which both strong and weak individuals have perished. The unnatural extinctions, to call them somehow, are the result of the predatory activity of humans, destroying forests for agriculture and grazing, overfishing and the methods used, turning the countryside into constructions that alter the ecological balance, covering the planet with cement, using harmful chemicals, polluting and heating the atmosphere as an effect of the operation of industry and transportation systems using coal, fossil fuels and uranium derivatives, polluting rivers, lakes and seas with toxic wastes, plastics and detritus, and many more actions, among them modern destructive wars. It is difficult to conceptualize these human actions as environmental or evolutionary pressures on animal and plant species especially, and it would be an understatement to attribute the ongoing and past extinctions to "natural selection" in this new period of the planet justly called the Anthropocene. For these reasons, we must not lose sight of the fact that the theory of evolution and the new evolutionary synthesis are not strictly speaking "pure science" (if there is such thing), but constitute a doctrine loaded with the ideology and social interests of the historical moment in which they arose.

Natural selection, who and what selects?

It is pertinent to critically examine the concept of natural selection and its implications for the study of animal behavior, its relation to human behavior, and the relevance of a comparative psychology. Although its logical scope is that of biology, the concept of natural selection assumes at two levels the fundamental role of the behavior of the individual organism in the process of adaption in the episodes of the acquisition of new functional traits (acquired characters), however they are built into the replicating soma, or in the episodes involved in sexual reproduction. Implicitly, the theory of natural selection supposes a covariation in the adaptive complexity of the soma and genome of species, as well as in that of their behavioral patterns. Therefore, evolution by natural selection occurs in a double plane: in the phylogeny of biological structure and in the phylogeny of behavior, which must covary and complement each other to a certain degree.

A first step is to examine the logic of the concept of 'selection'. To Darwin, natural election was the result of the struggle for life of organisms. It was a principle that accounted for the survival of the "fittest" that could sexually reproduce and thus maintain the species. The struggle for life, natural selection, and survival of the fittest were different ways of referring to the same aspect: some individuals survive, and others do not. The other two principles that accounted for evolution were logical corollaries of the first: only the survivors could reproduce, and they were fitter because they had possibly developed characteristics and behavior that had allowed them to adapt better, both as individuals and as a species. These acquired characteristics, following Lamarck's proposal, could be "transmitted" to the progeny, reproducing the aptitude of the survivors and thus allowing the perpetuation of the species. The struggle for life responds to what has been called "environmental pressure", the survival of the fittest to the development of somatic and behavioral characters at the individual and species level, and the perpetuation of the species to the sexual reproduction of the survivors, supposedly the fittest. This is the trinity of principles on which Darwin based the 'theory' of evolution, which are still relatively valid to a greater or lesser degree.

There are several logical and empirical issues in this explanatory trinity. Undoubtedly, the great impact and the initial difficulties in getting Darwin's view of evolution accepted had to do with two aspects. One, which contradicted the dominant fixist view that the existing species had been the only ones in history and had not been modified in any way. The other, which had to with the non-divine origin of humans (as in the case of animals and plants, but more socially problematic) and, consequently, the need to replace the creator or creators of the world (not only in the Judeo-Christian tradition) by "something" different, non-transcendent, that would give meaning to the evolutionary vision. The solution was to replace divinity by a "principle": natural selection. However, it was not a good solution in hindsight for several reasons, among them:

a) Firstly, mentioning or describing a 'selection' only means one outcome. Out of several options, one is "selected". Depending on the context of the expression, one may select a garment, a color, a dish, or a course of action. Selection always refers to the result of an act or behavior by which the selection occurs, but not to the act or behavior responsible for that result, for no one can identify acts consubstantial to selecting. Only circumstances under which selection can occur can be stipulated. From the viewpoint of its grammatical logic, the term "selection" only makes sense as a category of achievement or result. However, it does not include or imply in such logic the type of occurrences or activities involved for such an effect, achievement or result to occur. Natural selection does not describe or refer to a process, but to a result, effect or achievement and thus does not account for the achievement, but only states it. Natural selection, and natural means that this is the way it happens, that it is the given, is reduced to stating that existing species exist because they did not disappear. Thus, the extinct species (and the member organisms) were not selected. An educational metaphor would be to compare natural selection to an admission test, but in this case, the admission test and how it is solved is unknown. Maynard Smith (1979) was concerned that the tautological nature of the concept of natural selection cannot be ignored. He commented that "... the theory in at least some formulations is tautological. 'The survival of the fittest' appears to mean merely that survivors survive. There seems little point in trying to explain evolution by a tautology." (p. 83) Indeed, such an endeavor would be meaningless, but contrary to what he argues to justify its theoretical feasibility, the biological process that determines the survival and multiplication of some organisms and species (if it is a single, universal one) cannot be replaced by a statistical formula concerning the existing populations and their variations as the genetic theory of natural selection does.

The theory of natural selection was transformed into a genetic theory of natural selection (Fisher, 1930), in which the genes of the fittest were estimated based on Mendel's population genetics. In Mendelian genetics, rediscovered at the beginning of the past century, variation occurs from the differences contributed by each of the parents: instead of 46 chromosomes that characterize each of their cells, the sexual gametes, egg and sperm, contribute only 23 chromosomes each. The variation comes from the zygote, which shares half of the chromosomes of each of the parents and, to that extent, is distinct from each of them separately. Fisher's theory is a mathematical formalization of Mendel's laws to support natural selection as a process within the chromosomal variation of the zygote. Supposedly, through sexual reproduction of the different individuals of a species, what is selected are the "fit" genes that are expressed as variations of the adaptive phenotypes in the actual organisms. Sexual reproduction among survivors reproduces the genetic fitness to survive, a new tautology, but now transferred to genes and sexual reproduction within a population of the species. Selection occurs among gene variation and their mutations, and no longer among individual variation, so that evolution is determined by the survival of the fit genes, as it were. Genes become miniature organisms that replace the real organism and its effective interactions with other organisms and environmental conditions. It is important to always keep in mind that genes are the chains of nucleotide amino acids contained in the chromosomes of each and every cell of an organism. They are not a special heredity organ, as is falsely assumed, but are simply systems that participate in cellular metabolism by producing proteins and collaborating in energy release and cellular respiration.

Sexual reproduction (as opposed to mitosis) is a process in which half of the chromosomes of each parent and not the whole of them is replicated in the new organism, so that the new organism is only a partial replica of each of the parents, but the replicating cells, on the part of both, share the same functional structure that characterizes them as a species. Each cell, no matter what tissue or organ, contains the same chromosomes and genes. The functional differentiation of specialized cells (and the tissues and organs they comprise) is not replicated in sexual reproduction (nor in mitosis). Neurons do not reproduce neurons, nor do liver cells clone themselves. Thus, sexual reproduction can only account for variations within the same species, but it cannot explain the transformation into a new, distinct species (speciation as a biological emergent), species transmutation, which was what the theory of evolution was intended to address. Potential variation as an effect of sexual reproduction in a large population (as proposed by Malthus and Fisher), can only result in differences within the species, that is, subspecies or races as they are sometimes called. Mendel's peas never ceased to be peas, like the Drosophila of the fruit, although they "mutate" some characteristics, in the end they revert to the original characteristics.

b) Secondly, three issues concerning natural selection can be raised. The theory of evolution constitutes a history of living matter in one way or another. To give primacy to natural selection as the cause or determinant of evolution implies attributing to this 'principle' agency in evolution. Selection cannot be fortuitous or random. Someone or something is who or what carries out the selection, and that selection must be made on the basis of a criterion that cannot be identified with the selection itself. Three questions immediately arise: Who or what selects? What is selected? By what criterion or rule is it selected? Apparently, selection occurs naturally and spontaneously by itself as the term implies. If this were not so, one would have to suppose a reified entity in nature, which replaces divinities and creators and prescribes and applies its own laws: the struggle for life and the perpetuation of the species. Selection is aimed at individuals, assuming that there are "weak" and "strong" individuals, without previously specifying what this difference between "weak" and "strong" consists of. What is selected is established a posteriori: the survivors, and if they have survived, they must be the strongest because they are the most capable, the fittest to continue living. The circular argument is completed by assuming that when the fittest (of both sexes) reproduce sexually, the individuals who do so because they are the survivors, form, as a whole, a strengthened population of the species to which they belong (the theoretical basis of eugenics). It is important to note at this point that adaptive or survival "fitness" is the shared result of the fitness of each of the sexes in the act of reproduction. The natural question is, how can such fitness be identified in each sex? Is it limited to reproductive fitness in terms of the number of offspring they produce, and is it related to other aspects such as finding food, defending and delimiting territory, or to their predatory capacity? If so, what component of adaptative fitness does each parent contribute, and are non-strictly sexual fitnesses equivalent in both sexes? If what is selected are the genes contained in the chromosomes of the parents and common to the entire population comprising the species, given that there are no correspondences between genes, cell types, tissues and organs, or systemic and reactive behavioral functions, in which chromosomes and their nucleotide amino acid chains does each of these adaptive fitnesses reside? None of these questions seems to be clarified by the genetic theory of natural selection.

c) In considering the origin of species, the theory of evolution is an attempt to reconstruct and explain a history of life. Paradoxically, its three guiding principles describe and have been applied to only two of the life kingdoms: animals and plants. There is no mention of the origin of life, nor does it address how extant species, or their fossil ancestors originated, and the circumstances that account for the diversity of extant or extinct species. The theory of evolution attempts at best to show linage relations between fossils and extant species by morphological similarities, or between varieties in distinct secondary characters of individuals of the same species in different geographic locations, isolated from each other. The great void on the origin of life and of the three kingdoms with the greatest diversity of phyla, species and organisms (prokaryotes, Protoctista, and fungi), shifted the emphasis of the theory of evolution, and probably to call it in such a way, to account only for the ancestral origins of humans and of animals and plants correlatively. The history of life, like all history, is reconstructed from its ultimate point, the present time and the most complex form identified. Just as in the historical-social sciences the reconstruction is carried out starting from contemporary capitalist social formations, in biology the starting point for this historical return was taken as contemporary Homo Sapiens, and the Homo Sapiens represented by its Caucasian, European and "white" variety (or race, as it was thus established). From humans onwards, hominids, apes, mammals, and other vertebrates, as well as mainly arthropods, were identified. Plants were included because of the interest aroused by the techniques of domestication, hybridization, and crossbreeding, which provided an exemplary field for the application of natural selection, truly artificial in this case.

The concept of evolution, finally chosen over that of transmutation, assumes a directionality of the process of biological change and diversification. The terminal reference point is Homo Sapiens, and it is assumed that species have developed (evolved) to culminate in the human being as the terminal moment in the tree of life. Evolution represents the different changes or progressive advances in the appearance of the different species in the process of the rise of the human species, as the epitome of adaptive virtues. It is not god that creates man, but natural selection guiding his fitness for survival with respect to the environment. From an unknown origin and multiple divergent transformations, neither identified nor explainable, the theory of evolution is based on an unspeakable ultimate goal: the appearance of humans on Earth. This approach is pristinely expressed in Ralph Linton's (1936) comment that man is not a fallen angel but an upright anthropoid. This phrase sums up the meaning of the theory of evolution, which ultimately constitutes an anthropocentric view of the meaning of life and the reconstruction of its forms of organization. The search for the adaptation of organisms and species to the environment turns out to be the purpose of existence and of the whole evolutionary process. The danger of establishing the struggle for life and the perpetuation of the species as finality of existence, and its regulation by a misty natural selection, stamp a teleological mark on the theory of evolution. The absence of a creative, intelligent, planning being was replaced by an equally finalistic, but tautological principle, since the struggle for life and the perpetuation of the species are the circumstances in which existence takes place and not its reasons or determinants. The conditions of the phenomenon are confused with its determinants. Monod (1970) coined the term "teleonomy" to avoid any risk of transcendent finalism. He conceived teleonomy as an apparent quality of purpose and goal orientation of structures and functions of organisms to achieve reproductive success. As an antidote, Monod substituted random mutations for apparent purpose, a process difficult to prove and even more difficult to justify on the basis of available taxonomic data. The change of term from one of attribution to one of description does not cancel the logical confusion that evolution is driven by survival to reproduce.

d) The concept of environmental pressure is closely linked to those of adaptation and natural selection. Environmental pressure implies an environment, an ecology, or a habitat, separate and distinct from the individual organism (and by extension from its species). The environment does not constitute the set of circumstances that make life and its reproduction possible, but is represented as a hostile and threatening environment for organisms. The environment is an entity that is confronted, not one in which it is possible to live. It is a predatory environment, with conspecific competitors, with scarce nutrients and food, and permanently or potentially adverse conditions. This image is not a good representation of the circumstances of life on Earth, much less for all the existing varieties of organisms, from unicellular to higher primates, including humans. This view of Darwinian theory (and its new synthesis) represents a molecular view of the relation of organisms to their environment. Each organism is seen as a separate entity facing an undifferentiated block called the environment, which acts on it and to which it must adapt in the best possible or way or, otherwise, it is swiftly eliminated.

This molecular and "isolationist" conception of organisms is not exclusive to biology. It has also been and is present in other disciplines such as psychology and the historical-social science in which the concept of the 'individual' is prominent. In the case of bioecology (a more appropriate name than biology alone), ontological conceptions of its object of study are similar to some of those found in psychology. Due to its peculiar epistemological condition, psychology can historically identify three generic entities that have a different relation with the world as set of objects and events (Ribes, 2000). These entities are the mind, soul or cognition, instruments of consciousness, the brain, organ of consciousness, and the behaving individual organism. The latter entity will be addressed for reasons of similarity. In psychology, there are three ways of conceiving the organism or individual with respect to the world. Two of them conceive the individual as separate from the world. The first considers a reactive organism (for example, the conditional reflex theory), whose behavior corresponds to the characteristics and functional circumstances of objects in the world, in the style of Piaget's (1976) concept of accommodation offered in the context of his analysis of evolution. The second one, also considers the individual with respect to the world, but in this case, it is an active indi-

189

vidual who operates on the world (for example, in operant theory), affects it and is affected by the changes produced in turn, in the style of Piaget's assimilation, the basis of epigenesis as a process of evolutionary change. The third one, which is the one we wish to emphasize in the context under discussion, is that of the individual in the world, not in front of it, and which, to that extent, conceives the psychological as a relation between the individual and the entities of the world. This is the field conception of the psychological as interbehavior in a field of interdependencies. From this view, the individual who exhibits psychological behavior does not confront the world, react to it, or act upon it, but is part of it, and only in this way are the relations in which she participates understood.

In the case of bioecology, as in the historical-social science, it is even more discordant to separate or isolate the organism or biont and the individual from the world of which they are part: a habitat or a social formation. A compositional logic of the environment that molecularly isolates individual organisms from the environment would lead to proposing as many different environments, composed of heterogeneous elements or entities, as organisms of different species can be identified. The logical result of this formulation would be the existence of millions of different environments. This would not be a dynamic view of the environment, but only a tremendous confusion. There is no doubt at present that life on Earth appeared 4,000 million years ago, only 500 million years after the formation of the planet. There is also no doubt that the changing conditions that taken place on the planet are, at least partially, the result of certain physicochemical interactions that allowed the emergence of prokaryotes, archaebacteria, and cyanobacteria, which in turn modified the conditions of the planet's atmosphere, among others, transforming cyanide into oxygen and fixing nitrogen in the oceans. The origin and extension of life cannot be understood without conceiving it as a process of interdependence between the physicochemical conditions of the planet (including its inorganic and organic composition, as well as its temperature) and the appearance of the first cells with the capacity to metabolize, that is, to regulate their thermal conditions, their chemical composition (protected by a membrane, but without a nucleus), and to replicate by bipartition. The planet provided the conditions for the emergence of the first unicellular beings and these in turn modified the conditions of the planet, its atmosphere, its temperature, and after many millions of years, the characteristics of its crust populated by a great diversity of organisms that continue to transform it, among them humans.

The Earth constitutes a system that allows life and is affected by it. In this sense, it is said to be a "living" planet (Lovelock, 2000). It is a diversified habitat constituted by its changing geological and atmospheric condition since its origin, and the multiplicity of life forms harbored, in continuous interaction with each other, forming a symbiotic system, in which the inorganic environment affects and is affected by the organic or living environment. The diversification and increasing complexity of the different forms of life from the first prokaryotes onwards can only be understood on the basis of symbiotic relations. Margulis (1998) has documented how the first eukaryotes, nucleated protists, were formed from endosymbiotic fusions between different prokaryotes. She has also documented how the existence of organelles constituted by bacteria irreversibly fused in their cytoplasm can be identified in protoctists and fungi such as algae. Life could not have been developed and maintained under the fierce and adverse natural selection of the fittest, for adaptive fitness is meaningless when one examines the world of the prokaryote, Protoctista, and fungi kingdoms, which comprise almost all living variants on the planet. Though microscopy had existed since 1590, the formulation of the theory of natural selection was based on partial naturalistic observations of the animal and plant kingdoms only. Terrestrial animal life would not have been possible without the population of its crust by plant species that appeared, starting from some species of algae (fungi), 350 million years ago, after animal life in the seas. In fact, mycorrhizae are today an almost universal example of mutualist symbiosis between fungi and plants. Plants could not survive without the nitrogenation function of their roots, while fungi feed on the products of plant photosynthesis. Beyond the myriad examples provided by the various ecological chains between the five kingdoms of life, there is no clearer example of general symbiosis than this one. All species form an interdependent reciprocal environment. There is no total agreement in modern biology on a definition of symbiosis, but three general types of symbiosis are generally accepted: mutualism, commensalism, and parasitism. Loosely speaking, the latter would be the only case in which one species would take advantage of another, harming it, but obviously it would not fit the concept of predation proper to the most common characterization of the "struggle for life". All species nourish each other, directly or indirectly, and this circular or elliptical, multiradial and multidirectional chain allows them all to maintain their functions and to continue to reproduce. There are non-direct forms of symbiosis, such as the release of oxygen by plants and methane by cows, which allow the Earth's atmosphere to maintain stable (the methane/oxygen balance), making life as we know it possible (Matthews, 2000). Others constitute phenomena that we could call vestigial symbiosis, such as the fact that some million-year-old ancestors of the genus Homo fed on the waste of prey animals of other carnivorous species. Although unflattering to humans, early humans were at one time, due to the difference in physical strength and hunting tools, scavengers (Mithen, 1998), a form of vestigial parasitic symbiosis.

This is not a problem of selfish or altruistic genes as the neo-Darwinians now argue. It is simply a matter of recognizing the symbiotic structure of life and of its transformation on the planet, and of abandoning the genetic theory of natural selection and its corollaries of population struggles through competition of fit and unfit individuals. Life on Earth cannot be analyzed as a free market economy. In fact, all living beings constitute symbiotic units within an integrated system of the planet Earth and its geological and atmospheric conditions, which have been changing over the four and a half billion years of its existence. The planetary climatic changes brought about by localized ecological disturbances is further evidence of the generalized interdependence between the planet and all its life forms.

Alternative Perspectives and Gaps or Omissions in the Theory of Natural Selection

The Darwinian theory of evolution and its new synthesis not only have serious logical and conceptual problems, which are always crucial to evaluate the viability of a theory, but also confront a series of facts that cannot explain or account for them. Based on their survival and reproductive success criteria, one would have to conclude that the ideal of "evolution" is ultimately the prokaryotes, the bacteria, since they are the only species that have not become extinct during 4000 million years but have diversified and increased in population. This would be a paradoxical conclusion for a theory that tries to justify the superiority of Homo Sapiens as a species in the scale of life. Since perhaps one of the deficiencies or weaknesses of the Darwinian theory is that it does not start its analysis from the origin of life, but from the ancestors of humans, we will raise the issues and questions beyond a theory of the evolution of species, identified in the animal and plant kingdoms, but from an understanding of the transformations in complexity and diversity of life as part of the changes that have occurred on planet Earth.

The question of how to explain the different forms and functions that living beings have and have had is not a question exclusive to the problem of life, but is proper to the existing "reality", which is not the product or result of human activity. In the case of the Universe, there are different approaches to its origin, all agreeing that it occurred from a great concentration of energy, but it is not even possible to imagine the moment prior to this beginning. There are only two options: one, that of science, which consists of accepting that this was the beginning and no other, or a second, supposing a Creator of the Universe and all existing things, which simply constitutes another non-explainable, transcendent "beginning". Scientists attempt to understand what properties and processes occurred so that either the universe, living beings, or social formations changed in the course of known history based on the circumstances themselves. In the case of religion and transcendentalist thought, all that matters is an initial plan, an act of creation, to which everything created has been adjusted in various ways to fulfill the initial purpose of its existence. Although the logics of science and religion are not only different but incompatible, in the course of human history, paraphrasing Lynn Margulis, we could say that there has been a case of endosymbiosis of the religious organelles in the cytoplasm of science. Attempts to explain the functional morphology of all (previous and present) known species implicitly or explicitly, are not necessarily justified in terms of a predetermined environmental fit, but of a harmonious correspondence between the biological characteristics of the biont or symbiont and those of its environment. No theory can or will be able to explain the reasons why each species has its particular formation, nor why they occurred in the way they did and not in another way at the level of the great transformations. There is no intentionality in the Universe, nor is there intentionality in the domain of life (including, paradoxically enough, social formations). Intentionality is proper only to social coexistence and is difficult to disentangle even by its own participating members. Intentionality does not precede the acts of individuals, but is only a way of describing and justifying the acts of people that have effects and affect other people and, therefore, intentionality is always predicated after an act. Strictly speaking, unfulfilled intentions are not intentions, they are only desires. This is commented in order to rule out, as a problem of a theory of the history of life, having to elucidate the peculiar formation of each one of the extant or extinct species. It is the task of such a theory to account for the conditions that allowed the emergence and disappearance of these life forms, as well as their transformation into increasing complex bionts and symbionts. However, one must first accept that everything began on the basis of the conditions provided by the planet, and that the process of diversification of life assumed such a multiplicity of forms that is not possible, nor does it make sense, to try to account for each of them as part of a linear, branched or reticulated process. This would lead to such absurd questions as asking why there is such a diversity of eyes in the different phyla and animal classes and how they were formed, or, in a finalist sense, asking why the eyes were formed and trying to account for their characteristics based on their current functions. Similarly, one could ask why there are species with eyes. These are equivalent questions to those sometimes asked by comparative ethologists and psychologists as to whether flies, eagles, and humans see the world in the same way. These questions have no answer, as they are false questions and only lead to confusion and distraction.

A theory on the history and changes of living beings must begin with the origin, but it must cancel as an issue to be solved the question of the ultimate causes of the characteristics of the diverse forms of organization of life. This theory should only delimit the conditions under which life emerged and transformed, but not the "reasons" that determined their specific and peculiar forms. To posit the adaptative nature of the characteristics and functions of organisms or bionts is precisely the mistake to avoid. As already pointed out, the concept of adaptation ultimately assumes a finality in the adapting organism, so that it accommodates itself isomorphically to that which it adapts and, consequently, its morphology and function only make sense insofar as they meet that criterion of adaptation. However, the interdependent symbiotic nature, in the broadest sense of the term, does not require the concept of adaptation nor does it justify the adequacy of the organisms to their environment to account for their "survival" and reproduction. The functional morphology of each of the species (an ambiguous concept) comprising the five kingdoms is not a matter to be "explained" in the strict sense. There are two tasks to be fulfilled by a theory of the history of life: first, to identify the conditions under which all life forms have developed and, second, to trace the historical relation of possibility and transformation between these forms of life. The Darwinian formula was more concerned with justifying the supposed suitability of each species and the reasons that determined its specific characteristics. The hardest version of this formula, the genetic theory of natural selection, assumes a correspondence between the genome and the adaptative functions of organisms. This assumption cannot be corroborated since there is no localization of organs and functions "encoded" in the genome. In fact, the DNA (and RNA) do not constitute living matter. Nucleic acids are located outside and independently of living beings: viruses are the most conspicuous case of this fact. The genome, contained in chromosomes, only represents the various metabolic functions and characteristics shared by all the cells of a biont, and they replicate those characteristics and functions via reproduction. They do not reproduce organs, tissues, or traits, much less behaviors "contained" in genes. It is not surprising that molecular biology recognizes a universal genetic code, which consists of the different forms of composition and biochemical structuring of nucleic acid chains, and which is shared in practically all domains of life. This code allows the development of different metabolic functions in cells and, consequently, enables their functional differentiation and the formation of multicellular organizations of varying complexity, in interdependence with the environmental conditions and circumstances. There is no prefiguration of species in the universal genetic code. The genomes of each 'species' are in principle the result of the operation of this code shared by all living beings.

We will not provide a systematic analysis of feasible alternatives accounting for the transformation and increasing complexity of the different life forms, although some of them will be mentioned, possibly complementary to each other, and at different levels. As previously mentioned, the first step is to identify the conditions and circumstances under which cellular structures formed, that is, bodies with the property of self-generating energy and reproducing or replicating themselves. Archaebacteria and cyanobacteria seem to constitute the first life kingdom, that being the prokaryotes. Darwin, though not explicitly, assumed that the first life form on the planet "spontaneously" emerged, although he did not systematize his approach to speciation by natural selection and sexual reproduction from this primitive life form. Lazcano (2000) has described a succinct history of ideas about the history of life, including Hemholtz' panspermia, recently rekindled by Hoyle and Creek, which assumed the extraterrestrial origin of life, transported to earth by meteorites. Establishing the origin of the first organic molecules or even cellular forms outside the Earth only moves the problem of determining the conditions under which such organic or cellular structures formed to a space other than that of our planet. Oparin (1938) formulated the autotrophic origin of life, by identifying abiotic organic molecules, protected by a membrane, that could replicate and that could constitute the antecedent to the first forms of cellular organizations, with a cytoplasm and ribosome, like that of bacteria. Miller (1953) conducted an experiment that succeeded in synthetizing an organic molecule of these characteristics in the laboratory. Based on his findings, what are supposed to be abiotic structures, possible precedents of cellular structures, called protobionts or progenotes, have been identified. The latter structures constitute acellular aggregates of assembled organic polymers, surrounded by a membranous structure, such as liposomes and microspheres, similar to the phospholipid layers of cells. It is assumed that protobionts may have emerged as RNA (ribosomes) when surrounded by liposomes, or that they were structured from RNA transcription into DNA by successive RNA-supported enzymatic processes and perhaps satellite viruses. Regardless of the process of emergence of protobionts, they have the capacity of replication, like viruses, although they do not possess cytoplasm or the autotrophic possibility of cells and may be the precursors of cellular structures.

Butturini, García-Castellanos, Jordi, Ribas y Urmeneta (2020) state that it seems to be a fact that the "the solar system was colonized by organisms just some four hundred-five hundred million years after the beginning of the Sun's main sequence, and life has accompanied the Earth throughout almost its entire history. It could be said that the Earth not only met the requirements of habitability from almost its beginnings, but that life emerged and settled down as soon as these were shaped." (p. 187) Although the circumstances and special conditions in the history of the planet under which the first prokaryotes –unicellular beings with ribosome but no nucleus– emerged from protobionts or equivalents are unknown, there are well-founded approaches of how prokaryotes could have led to the appearance of the first unicellular eukaryotes or Protoctista. Based on laboratory evidence, Margulis (1998) has proposed the process of serial endosymbiosis as responsible for the emergence of the first eukaryotic organisms. According to Margulis, symbiogenesis results from living together, coexisting, cohabiting, a form of symbiosis, in which two distinct organisms merge into a new organism. Margulis says that "Symbiogenesis, an idea proposed by its Russian inventor Konstantin Merezhkovsky (19855-1921), refers to the formation of new organs and organisms through symbiotic mergers. As I will show it is a fundamental fact of evolution. All organisms large enough for us to see are composed of once-independent microbes, teamed up to become larger wholes. As they merged, many lost what we in retrospect recognize as their former individuality" (p. 33). To understand serial endosymbiosis I will quote Margulis at length:

> "My theory of the symbiogenetic origin of plant, animal, and other cells with nuclei employs four provable postulates. All four involve Symbiogenesis, incorporation, and body fusion by symbiosis. The theory precisely outlines the steps that must have occurred in the past, especially in relation

to the bright green cells of plants. Cells, of course, are familiar units of structure in mosses, ferns, and all other plants. The slender stamen hairs particularly visible in *Zebrina* and *Tradescantia* ('wandering jew') flowers are made of rows of such plant cells. Large, walled green cells preceded plants: they were already fully formed in the green algae, water-dwelling ancestors of plants. That organisms with nuclei evolved by merger is best appreciated in plants because in their large and beautiful cells, the integrity of their component organelles is easily observed. The idea is straightforward: four once entirely independent and physically separate ancestors merged in a specific order to become the green algal cell. All four were bacteria. Each of the four bacteria types differed in ways we can still infer. In both merged and free-living forms, the descendants of all four kinds of bacteria still live today. Some say the four types are mutually enslaved, trapped both in the plant and as the plant. Today each of the types of former bacteria provides clues about its ancestry; life is chemically so conservative that we can even deduce the specific order in which they merged. The term *serial* in *serial endosymbiosis theory* refers to the order in the merger sequence." (p. 34).

Each bacterium type, irreversibly merged in a mutual, sequenced fusion, results in a new cellular nucleated protist organism, the previously non-existent green algae. Each bacterium contributes a specific functional difference in the new unicellular organism: protein production, respiration, energy release, and movement. Likewise, the fusion of two bacteria types can explain the appearance of the nucleus in the new cell.

Margulis proposed that the first life forms consisted of chemoautotrophic and later photoautotrophic bacteria, according to the geological conditions of the planet at that time: without oxygen. In fact, she notes that the bacteria symbiotically coexisting in our soma correspond to this type of cellular structure, to the extent that our internal environment is similar to that of the Earth 3.5 billion years ago. To understand the origin of the first organisms, Margulis (1998) commented that "…The book of life is written in neither mathematics nor English: it is written in the language of carbon chemistry" (p. 55). Subsequently, heterotrophic cells emerged, which "feed" on external organic material, as opposed to autotrophic cells that produce their own "food". The serial endosymbiotic theory of phylogeny (Margulis, 2000) proposes four original bacteria types: photosynthetic (such as cyanobacteria), motile (such as spirochetes), fermenting, heat-producing and acid-resistant (such as thermoplasma), and respiring (such as paracocci). Cyanobacteria are direct ancestors of plants along with some protists (algae and aquatic molds), while the other bacteria types merged into protists, which in turn are ancestors of fungi and animals. The emergence of the various kingdoms began with the prokaryotes, then, in that order, the Protoctista (including protists), the fungi, the animals and the plants. The latter was the last kingdom 472 million years ago, after the appearance of the sponges and trilobites of the animal kingdom around 540-560 million years ago.

Obviously, the theory of natural selection cannot account for a sequence of life of this nature, for at least three reasons. First, it considers only two kingdoms, animals and plants, and in the case of the latter it could hardly branch out from animals as precedents. Second, sexual reproduction, as a process that leads to genetic variation (although only limited to the species itself) could not explain the sequence of life forms, many of them asexual, specially at the beginning. Lastly, random mutations in the genome (of a spontaneous nature, since they are assumed to be endogenous) could not explain the diversity of species, phyla and kingdoms, and their symbiotic relations with the habitat that stem from previous conditions and not from a process of survival given differential characteristics of individual species and organisms. It is also difficult for the genetic theory of natural selection to address the existence of a sixth extinct kingdom, the Ediacarans, which lived in the ocean in the Precambrian and Cambrian, characterized as metacellular organisms (McMenamin, 2000), shaped by the addition of bilateral, trilateral, and even tetralateral layers and symmetries. Even more challenging is to account for the so-called Cambrian explosion 540 million years ago, with deglaciation and changes in the continents and tectonic plates of the Earth's crust (Ward & Kirshvink, 2016), in which a great diversity of animal species suddenly appeared. The new geological conditions may help to understand the characteristics present in the new species, the extinction of 50% of them later, and a new expansion of the animal kingdom in the Ordovician-Devonian period, but not alleged genetic mutations due to environmental pressures on the fittest. The evidence provided by fossils indicates more a "life pressure" than an "environmental pressure".

In addition to symbiogenesis, epigenesis can contribute to the differentiation of cell reproduction and differentiation in the organism through DNA and histone methylation (Jaenisch & Bird, 2003). Epigenetic methylation (and acetylation) is activated by environmental factors during the embryonic process in animals and plants and can also alter cellular DNA activation-deactivation functions in fungal and bacterial genes. Methylation acts on the adenine and cytokine chains, in the case of histones, which are at the base of chromatin, also influencing their gene regulatory role, determining the expression of a stem cell as a differentiated cell, or deactivating the reproduction of certain cells or the somatic geography in which they are to be located. The molecular study of epigenetic processes has not only discarded any preformist hypothesis of a miniature representation of the embryo in the zygote but has also put back into perspective Baldwin's (1896) hypothesis of organic selection, environmental influences and learned adaptive activities in gene expression. It has indirectly led to a renewed appreciation of Lamarck's proposal of the possibility of transmitting to descendants functional characters (in use) developed ("acquired") in the process of interaction with the environment after several generations.

Research on bacterial resistance to antibiotics has also identified, for at least 30 years, processes of horizontal or lateral gene transfer and mutation, which do not occur from parents to offspring, but involve viral agents, plasmids, transposons, and satellite viruses, which somehow may also participate in symbiogenesis and epigenesis. These processes of horizontal transfer have modified the conception of genomic transformation and the organization of life, contemplating their metaphorical representation in the form of a network rather than a tree (Hilario & Gogarten, 1993).

Does a Comparative Psychology Make Sense as an Evolutionary Psychology?

The interest in a comparative psychology necessarily focuses on human psychological behavior and, consequently, on its two distinguishing characteristics with respect to any other species or life form: language and its social life constituted by conventional and institutional practices. The human being is undoubtedly a biont, but with very special characteristics, we might even say a mutualist symbiont, an active builder of its habitat. In the preceding section it has become clear that life comes from chemistry, but that it is not in chemistry. Similarly, it can be said that society, as a specifically human habitat, comes from biology, but is not in biology. This explicitly means that social formations cannot be understood on the basis of evolutionary biology. The strictly biological is the human soma and its functions, but its interindividual behavior (and psychological behavior) have no antecedents or ancestors in other species.

As previously discussed, comparative psychology was an immediate result of the Darwinian theory of evolution, with two clear objectives: first, to identify whether animals shared the same psychological processes as humans and, second, to demonstrate that these psychological processes were the key to account for the adaptation of individuals as a population of a species, and how through variation by sexual reproduction, given the survival of the fittest, natural selection promoted progressive changes in the species itself. In addition to Romanes' contributions already cited, two works conceived within the framework of comparative psychology are explicitly noteworthy. Not included among them is Behavior: An introduction to comparative psychology by J. B. Watson in 1914, as it is more of a theoretical and methodological work, which does not systematically review the various animal phyla. An outstanding work is that of Lloyd C. Morgan in 1903, entitled "An introduction to comparative psychology". Another is that of Margaret F. Washburn in 1908, entitled "The animal mind: A textbook of comparative psychology". Both works set out to examine whether animals, especially mammals, share some form of mental life with humans. Both authors concluded in the negative. Obviously, the formulation of psychological processes on the basis of terms such as consciousness, associative memory, reasoning, perception of relations or derived attention, did not constitute the most suitable logical framework for even systematically examining such phenomena in humans themselves. Aside from a considerable number of works studying animal behavior of different species from an experimental or ethological approach, another explicit attempt to formulate a comparative psychology is Gregory Razran's 1971 work, "Mind in evolution: An East-West synthesis of learned behavior and cognition". Razran extensively studied Russian experimental literature, as well as Anglo-Saxon literature to propose a comparative psychology, as the evolution of the mind from processes such as sensitization and habituation, through different levels of progressive complexity in conditioning procedures, to symbolization, as equivalent to thinking, planning and willing. The formulation is theoretically questionable in many aspects of its interpretation of the phenomena, but it constitutes an attempt to systematize the experimental procedures under conditioning theory as a comparative framework of the evolution of psychological life, to give it some neutral name.

Recently, another questionable criterion for comparison has been proposed by incorrectly implying the concepts of culture and society in the animal world. The concepts of cultural propagation of food consumption among animals, and of animal societies or social intentionality, either among insects or in primates respectively, have been discussed (Byrne & Whiten, 1998;

de Waal, 1982; de Luce & Wilder, 1983; Roitblat & Meyer, 1995; Wilson, 1975). A case in point is the attempt to merge sociobiology with operant theory –or behaviorology as some try to call it to distinguish it from psychology (Naour, 2009; Wilson, 2008; Wilson & Hölldobler, 2005). From this view, a coevolution of genetics and culture is proposed, based on epigenetics, a soft, multilevel version of natural selection, in which there is no longer a genetic determination of humans to be socially organized. In this case, some biological changes are accepted, but not explained, as allowing and being fostered by group selection, and not on an individual basis, and that this group selection, which allows the formation of culture as relations between individuals, is what epigenetically manifests itself in the modulation of the original genetic expression. From this perspective, selection by consequences of individual behavior would constitute the ecological and cultural "mechanism" of epigenetic regulation, and the final stage of evolution would be symbol formation or reification.

In this context, even the soft version of the multilevel theory of natural selection that incorporates epigenesis, two fundamental issues separately proposed emerge: the distinction between aggregation and society, and the distinction between population environment and culture.

In evolutionary biology and ethology, it is quite common the use the term 'society' loosely to refer to aggregations or groupings in some species. In fact, the concept of aggregation or grouping is difficult to delimit, because in the case of viruses, for example, these entities always appear in quantity (to use a neutral term), like crystals. There are a multitude of species in the different kingdoms that always live in colonies given their symbiotic relations, from Protoctista, fungi and plants, to animals, in which it would be more appropriate to consider insect groupings, such as those of termites, ants and bees, mainly as colonies rather than societies. Allee (1931) proposed the term 'aggregation' to describe the coexistence of groups of animals of the same species, an aggregation that provides mutual benefits to the participating organisms in terms of orienting movement, food localization, defense against predators, and timely reproduction. From this viewpoint, aggregations could be considered a form of intraspecies mutualistic symbiosis. Unlike animal aggregations, whether or not they are colonies with less or more functional differentiation among their members, societies are specifically human organizations and therefore the term will only be used in this sense. Unlike societies, animal aggregations (human aggregations can formed circumstantially and temporarily) are invariant in their organization, and the functions performed by the different members are directly determined by their morphological and physiological characteristics (Emerson, 1958). Only one type of bee can be a queen, another type of drone, and another type a worker. The functions are not interchangeable, nor are they modified in different generations. Simpson (1958) himself, one of the advocates of the new evolutionary synthesis, mentioned that one of the several reasons for the invalidity of social Darwinism was that "...to transfer to the study of cultural evolution within the species Homo Sapiens the principles dependent on genetic evolution is likely to be metaphorical or analogical and therefore misleading. Natural selection –a genetic process– between cultures or elements of culture is impossible." (pp. 534-535). A society, or social formations in general, are characterized by a specialized and diversified division of labor, which does not depend on particular biological characteristics as in animals. The social division of specialized labor translates into the deferred exchange and appropriation, in time and space, of goods produced or collected through the elaboration of special tools and the provision of mutual services among the different members of a community. Although some superficial analogies with insect aggregations can be drawn, insofar as social formations were originally established on the basis of parental ties (which does not occur in animals), gradually expanded and transformed into increasingly differentiated organizations, based on the new exchange relations that occurred in a dynamic process in history that has not yet concluded. Animal aggregations, which could be labeled as presocial or parasocial, are historically static and their only changes correspond directly to physiochemical and ecological changes in their habitat.

Culture is another concept employed very loosely. Obviously, culture is closely linked to the emergence of social formations. To speak of one without the other would be meaningless. Culture represents the set of conventional practices and products that emerge and interlace the individual members of a social formation. These shared practices include food practices, religious practices, political practices, labor practices, leisure practices, artistic practices, recreational practices, and many others that sometimes converge or separate. These practices are transformed as a consequence of their own dynamics, going from agreement to agreement or disagreement. Culture is thus constituted by the multiplicity and diversity of customs of a social community, among which are included the objects that are elaborated. The human habitat is a culturally constructed habitat: dwellings, roads, utensils, tools, books, musical instruments, the diversity of constructions, clothing, are all cultural products. It is not even possible to offer a remote comparison or a superficial analogy with respect to animal aggregations. Animals lack culture for one fundamental reason: they lack language, and language is the medium of all human social practice and, therefore, of all cultural practice. Language allows human beings to detach themselves from momentary and local properties and circumstances and allows them to relate to each other as a practice that transcends the strictly biological. It has nothing to do with its supposedly symbolic character, but with its referential, expressive and communicate character, which allows us to act as a whole, in relation to other circumstances and to other members of the social community. Language is so important that it is difficult to identify activities of any kind in which we do not participate linguistically, at the beginning, during or at the end of them. Moreover, human beings share a high proportion of our lives in activities directly or indirectly linguistic: conversing, reading, attending performances, writing, participating in meetings and assemblies, and many more.

One of the assumptions of the Darwinian theory is that the functions of the organism depend on its somatic morphology corresponding to the adaptive pressures of the environment. This assumption somehow justifies organic changes by genetic selection based on survival functions. Lamarckian acquisition (or "learning" as psychologists and ethologists would argue) would be the phenotypic expression enabled by genetic mutations in the organs and morphological structures of organisms. This assumption is not only implausible in the case of the human being, but also meaningless. Regarding Homo Sapiens and its comparison with Neanderthal (with whom we had offspring together more than 40,000 years ago, and with whom we share part of our DNA), Klein (1999) states that "...the fossil and archeological records suggest that the modern physical form evolved before them modern capacity for culture. From a behavioral (archeological) perspective, the earliest anatomically modern or near-modern people were not significantly different from their nonmodern predecessors and contemporaries...Although the basic human form did not change significantly in the ensuing 40 ky, cultural evolution accelerated dramatically. Plainly it was culture and not body form that propelled the human species from a relatively rare and insignificant large mammal 40ky ago to a geologic force today, impinging on all other species as an agent of natural selection" (p. 572). It is clear that the diversity of human life has no correlation with its somatic organization, not even that of the nervous system, which is very similar to those of its ancestors and contemporaries of the genus Homo. Practical life in society, constitutive of the culture in and through language, promoted humans to follow a divergent path from the rest of the other life forms. It seems contradictory, or at least not very coherent, to state that the one we are trying to explain as the result of natural selection is ultimately seen as the main agent of such a process.

A clear example of the complexity of the cultural process, as an exclusively human phenomenon, is that of feeding, one of the central aspects of adaptation for Darwinian theory. Unlike other higher primates, the genus Homo, by fully developing bipedal locomotion and walking upright, not only freed the upper limbs (and especially the hands) for other activities, but also changed its plant diet and cease to be, at least partially, herbivorous and a consumer of fruits. Humans went from living in the trees to the geography of the savannah. At first, humans and their direct ancestors of the genus Homo fed directly on natural edibles, that is, on unprocessed and unprepared food, just like all other living beings. This included the consumption of meat from large animals such as zebras and antelopes, the remains of which have been found together with lithic instruments probably employed to tear meat from bones and tendons by Homo Habilis between 2 and 1.5 million years ago. Our ancestors were not hunters but marginal scavengers. However, with the "discovery" and appropriation of fire, from 1.5 million to 790 thousand years ago (Cordón, 1980; Wrangham, 2009), already in Homo Erectus, the consumption of "processed" meat allowed the descent of the larynx into the throat and the development or articulated sounds, the reduction of the size of the teeth and the geography of the jaw to adapt the muscles that regulate the use of the tongue in the articulation of differentiated and complex sounds (Mithen, 1998). The increase in the size of human groups, and the social division of labor together with the probably simultaneous appearance of language, changed the nature of eating and drinking of the genus Homo with respect to the rest of living beings. Symbiosis, predation, scavenging, direct consumption of vegetables, characteristic of the obtaining of nutrients by all living beings, were gradually replaced by the genus Homo over hundreds of thousands of years. Food gradually ceased to be essential for survival and became the axis of subsistence and social organization of human life. Historically, human feeding followed a divergent course from that of other living beings. For this reason, the behavior of foraging, especially in animals, can shed little light on the feeding practices of human beings, and much less on those of our contemporaries. Human nutrition ceased to be an exclusively bioecological process and became a prominently sociocultural one.

Qualifying nutrition as a prominently cultural process in human beings applies to practically all spheres of life, including sexual behavior and agonistic forms of behavior. An understanding of human life in society, which is the only form of life we have ever had, requires a different perspective from those of other living beings. As a biont or symbiont, humans have emerged from successive and divergent transformations in the history of life on the planet. Moreover, its functional and many morphological characteristics do not lie fundamentally in a supposed evolution of its genome, but in the circumstances that its own social activity has allowed and continues to do so.

In examining the question of the evolution of psychological behavior and the meaning of a comparative psychology, one must start from the double dimensionality of the human being, as a biont and as a social being. Leaving aside the terminological issue of whether the changes in the Universe, including planet Earth, constitute evolutionary or transformative processes, it is clear that their comparative study has different meanings in each of the empirical sciences that can address them. It is difficult to think of a comparative physics or chemistry, although differences in the configuration of the various stellar and planetary systems can be identified from a historical viewpoint. However, the nature of the ingredients from which the whole history of existence has been "cooked" doesn't seem to have essentially changed. Therefore, the comparison only makes sense between emergents differentiated in function and complexity. These historical emergents in the existing reality correspond to bioecological systems and social systems. Comparative divisions can be established within each of these systems. Bioecological systems can be compared at the cellular, histological, embryological, anatomical, physiological, and ecological levels, including the corresponding paleontological levels. Social systems can establish both historical and cross-sectional comparisons between modes of production, political organization, types of institutions, legal regimes, and linguistic grammars, among other aspects. In all these cases, comparisons can be within a classificatory criterion or between classificatory criteria. The relevant question is what the scope of comparison of psychological behavior would be, and whether this comparison would be aimed at finding a correspondence between changes in the types of psychological behavior and transformations in the types of bionts, habitats, and social formations.

Before answering this question, it should be made clear that psychological behavior, as a functional process, cannot be identified with biological or with social behavior. The three types of behavior are concepts referred to at different levels of abstraction, although they share the term 'behavior'. Biological behavior can sometimes be reduced to physiological functions in the biont or organism, as when describing the behavior of a cell type or a subsystem such as the nervous system. But also, biological behavior is applied to descriptions of the complete reactions or actions of the biont –movements of the whole soma, as in the case of reflex, defense, or adaptive behaviors. In yet other cases, biological behavior describes interactions between bionts of the same species or with respect to different species, in any of the five kingdoms, but especially in the animal kingdom where it is customary to do so. Ethology is a case in point of this use of the term behavior in biology. Social behavior also refers to different descriptive levels in socio-historical science. The range of application of the term behavior in the social domain is wide and varied: ethnic behavior, religious behavior, institutional behavior, economic behavior, political behavior, and many others. Covariations are not necessarily found between the different types of biological behavior with genomic or somatic structure, nor are there necessarily covariations between the different types of social behavior and the general structure that identifies a given social formation. An unavoidable corollary is that psychological behavior does not evolve. It is an asymmetrical phenomenon in correspondence with biological and social behavior, but at the same time, it comprises different levels of organizational complexity, which cannot be represented by a linear criterion.

Psychological behavior, always identified from and in an individual, consists in the functional detachment of biological and/or social behavior. Psychological behavior lacks substance per se and always occurs as functional relations or contacts based on biological and social behavior. Psychological behavior is always identified at the level of an individual with respect to stimulus objects or other individuals, but these relations are always established in the context of the particular history of that individual alone and with respect to the variation of the functional contingencies in which these relations are configured. New contacts develop with new or recurrent variations in the contingency relations in the form of episodes that modify the mutually dependent circumstances between the individual's biological and/or social behavior and the properties of the stimulus objects and behavior of other individuals in his or her surroundings. From the field theory proposed elsewhere (Ribes, 2018), five general types of functional contacts are identified as psychological behavior, all of them as transitional episodes characterized by functional detachment from the initial behavior in the situation. Since psychological behavior is a functional coextension of biological and social behavior, specific to the history of each individual, it makes no sense to expect covariations of the individual with some criterion referring to species or social formation. The only assumption that can be made is that psychological behavior can occur in individuals with differentiated reactive systems and, consequently, with coordinating nervous structures, and that the functional detachability of biological and social behaviors are radically different because of the linguistic character of social behavior. This basic assumption limits psychological behavior to the exclusive domain of a fraction of the animal kingdom starting with the coelenterates (Loeb, 1900; Maier & Schneirla, 1964), and language establishes a qualitative cut-off between the psychological behavior of animals and humans, as Watson (1914) himself pointed out.

The first distinction that can be established is that the psychological behavior of human beings, due to their linguistic character, will not only exhibit greater detachability but also greater diversity and functional flexibility than the rest of the species of the animal kingdom. The other distinction established is that the linguistic reactive systems, exclusive to human beings, will allow functional contacts that cannot be developed by the rest of the species of the animal kingdom, given the restrictions imposed by the sensorimotor nature of their reactive systems. In contrast to attempts to establish a comparative psychology as a simile or analogy of the scale of life in evolutionary biology, from the current field perspective this purpose is meaningless for two reasons. The first reason is that human psychological behavior, coextensive with social behavior, is not comparable to animal psychological behavior, which is exclusively coextensive with biological behavior. Animal and human psychological behavior can be identified in the formation of functional contacts by coupling, alteration and, with restrictions, by comparison contingencies. However, the difference in the contact media that makes them possible does not facilitate their comparison. The spatial and temporal parameters of the contingencies structuring such contacts, as well as the nature of the stimulus objects and reactive systems, are not qualitatively or quantitatively comparable. In the case of contacts by extension and transformation contingencies, possible only via linguistic behavioral patterns, there is also no possible equivalent to compare. It is not even possible to look for points of comparison in the first months of life of the human infant because, with the exception of birds and mammals, the other species of the animal kingdom are practically born with their reactivity fully developed and, in the case of birds and mammals, the initial care corresponds to bioecological circumstances, whereas in humans it is structured on the basis of cultural patterns. To compare differences in ecological habitats in animal species with differences in cultural environments in human groups would be absurd: there is nothing to compare.

What Would be the Point of a Comparative Psychology?

Comparative psychology was originally conceived as the cross-species comparison, including humans, of phenomena or performances in experimental tasks possibly shared as a result of the bioevolutionary process. The purpose of such an analysis was to account for the so-called 'higher' processes as the culmination of the development of the nervous system that characterizes human begins and, therefore, to be able to establish correlations between phylogenetic structures and the appearance of processes at the ontogenetic level in the different species, even in the early stages of human life, based on the 'maturation' of the nervous structures. Unfortunately, it is impossible to show precise covariations between genome and nervous system structure, between genome and reactive patterns at the biological level (let us not even mention social behavior), and between nervous system structures and psychological behavior. Comparative psychology can only have a parallel meaning in the case of animal and human behavior, and it can adopt different modalities in both cases. In any case, two disciplinary "vices" should be avoided: choosing a species because is it easily available and economic, as in the case of the albino rat and the pigeon (or dogs and cats, all with some level of domestication), of doubtful comparative representativeness, as well as choosing a species that given its taxonomic proximity is assumed to exhibit psychological behavior analogous to that of humans (as in the case of apes and especially primates).

A first objective of a comparative study would be intraspecific in nature at two levels, observational and experimental, in which the circumstances of the habitat of the species could be reproduced, but manipulating variables that could systematically inform on the characteristics of the functional detachment processes that occur. An additional possibility would be observational comparative studies of varieties of the same species in different habitats. In all these cases, there should be theoretical reason justifying the selection of the species in terms of the possibilities of establishing generalizations at the genus, family, or even order level. Species representative of different 'phyla' and classes would probably have to be selected if the purpose is the development of a comparative theory. Moreover, the study of the functional detachment of biological behaviors of a species with a specific habitat (including other bionts) requires a well-grounded and deep knowledge of zoology, ecology, and physiology of the species in question, which is usually lacking. In the case of humans, similar comparison criteria should be used, referring to relevant dimensions of cultural practices and to the characteristics of behavioral patterns differential to those of other groups: religious beliefs, social rituals, language, food, and so on. In this case, it is necessary to be closely familiar with the knowledge of the social anthropology (in a broad sense) of the chosen groups, as manifest indicators of the medium of contact that enables psychological behavior in the context of interindividual interactions, and its possible comparative study between cultural groups (including ethnic criteria).

Two additional possibilities consist in the multidisciplinary collaboration between psychology and the sciences that endow it with empirical coextensiveness: bioecology and the socio-historical science. On the one hand, whether from bioecology or the socio-historical science, psychology can provide the methodology required to identify types of psychological behavior participating in conspecific or institutional interindividual relations, respectively. Although the explicit purpose is not to establish comparisons, it may be feasible under certain conditions. On the other hand, collaboration may take the form of psychobiology or psychosociology, whereby the relevant disciplines contribute criteria, methods, and information to help identify and make comparisons between reactive systems, shared behavioral patterns, potential dispositional properties of objects and events, and so on. Finally, a third additional possibility is the longitudinal study of the becoming of individuals of different species and/or cultural groups, in their natural habitats or in specially designed habitats in the case of animals, and in the different scenarios that make up a cultural space in the case of humans. From this perspective, psychological behavior would be studied longitudinally on the basis of the interactions of a "target" individual in the context of interactive episodes with his or her specific environment. Both longitudinal and cross-sectional comparisons can be made between individuals and between environments.

A final reflection has to do with the fact that conducting studies on animal behavior does not imply contributing to the formulation of a comparative psychology. Theoretical and experimental delimitation of the characteristics and conditions of the phenomena and processes configuring psychological behavior is required prior to any comparison. The comparison of processes in different species and their habitats (or environments) is always a second step, and cannot be replaced by mere comparison of tasks, procedures, or types of measures employed. It is essential to specify what is being compared and between which species and habitats it is being compared. Otherwise, animal and/or human research does not go beyond a mere technical-instrumental exercise, promoting speculations with fragile theoretical support and that usually do not go beyond what expert and systematic observers can tell about the species involved.

References

Allee, W.C: (1931). Animal aggregations: A study in general sociology. Chicago: The university of Chicago Press.

Baldwin, J.M. (1896). A new factor in evolution. American Naturalist, 30, 441-451.

Bentham, J. (1789). An introduction to the principles of morals and legislation. London: T. Payne.

Bekhterev, V.M. (1913/1953). La psicología objetiva [objective psychology]. Buenos Aires: Paidós.

Boakes, R. (1984). From Darwin to behaviourism: Psychology and the mind of animals. Cambridge: Cambridge University Press.

Brentano, F. (1874 German original, 1973, English edition). Psychology from an empirical standpoint. London: Routledge.

Butturini, A., García-Castellanos, D., Jordi, C., Ribas, I., & Urmeneta, J. (2020). Habitabilidad planetaria: fundamentos de astrogeobiología. [Planetary habitability: foundations of astrogeobiology] Barcelona: Marcombo.

Byrne, R., & Whiten, A. (1988). Machiavellian intelligence: Social expertise and the evolution of intellect in monkeys, apes, and humans. Oxford Clarendon Press.

Chomsky, N. (1975). Syntactic structures. The Hague: Mouton.

Cordón, F. (1980). Cocinar hizo al hombre. [Cooking made man] Barcelona: Busquets.

Darwin, C. (1871). The descent of man and selection in relation to sex. London: Down, Beckhenham, Kent.

Darwin, C. (1874). The expression of the emotions in man and animals. London: Murray.

Darwin, C. (1974). Methaphysic, materialism and the evolution of mind: Early writings. Chicago: The University of Chicago Press.

Dawkins, R. (1976). The selfish gene. Oxford: Oxford University Press.

De Luce, J., & Wilder, H.T. (1983). Language in primates: Perspectives and implications. NY: Springer Verlag.

De Waal. F.M.B. (1996). Good natured: The origins of right and wrong in humans and other animals. Cambridge, MA: Harvard University Press.

De Waal, F.M.B. (1998). Chimpanzee politics: Power and sex among apes. Baltimore: The John Hopkinss University Press.

Dunn, L.C., & Dobshansky, Th. (1946). Heredity, race, and society. NY: Penguin Books.

Emerson, A. (1958). The evolution of behavior among social insects. In, A. Roe & G.G Simpson (Eds.): Behavior and evolution (pp. 311-335). New Haven, MA: Yale University Press.

Everett, D.L. (2017). How language began: The story of humanity's greatest invention. NY: Liveright Publishing Corporation.

Fisher, R.A. (1930). The genetical theory of natural selection. Oxford: Clarendon Press.

Galton, F. (1889). Natural inheritance. London: MacMillan.

Galton, F. (1969). Hereditary genius. London: MacMillan.

Gould, S.J. (1981). The mismeasurement of man. NY: W.W. Norton & Co.

Guthrie, E.L. (1935). The psychology of learning. NY: Harper & Row

Herrnstein, R.J. (1977). IQ and the meritocracy. Boston, MA: Little, Brown.

Hilario, E., & Gogarten, J.P. (1993). Horizontal transfer of ATPase genes: The tree of life becomes a net of life. Biosystems, 31, 111-119.

Hilgard, E.R., & Bower, G H. (1973). Teorías del aprendizaje. [Leaning theories] CDMX: Trillas.

Hull, C.L. (1943). Principles of behavior. NY: Appleton Century Crofts.

Jaenisch, R., & Bird, A. (2003). Epigenetic regulation of gene expression: how the genome integrates intrinsic and environmental signals. Nature Genetics, 33, Suppl. (35), 245-254.

Jensen, A.R. (1973). Educational differences. London: Methuen.

Kamin, L. J. (1974). The science and politics of IQ. London: John Wiley.

Klein, R.G. (1999). The human career: Human biological and cultural origins. Chicago: University of Chicago Press.

Kropotkin, P. (1902). Mutual aid: A factor of evolution. London: William Heinemann.

Kuo, Z. (1967). The dynamics of behavior development: An epigenetic view. NY: Random House.

Lamarck, J.P. (1809). Philosophie zoologique. Paris.

Lazcano, A. (2000). Origins of life: History of ideas. In L. Margulis, C. Matthews, & A. Haselton (Eds.): Environmental evolution: Effects of the origin and evolution of life on planet Earth (pp. 83-94). Cambridge, MA: MIT Press.

Lehrman, D.S: (1962). Ethology and psychology. In Recent advances in biological psychiatry, Vol. 4, pp. 86-94. NY: Plenum.

Linton, R. (1936). The study of man: an introduction. NY: Appleton Century Crofts.

Loeb, J. (1900). Comparative physiology of the brain and comparative psychology. NY: G.P. Putnam's Sons.

López-Beltrán, C. (2004). El sesgo hereditario: Ámbitos históricos del concepto de herencia biológica. [Hereditary bias: historical remarks about the concept of biological inheritance] CDMX: Universidad Nacional Autónoma de México.

Lorenz, K. (1965). Evolution and modification of behavior. London: Methuen.

Lovelock, J.E. (2000). The Gaia hypothesis. In L. Margulis, C. Matthewus & A. Haselton (Eds.): Environmental evolution: Effects of the origin and evolution of life on planet Earth. (pp. 1-27). Cambridge, MA: MIT Press.

MacKintosh, N. J. (1994). Learning and cognition. NY: Academic Press.

Maier, N.R.F. & Schneirla, T.C. (1964). Principles of animal psychology. NY: Dover.

Malthus, T. (1798). An essay on the principle of population. Anonymous edition.

Margulis, L. (1998). Symbiotic planet: A new look at evolution. NY: Basic Books.

Margulis, L. (2000). Symbiosis and the origin of Protists. In L. Margulis, C. Matthews & A. Haselton (Eds.): Environmental evolution: Effects of the origin and evolution of life on planet Earth (pp. 141-157). Cambridge, MA: MIT Press.

Matthews, C. (2000). Chemical evolution in a hydrogen cyanide world. In L. Margulis, C. Matthews & A. Haselton (Eds.): Environmental evolution: Effects of origin and evolution of life on Planet Earth (pp. 47- 65). Cambridge, MA: MIT Press.

Maynard Smith, J. (1979). Acerca de la evolución. [About evolution] Madrid: Blume.

McMenamin, M. (2000). The antiquity of life: From life's origin to the end of the Lipalian period. In L. Margulis, C. Matthews, & A. Haselton (Eds.): Environmental evolution: Effects of the origin and evolution of life in planet Earth (pp. 159-169). Cambdrige, MA: MIT Press.

Mill, J.S. (1848/1885). Principles of political economy: with some of their applications to social philosophy. NY: Appleton and Company.

Miller, S.L. (1953), Production of amino acids under possible primitive Earth conditions. Science, 117, 528.

Mithen, S. (1998). Arqueología de la mente. [Archeology of the mind] Barcelona: Crítica.

Monod, J. (1970). Le hasard et la necéssité: Essai sur le philosophie naturelle de la biologie moderne. Paris: Editions du Seuil.

Morgan, C.L. (1890). Animal life and intelligence. London: Edward Arnold.

Morgan, C. L. (1903). An introduction to comparative psychology. London: The Walter Scott Publishing Co.

Mowrer, O.H. (1960). Learning theory and the symbolic processes. NY: John Wiley.

Naour, P. (2009). E.O. Wilson and B.F. Skinner: A dialogue between sociobiology and radical behaviorism. N.Y.; Springer.

Neisser, U. (1967). Cognitive psychology. Englewood Cliffs: Prentice Hall.

Oparin, A.I. (1938/1968). El origen de la vida. [The origin of life] CDMX: Grijalbo.

Pavlov, I.P. (1927). Conditioned reflexes. Oxford: Oxford University Press.

Piaget, J. (1977). El comportamiento: motor de la evolución. [Behavior and evolution] Buenos Aires: Nueva Visión.

Pinker, S. (1994). The language instinct: How the mind creates language. NY: W. Morrow.

Razran, G. (1971). Mind in evolution: An East-West synthesis of learned behavior and cognition. NY: Houghton & Mifflin.

Ribes, E. (2000). Las psicologías y la definición de sus objetos de conocimiento. [Pscyhologies and the definition of their objects of knowledge] Revista Mexicana de Análisis de la Conducta, 26, 365- 382.

Ribes, E. (2011). Perception and conciousness as behavior-referred concepts. In E. Ribes & J. Burgos (Eds.): Conciousness, perception, and behavior: Conceptual, theoretical, and methodological issues (pp.191-223). Nueva Orleans, LA: University Press of the South.

Ribes, E. (2018). El estudio científico de la conducta individual: Introducción a la teoría de la psicología. [The scientific study of individual behavior: An introduction to the theory of psychology] CDMX: El Manual Moderno.

Ribes, E. (2018a). The inexistent link between the logic of reflex and the ideology of natural selection: Comments on Carneiro and Bentes "Successive approximations to selectionism: Skinner´s framework for behavior in the 1930's and 1940's". Revista Mexicana de Análisis de la Conducta, 44, 233-242.

Roitblat, H.L., & Meyer, J.A. (1995). Comparative approaches to cognitive science. Cambridge, MA: MIT Press.

Romanes, G.J. (1883). Mental evolution in animals. Londres: Kegan Paul, French & CO.

Romanes, G.J. (1884). Animal intelligence. NY: Appleton and Company.

Schneirla, T.C. (1956). Interrelationships of the "innate" and the "acquired" in instictive behavior. In P.P. Grassé (Ed.), *Instincts dans le comportement des animaux et de l'homme*. Paris: Masson.

Schoenfeld, W.N. Notes of a bit of psychological nonsense: "Race differences in intelligences". The Psychological Record, 24, 17-32.

Simpson, G.G. (1958). Behavior and evolution. In A. Roe & G.GF. Simpson (Eds.), Behavior and evolution (507-535). New Haven, MA: Yale University Press.

Skinner, B.F. (1938). The behavior of organisms. NY: Appleton Century Crofts.

Skinner, B.F. (1966). The phylogeny and ontogeny of behavior. Science, 153, 1205-1213.

Skinner, B.F. (1981). Selection by consequences. Science, 4507, 501-504.

Spencer, H. (1855). Principles of psychology. London: Longman.

Thorndike, E.L. (1898). Animal intelligence: An experimental study of the associative processes in animals. Monograph Supplement No. 8, Psychological Review, 68-72.

Thorndike, E.L. (1911). Animal intelligence. NY: MacMillan.

Thorpe, W.H. (1966). Learning and instinct in animals. Cambridge, MA: Harvard University Press.

Tinbergen, N. (1951). The study of instinct. Oxford: Oxford University Press.

Tolman, E.C. (1932). Purposive behavior in animals and men. NY: Century.

Tomasello, M. (1999). The cultural origins of human cognition. Cambridge, MA: Harvard University Press.

Tomasello, M. (2003). Constructing a language. Cambridge. MA: Harvard University Press.

Wallace, A.R. (1871). Contributions to the of natural selection: A series of essays. NY: MacMillan.

Ward, P., & Kirschvink, J. (2015). A new history of life: The radical new discoveries about the origins and evolution of life on earth. NY: Bloomsbury Press.

Washburn, M.F. (1908). The animal mind: A textbook of comparative psychology. N.Y.: MacMillan.

Watson, J.B. (1914). Behavior: An introduction to comparative psychology. NY: Henry Holt.

Watson, J.B. (1916), The place of conditioned reflex in psychology. Psychological Review, 23, 89-116.

Wilson, E.O. (1975). Sociobiology: The new synthesis. Cambridge, MA: Harvard University Press.

Wilson, E.O. (2006). The creation: An appeal to save the life on earth. NY: W.W. Norton.

Wilson, E.O. (2008) "One giant leap: How insects achieved altruism and colonial life". Bioscience, 58,17-25.

Wilson, E.O., & Hölldobler, B. (2005). Biosociality: Origin and consequences. Proceedings of the National Academy of Sciences (USA), 102 (38), 13367-71.

Wrangham, R. (2009). How cooking made us human. New York, NY: Basic Books.

ESSAY SEVEN: REFERENTIAL BEHAVIOR, LANGUAGE FUNCTIONS, AND MODES OF KNOWLEDGE

This essay proposes to examine the relations between referential behavior, as a paradigmatic practice of ordinary language, the various language functions (living and dead), and the various modes of knowledge involving special technical languages. In this vein, the previously established distinction between morphological and functional linguistic behavior (Ribes & López, 1985) will be revised. In the previous work, the functional character was applied exclusively to the then-called contingency substitutive functions.

Social practices of ordinary language and behavior

'Behavior' and 'language' are not technical terms, although they can be employed technically for certain purposes. This is one reasons for the frequent confusion in psychology. When people talk about "psychological" terms, they undoubtedly think they are talking about the same things because they are using the same words, but this is usually not the case. Words in ordinary language have multiple meanings because they are used in different situations and contexts. Ryle (1962) pointed out that people often assume they are discussing a common subject, when actually two simultaneous monologues about different topics are occurring. In ordinary language, words do not have a specific and constant referent or a one-to-one correspondence with things. However, in technical languages some words have specific uses only for some things. This is a clear distinction between ordinary and the technical language of the sciences and other modes of knowledge.

'Behavior' and 'language' are not univocal terms even in scientific domains and in psychology. The ways in which these terms will be employed hereafter will now be explained. 'Language' as a term always directly or indirectly pertains to social practices of human beings. In fact, 'language' is the only inherently reflexive term since we can talk about language in language or through language. Language originates with human society, the organized division of specialized labor, and shared (not necessarily symmetrical or equitable) appropriation of mutual goods and services among individuals (Ribes, 2001). This explains why communication in some animal species does not constitute genuine language, and why it is absurd to postulate "private" languages of different kinds. Language emerged socially as a conventional practice, and cannot be construed as an individual product or process. On the contrary, human individuals are differentiated from one another, not by language, but in language, as will be argued later. Language is not external to human life and practice; it is not an instrument or way for individuals to relate to each other, but is the very medium in which human practice and social relations take place and, therefore, where they have meaning. Language and human social practice are one and the same thing, and are intrinsically interlaced with each other. There is no known human society without language. In this sense, language is not just talking or the like, but as Ludwig Wittgenstein (1953, p. 19) put it: "to imagine a language is to imagine a form of life". Any form of social life as language constitutes multiple activities, relations, products, and dispositions. It would be impossible to establish a single framework to classify them. Nevertheless, following J. R. Kantor (1936, 1977), a first step may be to distinguish between "dead" and "living" language, that is, to distinguish between the language that takes place as an act or practice between individuals, and that which constitutes vestiges of such acts.

"Dead" language is related to vestiges and products of actual practices, such as records of all kinds: marks, drawings and paintings, inscriptions, letters, books, recordings, codes, and so on. Dead language, as products, is not equivalent to the practices of which it is the result, although it may sometimes provide clues from which to partially infer the conditions under which the actual practices took place. Nevertheless, linguistic vestiges should never be confused with the actual practices of which they are outcomes. As words and expressions do not correspond to things or events, so linguistic vestiges do not correspond to the practices of which they are the result or product. In contrast, "living" language is always part of a social practice involving more than one individual, which is always articulated with the multiplicity of interindividual relations that occur in society. Relations thus established need not necessarily to be simultaneous in time and space, especially when some sort of graphing or writing is involved.

In behavior analysis language has been considered a special type of operant behavior (Skinner, 1938, 1957), and has been equated with so-called verbal behavior, as a uniquely human "topography". However, this is a conceptual mistake that inevitably leads to confusion. Verbal behavior has to do with speech, that is, with language emitted orally, which is not the only modality nor the most important in all situations, albeit its predominance in language practices. Further, it does not share the same functional properties with gesturing and writing. For this reason, the term linguistic behavior will be employed to refer to any type of individual language activity; and "verbal" will be reserved to speech. All linguistic behavior is social behavior. From an individual analytic viewpoint, linguistic behavior only has meaning as a segment of social behavior, and not by itself. Therefore, it is incorrect to analyze 'language' as an individual, psychological phenomenon (Ribes, 1999). Language, and its individual manifestation as linguistic behavior, always originates and is functionally regulated in social practice. All linguistic behavior is social behavior, and all human behavior is linguistic behavior, including sensorimotor behaviors that, as biological behavior, support the development of all possibilities of social and psychological behavior.

Living language is the practice that underlies social relations between individuals and consists of different modes or modalities of occurrence as behavior. Linguistic modes can be identified as active or reactive, although they commonly occur simultaneously, not only between individuals, but also within a single individual. Some active and reactive modes constitute inseparable pairs, while some active modes usually occur together as functional patterns. They are characterized in their biologically arbitrary conventional morphology and, therefore, diverse across social formations. In turn, biological modes of behavior are shared by all human individuals, in the form of reactivity and sensory and motor activity in different modalities and modes of occurrence. Conventional behavioral patterns are always explicitly established by the specific groups participating as social practice, whether of an arbitrary nature such as the articulated sounds of each language, accents, styles, intonations, facial and body expressions associated with speaking, as well as reactivity to specific patterns of visual, auditory, olfactory, gustatory, and proprioceptive stimulation, or the development of articulated forms of orienting, manipulation, contact, displacement, and other movements. In colloquial terms it could be said that all conventional behavior is "learned" under the criteria of the corresponding social group, independently of the similarities of the morphological properties of the active/reactive components shared with other groups. The fact that everyone must learn conventional behaviors as circumstantially structured patterns does not mean that language or other dimensions such as musical or mathematical competencies constitute individual processes. All individuals of a social group learn these behaviors, but the very processes of language practices, of the arts and of all domains of knowledge are always social in nature: they are conventional in origin and in practice.

The active linguistic modes are gesturing, speaking, and writing, the reactive modes are observing (not in the sense of looking) listening (not hearing), and reading (not texting). Gesturing-observing, speaking-listening, and writing-reading are obviously complementary pairs, and they usually occur at the same time even in a single individual or between relating individuals: gestures are observed (sometimes in a mirror or as proprioceptive observation), speech is listened to, and writing is read. These relations are synchronous and most of the time we are not aware of them, but as developmental studies show studies (King & Quigley, 1985; Marschark, 1993; Marschark, Mourandian, & Halas, 1994), children with vision and/or hearing impairments are seriously affected in learning to speak, in developing conventional social gesturing, and obviously in learning to read. Individuals who do not read are not able to write, even if they copy letters or words. Delayed feedback as listening to one's own speech induces stuttering (Flanagan, Goldiamond, & Azrin, 1958). On the other hand, when individuals interact through active modes of linguistic behavior, each mode does not occur in isolation from one another. While speaking and reading, we perform gestures, and while writing we speak "silently" or read aloud while reading simultaneously. Not only do linguistic modes not occur in isolation, but they are always part of an act or activity of the individual in a given circumstance, so that they are structured as components of patterns of situational interactions.

From this viewpoint, linguistic behavior includes molar patterns of behavior of the individual as part of a social practice, although some components of such patterns do not appear linguistic given their morphology consisting of movements of a different nature. Behavioral response systems include natural biological reactions and actions common to all individual members of the human species. In fact, psychological behavior consists of the development of new functions and ways of organizing biological response systems (Kuo, 1967). This is the result of the interaction of the individual with different types of environmental contingencies related to objects, events, and other individuals. But human beings develop not only biological response systems, but also new forms of response from them, morphologically arbitrary. These new response systems are precisely the linguistic response systems. From a biological viewpoint, the arbitrariness of their morphology means that there is no necessary relation between the form of the responses and the physical and chemical circumstances in which they occur. However, arbitrariness in form does not mean arbitrariness in function. On the contrary, inasmuch as linguistic response systems are conventional and shared, their functions are delimited and established by social practice. Social practices constitute the rules that "govern" the functions of language. Grammar as a set of formal rules appeared after writing, as an apparently prescriptive descriptions of the uses and functions of language. However, these "grammatical" functions are always the result of living practices among individuals, and necessarily involve and imply social relations articulated with objects and environing events.

In contrast to purely biological response systems, linguistic response systems are in principle detachable from all the conditions in which they first occur or are "learned" given their conventional nature and morphological arbitrariness. This feature of linguistic response systems allows individuals to act similarly under different conditions, and to respond in the "absence" of the circumstances (including objects, events, and individuals) in which the linguistic behavior has previously occurred. Human beings can relate to past and future times, to different places, to absent objects and persons, and to conventionally "constructed" objects (concepts, myths, non-existent beings, and so on), given the detachability of linguistic response systems. It is also possible to relate to the linguistic behavior of absent individuals, be it dead or living language. In the becoming of human individuals in the history of humanity, the first modes of language are (were) gesturing and speech, with writing being the last to appear (6500 years ago in Mesopotamia, and today when children are taught to read and write). Words were created with the emergence of writing as transcriptions of the articulated sounds of speech. Words do not represent objects or events. Words (always written) represent the articulated sounds of speech, and as grammatical units, they did not exist as independent "entities" before writing. Words, like speech itself, as graphic representations, are human constructions. Thus, the emergence of writing also represented the existence of new objects: (conventional) linguistic objects in the form of words, hieroglyphs, pictograms, and others. Linguistic objects have coexisted with natural objects since the creation of writing. They are graphic representations, but they do not constitute symbols of natural objects, nor of those human artifacts created through craftsmanship and technology. Writing allows connecting temporal and spatial distances between individuals, so that interpersonal relations can be established through the conventional presence, as dead language, of the behavior of physically separated individuals participating in a common episode. Writing also includes complex linguistic stimulus objects in different modes of knowing (ordinary, scientific, artistic, formal, religious, technological, and others). Individuals can interact with said linguistic stimulus objects in different places and times (impersonal interactions) without contacting the circumstances that were contacted by the writer.

Considering what has been said thus far, it is convenient to rectify a previous distinction (Ribes, 1986; Ribes & López, 1985) whereby language, as a psychological behavior (or interbehavior), was identified only with episodes of substitution, referential, and non-referential contingencies. This distinction is meaningless insofar as all human behavior is conventional and linguistic in nature. The morphological arbitrariness of conventional reactive systems, the imposed criteria and circumstances, and the formal and informal institutions of the social group of reference are the basis for the detachability of psychological behavior. In this sense, the characteristic detachment of those functional contacts shared between humans and other animals is qualitatively different in complexity, flexibility, and possible transitions. Comparisons of intrasituational psychological contacts (by coupling, alteration, and comparison contingencies) between humans and animals are very limited. Given the fact that human psychological behavior is always a component of social behavior and thus occurs in a conventional medium, allows a greater detachability in principle than that which can develop in situational psychological contacts. Moreover, the abovementioned human intrasituational psychological contacts always occur as personal social contacts, whereas contacts by extension occur as interpersonal social contacts, and contacts by transformation occur as impersonal social contacts. The reasons to dismiss the concept of substitution contingencies will not be reviewed here as these arguments have been explicated elsewhere (Ribes, 2018).

Psychological behavior and reference

'Comport' (as translation of 'behavior' -be-have) and 'conduct' are neither technical terms, nor are they exclusive to psychological descriptions or attributions. These terms are used in everyday language, and in Romance languages are derived from the Latin words comportare and conducere, which mean "to bring with oneself" and "to lead to". They are ordinary terms, used not only in reference to the acts of persons, but also to changes related to 'direction' in events or inanimate objects.[1] Disciplines other than psychology also use the term 'behavior' to describe changes in conditions of particles, physical bodies, electricity, molecules, cells, groups, institutions, markets, surveys, and many others. The terms conduct and behavior are generic terms that apply

---

1 For Anglo-Saxon speakers, to behave is the reflexive form of these terms and carries the same meanings in ordinary language practices (*translator's note*).

not only to the movement of organisms, but to changes in the activity or conditions of a diversity of entities or things. In the case of psychology, behaviorism (Watson, 1913) naturalized the term to define its object of knowledge (or at least to establish an index). For Watson, behavior was everything that individuals do and say. However, behavior has no single meaning even within behaviorism itself.

Kitchener (1977) identified a diversity of definitions of 'behavior' among the various behaviorist schools, which point to different concepts of the object of study despite the use of the same term. This should not come as no surprise given that words and concepts are not the same thing. Words are morphological units that constitute the lexicon of a natural language, while concepts are the functions performed through words in practice. The same word can have different meanings, that is, belong to different conceptual frameworks, and at the same time different words can be conceptually similar. Previously it has been stressed (Ribes, 2004) that the term 'behavior' is not an ostensive, neutral, descriptive term corresponding to or denoting "psychological" phenomena or events. Rather, as "technically" employed in psychology, the term is an abstraction related to different uses of the word and other similar terms, which show 'family resemblance' (Wittgenstein, 1953) according to an explicit or implicit criterion. Although other disciplines employ the term 'behavior' in their descriptions, the term is always adopted by these disciplines in its ordinary use, related to activities and changes in conditions: movements, temperature, pressure, direction, among others depending on the object of study. Only in psychology is 'behavior' considered to be a term "indigenous" to its object of knowledge, without the conceptual clarity needed to realize that this is not the case.

Kantor (1963) pointed out that 'behavior' is a term employed by different disciplines, and that psychology incorporated it from biology through the conceptual tradition of reflex physiology. Kantor was especially critical of the organocentric conception of behavior as an activity emanating from the organism, either as a reaction (provoked or elicited), or as an action (emitted). He proposed to distinguish between biological and psychological behaviors in order to move away from this reductionist conception, and later added institutional or cultural behavior. Psychological behavior consists of functional contacts constituted by an active/reactive individual and the stimulus properties of objects and environing events, including other individuals and the individual herself interacting with her own linguistic behavior in some cases. Psychological behavior is not identified with movements or actions, but with functional relations between individuals and particular stimulus objects (sometimes other individuals). In any case, movements or actions can be identified as forms of physical, chemical, or biological behavior depending on the circumstances.

However, psychological behavior is always conceived from the viewpoint or perspective of the individual and not of the stimulus object or event, especially when the latter is another behaving individual. The analysis of relations between individuals (interindividual), as functional unit, belongs to the domain of social science. Interindividual relations constitute institutional behavior and can be studied as a multidisciplinary enterprise between social science and psychology (Ribes, Pulido, Rangel, & Sánchez-Gatell, 2016). It is always important to consider that psychological behavior occurs only as individually delimited episodes part of bioecological relations in animals specially (survival) or of social relations in human exclusively (covival[2]). There are no autonomous psychological contacts, unrelated to ecological and conventional contact media. Psychological contacts constitute a special set of relations between individuals having differentiated reactive systems and stimulus objects or events or other individuals. However, only some of these relations, between individuals and stimulus objects and/or other individuals, qualify as psychological, always being components of ecological or social relations. Psychological behavior consists of transient episodes varying in length, of functional detachment from the biological and/or social behavior of a particular individual.

Not surprisingly, psychological relations are usually identified from those practices of ordinary language that include terms or consist of "mental" expressions. "Mental" terms and expressions do not occur in isolation. They are always part of social episodes characterizing the circumstances of the individual's actions with reference to other individuals, objects, or events. "Mental" terms do not describe, denote, or refer to special activities occurring "within" the individual. So-called "mental" terms and expressions are constitutive of social practice and are part of the circumstances configuring the episode of which they are a part. Psychological behavior always consists of an episodic relation in ordinary language (Ryle, 1949), and comprises episodes in which an individual can be characterized, by others or by herself, as remembering,

---

2 The word is a neologism derived from the Spanish word *convivencia*, meaning "coexisting in harmony", and a modification of the English word survival *(translator's note)*.

learning, feeling, perceiving, and so on. These references are not about something happening in the individual, but about something that occurs between the individual and other individuals, stimulus objects, or events as circumstances of the relation. This is why psychological behavior can be considered as episodic segments of the and in ordinary language practices and not as isolated occurrences (Wittgenstein, 1953). These segments are part of the referential nature of ordinary language. Reference is not a correspondence between words and things, it is not a matter of names and identity, as will be examined later. On the contrary, referring means that when we speak (or write) we always speak (or write) about something (not necessarily of things, actions, or entities) to someone (and in special circumstances to ourselves). Speaking, gesturing, and writing are not a mere denotative or descriptive accompaniment of the reactions and actions occurring when individuals behave. Language as a mere denotative accompaniment would be redundant and dispensable.

Behavior is functional in human beings because it is integrated with language, even in its reactive modes. Thus, the language of the "psychological" should be understood as language about the individual circumstances involved in social episodes, and nothing else, regardless of whether the talk of the individual in the relation occur in the first, second, or third person (I, you, she/he). For example, when mentioning or talking about "remembering", remembering consists of the relation that is taking place in that episode. Talk of "remembering" is not an index, a description, or a "reference" (in the sense of the theory of signs) that something is occurring in the individual. The way in which one speaks of "remembering" is precisely what remembering consists of in that circumstance. The same can be said of any "mental" term or expression relating to psychological phenomena ordinary language practices.

Psychology is a special case because of its incorporation of "psychological" words and expressions employed in ordinary language as if they were technical terms, with denotative properties. Wittgenstein (1953) commented in this regard that psychology possessed experimental methods and conceptual confusion, pointing to the fact that psychologists have incorrectly identified ordinary "psychological" terms with supposedly univocal references to reports and descriptions of events or experiences that are supposed to occur within individuals. In contrast to other sciences, psychology has assumed that terms employed in ordinary language, such as perception, feeling, sensation, memory, thought, imagination, and the like, constitute reliable references to certain types of experiences, activities, or events that occur "in" or "by" the individual (as agent), hence the initial use of introspection as an "experimental" method. A legacy of this historical condition is the tendency in psychology to "borrow" technical terms (and models) from other disciplines, with a false desire for apparent scientificity. At the same time, unsuccessful attempts have been made to give technical status to ordinary language terms using operational definitions and construct validity techniques (of a statistical nature). Conditioning theory, theories of cognition based on informational and computational models, and psychometric theories are prominent examples of this historical trend.

Referential behavior, language functions, and understanding

All classifications of language, even those close to pragmatism, have been offered on the basis of dead language, that is, direct or indirect transcriptions of speech-acts, either as written vestiges or as recordings of what individuals have said. Such classifications usually emphasize two aspects: the grammatical components and the communicative segments in an expression. Both aspects assume a theory of reference, as units of predication (verbs, nouns, adjectives, adverbs) that somehow denote, name, or describe objects and actions, or present or report about the situation as symbolic segments. They differ from the expressive segments, which also inform, although in this case of the conditions of the individual or speaker, and from the appellative or connotative segments that ensure the effect of the utterance on the listener or recipient (the acts of locution, illocution, and perlocution in Austin, 1955/1962). Traditionally, reference also includes deictics or index words (Bühler, 1934/2011; Ryle, 1949) constituting contextual indices of the reference in relation to the speaker, however, meaningless in themselves (I, here, after, above, etc.).

The concept of reference in linguistics, grammar, communication theory, and social and cognitive theory is framed in a denotative conception of the relation between words and expressions in relation to "that" of which they speak. In this dominant tradition, reference is determined by the correspondence between what is said and that of which it is said. The meaning of what is said directly depends on this correspondence. In this sense, communication constitutes an act of notification or information about things, actions, or events as acts of reference, including the intentions, ideas, and feelings or emotions of the speakers. Following Wittgenstein (1953), Canfield (2007) has criticized this perspective of reference. In *Philosophical Investigations*, Wittgenstein emphasized that, according to the Augustinian conception, the foundation of most of the theories on language, words and language are denotative representations of reality (and, to that extent, are erroneously considered symbols). Thus, Wittgenstein continues, the meaning of words and expressions is supposed to lie in their correspondence with what is named, identified, or described. In the Augustinian tradition, language consists of names representing objects and their corresponding ideas, so that the meaning of words lies in the association of ideas and objects. A corollary of this conception of language is that the words referring to the speaker herself represent ideas (conscious, obviously) of activities and events that occur within her, so that language is a system of symbolic representation of the world in correspondence to the internal representations of that world in the speakers as conscious experience. As we already pointed out, a language of names would be redundant or confusing, and paradoxically, not very communicative. Conceiving language as a symbolic system of names of reality in correspondence with the conscious experience of the speaker raises another of the problems that entertain psychologists and philosophers: the knowledge of other minds and how the same word can correspond to the same conscious experiences of two different speakers and their reciprocal understanding. A denotative conception of language, even a non-mentalist one, cannot account for the collective concordance in language practice as a social convention, nor for the resulting effectiveness/affectivity in the behavior of the participating individuals in any linguistic episode.

The term 'reference', even in its Latin origins, is not "tied" to the theory of name-object-idea correspondence. On the contrary, to refer means to bring something to present, to mention, to cite, to return, and other types of "actions" that always involve at least two individuals related to something in common. Reference is always an episodic interrelation between individuals with respect to their activities and the relevant circumstances, persons, objects, and events. In this sense, we intend to rescue the term 'reference' and its derivations, especially 'referential', as the predominant characteristic of the active/reactive patterns of psychological behavior in human beings. What is referred to and to whom when referential action/reaction patterns occur in psychological behavior? What is referred to is what is done and said, with respect to what and to whom it is done and said, and the circumstance in which it is done and said and, also, for what or why it is done and said. And this reference is always directed to the other individuals participating in the same episode. In this sense, reference represents only the functional correspondence of the individual's behavior in and with the collective practice in a given episode. Reference is to make explicit the concordance of what is done and said with the conventional practices in which the behavior occurs in a given circumstance. What, then, is the meaning of language as reference? As Wittgenstein emphasizes, words and expressions mean what occurs as practice in circumstance or, in his metaphorical terms, meaning is use in context.

This circumstantiality of reference as meaning adjusts to the multivocality of words and expressions in the practices of ordinary language. Linguistic words and expressions by themselves are meaningless, for they do not bear a univocal or unique relation of correspondence to what is being done whilst being said or to what is being said while being done. Therefore, the referentiality of linguistic behavior patterns is multiple, diverse, and in accordance with the circumstantiality of their occurrence in a practice always conventional and in relation to others. The notion of 'language game' formulated by Wittgenstein underscores the practical, social, and circumstantial nature of language as a shared activity with others, whether in the various learning stages as a reactive system or part of a conventional practice, or during the course of all individuals' life stream. A language game represents a grammar (in a metaphorical sense) for the words and expressions that occur together with the activities proper and specific to a social practice in situation. The notion of language game suggests the existence of as many "grammars" (and "systematics", one might add) as there are types of social practice in circumstance, situation and/or context that can be identified. Different language games may use the same words or expressions, and the same language game may involve different words and expressions. Language games can be articulated on the basis of family resemblances of the circumstances, not of the "employed" words or expressions. For this reason, the functionality of the linguistic behavior patterns in psychological behavior depends on the circumstantiality of their occurrence, not on their morphological properties per se. Each time the circumstantiality in which an individual participates in the context of a situational social practice changes, linguistic patterns adjust to a new functionality, thereby participating in a functional detachment process. Once the individual's participation in the new circumstance or context (or the new language game) adjusts to the constitutive criteria of that social practice, functional detachment is complete, and the psychological behavior involved dissolves into the social behavior characteristic to that situation. Thus, it is clear that different language games constitute different practices with the meaning of what is said while doing and vice versa, and not just different words or expressions.

The functional detachability of linguistic behavior patterns endows human beings with the situational flexibility implied in the practical diversity of possible language games. Wittgenstein's metaphor of language as a toolbox with a multitude of uses emphasized the detachable character of speaking (and, in parallel, of gesturing and writing) with respect to the situations and meanings in which it always occurs as an integral part of a social practice. Words, expressions, and concepts interlace in different ways and relations, based on their participation as an activity between individuals. For this reason, as opposed to animal behavior, where it is only detachable within the situation on the basis of sensory and motor distancing, human behavior is also detachable between situations and from circumstances and criteria. The various functions that can be identified in language practice are all referential dimensions (in the sense proposed here) of social practice and not characteristics of the linguistic individual. What are the functions of language? The answer is as follows: there are as many functions as language games can be established. We can mention countless functions, all of them identifiable as forms of language games: asking, demanding, investigating, questioning, persuading, narrating, praising, remembering, planning, ordering, seducing, recognizing, naming, lying, and so many more that are part of the different episodes of human life. Denoting, naming, describing, expressing, convincing, and indicating are not characteristics of language that occur by themselves in isolation. They are in fact of various language games, and only in them do such functional forms or features make sense. But in each language game there are different meanings, so that they do not constitute universal language units. They may or may not occur, and do so in different ways, so that sometimes, for example, an interrogation functions as an affirmation when it occurs in the context of a relation of domination or coercion. A compliment may be a mockery, and an affirmation may consist of a de facto denial. Language games are always structured in the context of the social practice of the participants, so that the language game of remembering in a psychoanalyst's practice is not the same as in a competitive exam, in a "memory" game, or when testifying in a court trial. Language games exemplify the possible practical referential domains in which individuals participate and constitute ways of 'acting as' in situation and circumstance (Ribes, 2012). Language games are living language and the functions that have been proposed in grammar, linguistics, and semantics have been 'extracted' from dead language. However, a limited set of movements and sounds produced by the human body, which actually constitutes an infinite diversity of customs and languages as forms of life, functionally integrating the different episodes and relations in which the life of individuals unfolds, always as a social practice. The functions that delimit each episode or circumstance of social practice are manifested as language games, that is, the fusion of what is said or written with what is done in relation to others in the context of a given situation or circumstance.

A special section related to referential behavior has to do with understanding. Traditionally, understanding is conceived as a moment or "process" different from speaking and writing. Separating understanding from the active modes of language is a misconception, which usually leads to the assumption that understanding is a special kind of covert (non-implicit) behavior, usually consisting of some kind of self-speech, or self-observation, as in introspection (Schlinger, 2008). Understanding actually always involves conventional "overt" behavior, both in linguistic and non-linguistic forms. Understanding implies completing an episode in which one participates consistent with a social convention. Understanding is nothing more than a social practice shared by at least two individuals. Linguistic behavior always occurs in episodic situations, involving at least two individuals, although sometimes one individual may play two different functional roles, as in a soliloquy. In the latter case, it would be absurd to predicate some form of "self-understanding". Language involves all human relations and interactions given its inseparability from social practice. It is the medium in which all human behavior occurs. Extending the concept of medium of contact (Kantor, 1924-26), it could be said that language, in articulating institutional practices as interindividual relations, is unique to human behavior as a conventional medium of contact. Wittgenstein (1980, p. 678) emphasized this link between language and human life in saying, "W are used to a particular classification of things. With language or languages, it has become a second nature to us". Linguistic behavior (as an equivalent of human behavior) is conventional by nature (Ribes, 1993, 2006) and, as such, always occurs in concordance with those participating in any interaction or relation. Concordance, which is inherent to convention, presupposes understanding. No one speaks, gestures, or writes trying to be understood, but actually does so because she is always understood and understands at the same time. When a person speaks, gestures, or writes to another person, she is sure that she is understood. Otherwise, people would constantly probe before contacting another person. Understanding is not a special form of "referential correspondence" in which the listener, observer, or reader reacts internally to the meanings of what is said, written, or shown, and once this correspondence of meanings has been established, she acts or does not act. Understanding consists in behaving consistent with the criteria of practice in a situation. These criteria are not rules external to the situation, but are rooted in the practice itself as shared participation. The one who understands what is said to her does so because she can also say it in the same situation. Subjective 'meanings' are not shared, but the same practices are shared. In fact, 'understanding' is used in ordinary language practices only when, for special reasons, individuals show inappropriate behaviors in relation to what is indicated, said, or written to them. Philosophers and psychologists, who have created and followed the myth of the "cognizant" individual as the origin of knowledge and language, are responsible for posing the false problem of understanding.

Technical languages and modes of knowledge

The practices of ordinary language are the foundation from which the diversity of activities constituting social life are developed (Wittgenstein, 1969). The different modes of knowledge have developed special technical languages from ordinary language and articulated in their diverse "grammars". The modes of knowledge differ from the games of ordinary language insofar as they do not constitute referential practices in a situation between individuals. The technical languages of the various specialized modes of knowledge (scientific, formal, technological, religious, artistic, and ethical/juridical) conform to specific social validity criteria, that is, to the "certainty" of their results. These are always reported as written impersonal communications, although the process of obtaining and searching them always involves interpersonal relations in which speech predominates.

The technical language of modes of knowledge is denotative by definition, descriptive of procedures, informative of "facts" and results, and interpretative of the described relations; therefore, it is hermeneutic within the limits established by its own concepts. Although these characteristics make all technical language an impersonal language, insofar as it employs extensions of ordinary language in the form of distinct figures (metaphors, analogies, metonymies, allegories, and others), it can also be included into ordinary language on the basis of the same type of figures of speech. Technical impersonal language adapts itself as interpersonal language in various social situations. In this way, the practices of ordinary language expand, transform, and diversify always according to the dominant ideological practices in the corresponding social formation.

Although the different modes of knowledge start from the phenomenal "reality" of the practices of ordinary language, they construct —in the strict sense of the term— a transversal reality to these phenomena based on the criteria defining their social objective or end. This is a reality consisting of different ways of naming, recognizing, and interacting with its constituent entities and events. It is a reality in which others participate, but not as direct episodes in it, but as indirect contacts based on what is referred to or how it is conceived. However, the results and products of these specialized modes of knowledge are always materialized in situations with which one can interact indirectly, that is, personally and interpersonally. Every mode of knowledge delimits different domains of possible direct or indirect interaction, yet given their ultimate articulation with the practices of ordinary language and, consequently, with the everyday world of interpersonal relations in society, the different modes share criteria, objects, events, as well as procedures. The social nature of the various modes of knowledge brings them together at different moments of their operation or occurrence.

There are two strictly linguistic dimensions in the conformation of technical languages: one, related to definitions, and the other, related to the interpretation of what is 'known'. Both dimensions are always framed within the logic of a general conception of the domain of knowledge and the nature of the mode employed. These conceptions are not necessarily unalterable, and in some modes of knowledge they undergo profound transformations (scientific, artistic, technological), in some others only partial or added (formal, ethical/juridical), and in others the conceptions are unalterable or can be brought together with similar conceptions (religious).

Unlike the names and descriptions in ordinary language, whose meaning is always directly linked and merged with the acts and activities performed with respect to objects, events, and persons in situation, in technical languages such linguistic components are defined beforehand. In ordinary language one learns, recognizes and mentions the names of things and events by listening to what others say, asking what they are, reading, and being corrected when incorrectly named. Names are not learned by dictionary definitions, which commonly refer to names in terms of their descriptions and uses — often circular, incomplete, or ambiguous. It is no overstatement to say that most people who speak a given language and participate daily in all the activities of their group in that language can hardly give "definitions" of the words they use, especially of the names of objects and activities (for activities are also named).

On the contrary, any specific object proper to that language is defined in advance in technical languages. Definitions can be of different types: specifying observable or measurable characteristics or properties, in terms of their effects, based on the procedures or criteria we use to identify them, by their relational character between two things or events, or by their differential origin, among many others. In all cases, definitions constitute the way in which the objects, events, and/or processes dealt with by a mode of knowledge in a given domain are recognized or identified. For this reason, unlike the meaning or sense of words and expressions in ordinary language, technical terms and expressions are univocal, that is, they have only one meaning, the one that delimits their definition. In the different modes of knowledge, technical terms can only be understood in one way, which is precisely their functional reason: not to induce confusion or ambiguity. When physics defines 'mass' there is only one way to understand the term, just as in music when one speaks of an 'arpeggio', in mathematics of an 'algebraic sum', in jurisprudence of 'intentional homicide', in engineering of 'polarity', and in every religion of 'paradise'. Only in psychology does a permanent state of conceptual confusion seem to prevail due to the uncritical use of ordinary language terms as if they were univocal denotative terms. Definitions never constitute the identification of the essential properties of an object, activity, or attribution. They are instruments that delimit the way in which we relate practically to "reality". They are not conceptual portraits of that "reality", but rather, quoting Wittgenstein, they are "conceptual glasses" for seeing it in a single predetermined way. To the extent that specialized modes of knowledge constitute "restricted" social institutions, those who participate in such knowledge processes require explicit training in the lexicon and use of the corresponding technical languages. Unlike the integration of practices of ordinary language in which individuals gradually develop linguistic behavior patterns "spontaneously" or informally, there is a structured process of training prior to incorporation into the activities of a specialized mode of knowledge in a particular domain. Only the mastery of the technical language allows incorporation and access to rituals and specialized practical procedures.

As noted, the definitions of the technical terms in the different domains in which the special modes of knowledge are developed conform to the criteria of a general logic or conception of those domains, and to the ultimate function or purpose that is pursued by each special mode: comprehensive discovery (scientific), symbolic representation (formal), utilitarian elaboration (technological), induction of enjoyment and interest (artistic), cohesion through the non-apparent (religious), and justification and judgment (ethical/juridical). Thus, it could be pointed out that the different criteria that underlie and frame the logical criteria of the definitions are empirical contrast (scientific), postulation of properties (formal), precision and effectiveness (technological), dogma and mystery (religious), representation (artistic), and interest (ethical/juridical). Each of these criteria has undergone and will continue to undergo specific adaptations in the course of the history of changes in the various social formations. However, it is important to underline that the criteria regulating the formulation of technical language can also intermingle and bias the operation of the modes of knowledge and their concepts insofar as the latter intertwine and merge in particular domains at different historical moments. History provides us with examples of the fusion of religious, artistic, and ethical/juridical modes, of scientific, religious, and technical modes, of formal, artistic, and technological modes, among others. Social practices never occur in neutral spaces or in spaces of specific purity.

The second dimension of all technical language is its interpretative, hermeneutic character of reality, insofar as it is directly linked to the practices of ordinary language and to the interindividual relations sustaining these practices, whether as interpersonal or impersonal. In each mode of knowledge, the interpretative formats are different and adjusted to the specific purposes of each one of them. However, each and every one develops as a narrative permeated with metaphors and allegories articulating its arguments, procedures, and results. Particular metaphors and allegories may be periodically replaced at different historical moments, but in one way or another they always hold a relation to an original assumption or myth of all human knowledge practice: the possibility of endowing everything in existence, including human life itself, with some form of rationality and order. This root-myth manifests itself as an act of creative will in the religious mode, as rational order—even in chaos— in the formal mode, as laws of nature and society in the scientific mode, as conflict between rationality and irrationality in the artistic mode, as rational mastery of nature in the technological mode, and as rational justification of human acts in the ethical/juridical mode. In each historical epoch, the underlying concept of rationality adapts to the circumstances, and this determines to a certain degree the more or less transitory fusion and articulation between the different modes of knowledge. In any case, paraphrasing André Breton, the hermeneutic dimension of technical languages and their root-myth of rationality constitute the permanent communicating vessels between the historical continuity of the practices of ordinary language as the original mold of all knowledge and form of social life, and the relative transience of the different forms of specialized knowledge and their technical languages. For the purposes of this essay, it is sufficient to note this fact. To delve deeper into these relations is an epistemological endeavor that recognizes the fundamental role of language as a social practice in the various forms of knowledge.

References

Austin, J. L. (1955/1962). How to do things with words. Oxford, England: Oxford University Press.

Bühler, K. (1934/2011). Theory of language: the representational function of language. Amsterdam: John Benjamins Publishing Co.

Canfield, J. V. (2007). Becoming human: The development of language, self, and self-consciousness. NY: Palgrave MacMillan.

Flanagan, B., Goldiamond, I., & Azrin, N. (1958). Operant stuttering: the control of stuttering behavior through response-contingent consequences. Journal of the Experimental Analysis of Behavior, 1, 173-177.

Kantor, J. R. (1924-1926). Principles of Psychology (vols. I & II). New York, NY: Alfred Knop.

Kantor, J. R. (1936). An objective psychology of grammar. Granville, Ohio: Principia Press.

Kantor, J. R. (1963). Behaviorism: Whose image? The Psychological Record, 13, 499-512.

Kantor, J. R. (1977). Psychological Linguistics. Chicago, Ill.: Principia Press.

King, C. M., & Quigley, S. P. (1985). Reading and deafness. San Diego, Cal: College Hill Press.

Kuo, Z. Y. (1967). The dynamics oof behavior development: An epigenetic view. New York, NY: Random House.

Marschark, M. (1993). Psychological development of deaf children. New York, NY: Oxford University Press.

Marschark, M., Mourandian, V., & Halas, M. (1994). Discourse rules in the language productions of deaf and hearing children. Journal of Experimental Child Psychology, 57, 89-107.

Ribes, E. (1986). Language as behavior: Functional mediation versus morphological description. In H. W. Reese, & L. J. Parrott (Eds.), Behavior science: Philosophical, methodological, and empirical advances (pp. 115-138). Hillsdale, NJ: Lawrence Erlbaum.

Ribes, E. (1993). Behavior as the functional content of language. In S. C.

Hayes, L. J. Hayes, T. R. Sarbin, & H. W. Reese (Eds.): Varieties of contextualism (pp. 283-297). Reno, NV: Context Press.

Ribes, E. (1999). Teoría del condicionamiento y lenguaje. Un análisis histórico-conceptual. [Theory of conditioning and language: A historical-conceptual analysis]. México: Taurus.

Ribes, E. (2001). Functional dimensions of social behavior: Theoretical considerations and some preliminary data. Mexican Journal of Behavior Analysis, 2001, vol. 27, monographic issue, 285-306.

Ribes, E. (2004). Behavior is abstraction, not ostension: Conceptual and historical remarks on the nature of psychology. Behavior & Philosophy, 32, 55-68.

Ribes, E. (2006). Human behavior as language: Some thoughts on Wittgenstein. Behavior & Philosophy, 34, 109-121.

Ribes, E. (2012). Función heurística de algunas nociones wittgensteinianas para la psychology [Heuristic function of some Wittgensteinian terms for psychology] In A. Tomasini (Ed.), Wittgenstein en español [Wittgenstein in Spanish] (pp. 95-120). Xalapa: Universidad Veracruzana.

Ribes, E. (2018). El estudio científico de la conducta individual: introducción a la teoría de la psicología. [The scientific study of individual behavior: An introduction to the theory of psychology]. Ciudad de México: El Manual Moderno.

Ribes, E., & López, F. (1985). Teoría de la conducta: Un análisis de campo y paramétrico [Theory of behavior: A field and parametric analysis] C DMX: Trillas

Ribes, E., Pulido, L., Rangel., N., & Sánchez-Gatell, e. (2016). Sociopsicología: Instituciones y relaciones interindividuales [Sociopsychology: Institutions and interindividual relations]. Madrid: La Catarata.

Ryle, G. (1949). The concept of mind. New York, NY: Barnes & Noble.

Ryle, G. (1962). Dilemmas. Cambridge, England: Cambridge University Press.

Schlinger, H. D. (2008). Consciousness is nothing but a word. Skeptic, 13(4), 58-63.

Skinner, B. F. (1938). The behavior of organisms. NY: Appleton Century Crofts.

Skinner, B. F. (1957). Verbal Behavior. NY: Appleton Century Crofts.

Watson, J. B. (1913). Psychology as the behaviorist views it. Psychological Review, 20, 158-177.

Wittgenstein, L. (1953). Philosophical investigations. Oxford, England: Basil & Blackwell.

Wittgenstein, L. (1969). On certainty. Oxford, England: Basil & Blackwell.

Wittgenstein, L. (1980). Remarks on the philosophy of psychology (Vol. 2). Oxford: Basil & Blackwell.

ESSAY EIGHT: THE POLITICAL DIMENSION OF INTERINDIVIDUAL BEHAVIOR: ACTING *AS IF* AND IDEOLOGICAL PRACTICE

In an essay in this work, I have argued that the psychological, as an object of knowledge, is a coextensive abstraction of the substantive objects of knowledge of two borderline disciplines: ecobiology and socio-historical science. This approach means that the psychological, as an individual dimension of animal behavior, including human, only takes place as a segment or fraction of a continuum represented by biological behavior and social behavior, that is, by the interrelations between individuals of a species with their ecological niche and by the interrelations between individuals as constituents of social institutions. In the case of human behavior, this takes place at three levels, the ecobiological (linked to survival), the sociocultural (linked to covival), and the psychological, as a personal transitional segment always in situation (as a process of functional detachment —Ribes, 2018). Psychological behavior, as an individual dimension, occurs most of the time as part of relational episodes between individuals. Psychological behavior, it follows, participates in but doesn't determine the interactions that occur at the interpersonal and impersonal level between individuals in social life, whether in the sphere of informal institutions constitutive of culture as a custom of formal institutions constitutive of the hierarchical organization of a social formation such as State (Ribes, Pulido, Rangel, & Sánchez-Gatell, 2016).

Human covival, unlike animal survival in their ecological habitats, is based on collective and not individual subsistence, based on the organization of labor as complementary but asymmetrical and frequently inequitable activity, both in relation to the nature of specialized labor division as to its contribution and retribution to the welfare of the totality of individuals in the social formation. The social division of labor and its complex exchange relations between sets of individuals is only possible in language (Ribes, 2001). Language is consubstantial to all social practice, as a system of relations between individuals that makes it possible to detach itself from the concrete situations in which the various moments of the social work process occur as a subsistence process: Production (locating and storing resources, creating tools, developing skills and techniques at work and generating goods and services) and appropriation (distributing the products of labor as goods and satisfiers through services). The complex forms of organization of human life, of increasing and progressively indirect interdependence between individuals and situations, can be woven and in and through language, as an exclusive and eminently human form of relation. Specialized work is the foundation of the complementation between individuals and groups that allows their subsistence, and is structured in diverse exchange relations between what is produced with what is appropriated and distributed, as well as between the services that articulate these production-appropriation relations. Exchange relations, sustained by the modes of social production and material life that characterize them (Braudel, 1986), generate and feed concomitant power and sanction relations in all past and contemporary social formations, and in their corresponding formal and informal institutions (Ribes et al., 2016). Power relations always appear linked to exchange relations, such as being able to do and to have, and being able to make others able or not to do and able or not to have. Power always consists in entitling, allowing, or impeding. Expertise, physical strength, "knowledge", and accumulated or available wealth are the immediate sources of power, its sustenance, and its *raison d'être* to preserve and maintain the privileges (and the consequent inequality) that certain forms of social life protect and permit.

The rise of political institutions

Complementation, domination, and constraint of the activities and requirements of individuals in archaic and tribal societies were articulated horizontally and in an overlapping manner (Sahlins, 1972, 1974; Scott, 2009). As exchange relations became more complex (the emergence of trade, market, and corporate specializations, shaped by the division into hierarchical classes), mutuality, as the articulating axis of interindividual relations and social life, was gradually replaced by the three institutional axes that have characterized later social formations: the economic axis, the political axis, and the ethical/juridical axis. Subsidiarity originally took place in the form of mutual complementation within the kinship group and within the clans that made up the tribal formation. Power and sanction relations were intrinsic to the specialized division of labor as mutual complementation and sharing, and were manifested on the basis of specific expertise and knowledge from experience. Not only the material life directly linked to common subsistence was organized horizontally, but also additional manifestations such as singing, dancing, handicrafts, and the first forms of religious expression. The etymology of the word religio (Müller, 1889) is linked to the gathering of the collective to worship, show respect, take care of all those natural elements beneficial to the group and that favored its subsistence, either by being available or by not happening. Religious functions in tribal societies merged with the knowledge of healing procedures and the interpretation of events and circumstances, giving rise to the so-called sorcerers, shamans, and healers. However, it is with the rise of cities that the horizontal articulation of mutual complementation and power and sanction relations is lost. Social leadership and covival rites were supplanted and usurped by "representatives" of divine and natural forces, establishing subordination relations, serfdom and intermediation in all areas of social life. There emerged the religious institution and the State integrated as instruments of domination in the new social formations stratified into classes and castes. The first despotic states were theocratic states, in which divine laws and human laws were one and the same, whether written by man, as in the code of Hammurabi, or directly written by the particular god, as in the ten commandments collected by Moses. In all cases, the religious worldviews constituted a projection of the organization of the constituted or to be constituted State proper. Thus, the relations between the elements of the cosmos, including the different divinities, represented the virtues, defects, privileges, and subjugations that characterized these social formations (Frankfort, Wilson, & Jacobsen, 1967). An eloquent example is that of the catholic church. Anderson (1979) amply documents how the official institutionalization of the Christian religion at the end of the Roman Empire, as a State religion, was a fundamental, catalyzing factor in the incorporation of the Germanic, Scandinavian, and Slavic peoples, among others, into the process and consolidation of the feudal mode of production.

From the first centuries of sedentary populations dedicated to agriculture, pastoralism, and fishing (12000 or 10000 B.C.E.), the material life related to subsistence (food, clothing, various household goods and habitation) was autarchic and based on self-sufficiency (Braudel, 1989; Polanyi, Arensberg & Pearson, 1957). As populations based on kinship and lineage relations grew, the exchange of complementary goods between them took place, without actually constituting a commercial activity. Appropriation by force and plunder also emerged, carried out by semi-nomadic populations, which was later adopted by despotic States to extend their domains, establish serfdom, and increase their wealth, resources, and the availability of slaves. Warfare, as Clastres (1987) points out, preceded politics. He disagrees with the usually accepted view formulated by Clausewitz (1832), who, from a purely military perspective, considered that the ultimate end of all war was political, and war primarily a means to seize power. Instead, Clastres suggests that politics has been an extension of war and not the opposite. War was, and still is, a violent way to appropriate the wealth produced, the resources, and the labor force (the origins of slavery) through dispossession and extraction. In fact, politics became important, first as an instrument of control of vassals dominated by armed force and, later, within social formations (in conjunction with religion), to articulate relations of internal subjugation and serfdom as forms of hegemonic domination based first on persuasion and later on coercion. Anderson (1979) stresses that diplomacy —politics between states— emerges very late, in the sixteenth and seventeenth centuries with the consolidation of absolutist states. Aristotle himself (English translation 1995) argued, in the Politics and Nicomachean Ethics, about the complementary nature of the City-State for the welfare of individuals, and about the need to maintain the healthy balance of wealth and property through the application of criteria relating to the virtues and the just, but only in relation to citizens, who were educated men with goods and properties. The rest of society was excluded from these criteria, so that politics, conceived as the management of the welfare of the inhabitants of society, distinguished two levels: one, for the real citizens, and the other, for the rest of the individuals who lacked the rights of citizens, while having more obligations than them. It was thus that productive activities of complementation for subsistence in the form of interpersonal collective communal mutuality became collective class duties and rights in the tributary retributive formations. These relations between classes were not assumed "voluntarily", but ultimately always imposed through coercion.

Interpersonal segmentary relations, based on kinship and lineage, were formalized in impersonal institutions with the emergence of the State and, later, of private ownership of land and slaves as labor force. From despotic states to feudal states, interpersonal segmentary relations were gradually formalized into money as currency, exchange markets and intermediation markets (and with the latter, what we now call the market economy), the first forms of banking, public finance, delegated authorities of formal political power, as well as judges, courts, and various religious organizations and their priests. Thus, exchange, power, and sanction relations originally interwoven in situations with less differentiation and organization of social activities and practices became "fragmented" into two distinct but overlapping spheres: formal and informal institutions. In the former, the relations are structured in a vertically, while in the latter they are structured horizontally or transversally. From the point of view of interindividual relations, the political dimension of behavior should be examined in informal institutions, since it is in them that ideological practice –a subtle way of preserving power– occurs as a hegemonic practice of subjugation or submission. Ideological practice, eminently political, makes it possible to maintain the hegemony of some social classes over others without the need to use force (the so-called legitimate violence of the State or the defense of social or religious values), and without the need to promote a fair distribution of wealth in an effective way. The practice of custom, and the tacit acceptance of its *raison d'être* and its justification, is sufficient. Ideological practices naturalize the ways and ends of social inequality in and through customs. Economic criteria foster ambition, profiteering, accumulation, consumption, benefit, and profit. Political criteria foster complicity, negotiation, lobbying, clientelism, coercion[3], adhesion and opposition. Ethical/juridical criteria foster appraisal, justification, qualification and disqualification, guilt, shame, resignation, and many others.

Two texts will be cited, both from the mid-sixteenth century, at the height of the consolidation of absolute monarchical States as part of the transition begun in the fourteenth century from feudalism to nascent mercantile capitalism. Both texts underscore the oppressive nature of customs and laws as forms of domination and subjugation of the power of the State and its economic interests. The first text is by Girolamo Vida in 1556 (reproduced from the *Introduction to the Discourse on Voluntary Servitude* by La Boétie):

> What are laws for? To constitute servitude, which the wise say is worse than death; to force us to live under the domination of others; to give us an artificial nature and to make us rebel against ourselves; to make us, not better, but more cunning; to teach us, not justice, but the art of litigation… Have you ever seen a single grouping of men in which justice is served and in which each is rewarded according to his merit? [...] And how do States arise? With larcenies, with usurpations, with invasions, and they live by oppressing an innumerable multitude of workers and domestics, not citizens, but slaves, who are forbidden as a crime what constitutes the delights of their masters… happy the age when there were no laws, no plebiscites, no fictions, no frauds, no taxes, no greed, no ambition, no glory, no rich, no poor, no sieges, no ravages, no wars, no revolutions! Let us free ourselves from this corrupt and perverse society, and let justice descend upon the earth for the second time (p. 33).

The second text is by La Boétie himself (circa 1580):

---

3 Ribes uses the word *coacción*, from the Latin coactio, meaning "to force someone to do something". Coercion is much broader, meaning "to control, restrain" (*translator's note*).

It is incredible how as soon as a people becomes subject, it promptly falls into such complete forgetfulness of its freedom that it can hardly be roused to the point of regaining it, obeying so easily and so willingly that one is led to say, on beholding such a situation, that this people has not so much lost its liberty as won its enslavement. It is true that in the beginning men submit under constraint and by force; but those who come after them obey without regret and perform willingly what their predecessors had done because they had to. [...] Nevertheless it is clear enough that the powerful influence of custom is in no respect more compelling than in this, namely, habituation to subjection. It is said that Mithridates trained himself to drink poison. Like him we learn to swallow, and not to find bitter, the venom of servitude [...] yet it must be admitted that she has less power over us than custom, for the reason that native endowment, no matter how good, is dissipated unless encouraged, whereas environment always shapes us in its own way, whatever that may be, in spite of nature's gifts (pp. 62-63).

It is noteworthy that these texts are contemporary and contrary to what the traditional academy considers foundational texts of political science: *The Prince* by Niccolo Machiavelli (1513), and *Education of the Christian Prince* by Erasmus of Rotterdam (1516), which are compendia of advice and recommendations to the monarch to stay in power and fulfill its objectives. Rather, they can probably be considered the foundation of politics as a formal institution, that is, of the power relations to be cared for and fostered within the structure of government as a State to ensure the continuity of the existing domination relations in the social formation. The culmination of this tradition occurs with Montesquieu, in *The Spirit of the Laws* (1784), in which he proposed division of powers, similar to the England of his time, as an alternative to the absolute, despotic monarchy of the France of his time. Attempting to recover the ideal of the Roman republic, Montesquieu laid the foundations in the Enlightenment of the bourgeois republic and the burgeoning mercantile capitalism suffocated by monarchical centralism. His ideal led to the illusion that in a class society the powers of the State (executive, legislative, and judicial) could be separated from the influence and domination of the holders of wealth (and real power). He transformed politics into a search for and pursuit of just laws. These laws, however, had to be based on the prevailing customs and circumstances, that is, they had to formalize as a rule what was already a social reality. He says at the end of his author's warning:

Finally, the good man of whom we are dealing in Book III, Chapter V, is not the good Christian man, but the good political man, who possesses the aforementioned political virtue. He is the man who loves the laws of his country and who acts out of love for it.

He is, in short, the man identified with the State.

Political practice as ideological practice

Political practice as the exercise of institutionalized power is an emergent of the polis, of the city as an articulated population center that is the focal point of the division and specialization of labor in a social formation. Power as a functional dimension of social relations is found in political institutions, and can be differentiated into two types: substantive power and formal power. Political institutions correspond to the government and governance of relations between individuals in the set of institutions that make up a given State as a social formation. They constitute what is called the State apparatus (which includes bureaucracy, the armed forces, the media, and others). In contrast, substantive power deals with actual administration based on coercion and the use of force, monopoly and distribution of wealth and knowledge, while formal power deals with the regulation, surveillance, and prescription of power contingencies. The State constitutes the complete system of social relations, while the government is a macro-institution in charge of maintaining and managing domination relations supported by substantive power. Government is formal delegated power. Politicians assume a doble representation, contradictory in principle: that of substantive power and that of the polis, as a group of citizens. Thus, politics as governance management turns out to be an ideological and "mediating" practice of relations between the powerful themselves and between the powerful and the dominated. There is no social formation or political system that in principle allows transforming its constituent foundations, in particular those relating to the production and appropriation of wealth. Political relations are always relations between individuals, who manage their possibilities, their operations as social acts, and their results and effects, always within the framework of a hierarchical system of classes.

I will quote Wallerstein (2007) at length regarding how ideology, as a political practice, is fundamental in the domination relations exercised in the current capitalist world-system:

> The modern world-system could not have been created and institutionalized without the use of force to expand its boundaries and control large segments of its population. Nonetheless, superior, even overwhelming force has never been enough to establish lasting dominance. The powerful needed to gain this legitimation first of all from their own cadres, who were the essential human transmission belts of their power, and without whom they could not have imposed themselves on the larger group who are the dominated. But they also needed to obtain some degree of legitimation from those whom they dominated, and this was far harder than obtaining the consent of the cadre, who after all received some degree of immediate reward for playing the role that was asked of them. If one looks at the arguments encrusted in the various doctrines that were put forth, they always ended up by seeking to demonstrate the inherent superiority of the powerful. And from this inherent superiority, these doctrines derived not merely the capacity to dominate but the moral justification of their domination. Gaining acceptance for the moral right to dominate has been the key element in achieving the legitimation of power. And in order to do that, it had to be demonstrated that the *long-run* effect of the domination was to the benefit of the dominated, even if the *short-run* effect seemed to be negative. (pp. 71-72)

Politics is consubstantial with the mutually affecting asymmetrical power relations between individuals of different classes in a hierarchical society. Therefore, politics, as the management and intermediation of power relations, can occur informally or formally. On the one hand, politics at the formal level, as government and governance, is embedded in the interests of one or more social classes, and always has an impersonal character. Political relations have historically been characterized by fostering the illusion, through laws and myths, that the representatives of power and in power are so by a direct or indirect delegation, first from the divinities and then from the people. This delegation was restricted until recently by criteria of race, sex, and education, and was always based on some form of consensus of a part of the population, as a contract or by vote. However, the options for political representation never directly include the possibility of transforming the State and its economic foundation. On the other hand, politics at the informal level can be identified in the power relations constitutive of life customs, for example, in sexist, patriarchal, religious, racial, and other relations. These customs are maintained regardless of the historical circumstances that gave rise to them, as long as they don't affect, or better yet, if they strengthen the hegemonic practices of the social formation. Politics, as the management of power relations in the social formation, as in *Leviathan* (Hobbes, 1651) is offered as the only possibility of establishing and maintaining forms of covival that are convenient and affordable for all individuals. This is why the politics in a class society is an omnipresent axis in the relations between individuals. One always lives in politics, and the members of the dominant classes and their delegates or representatives also live from politics.

As social formations become more complex, production and appropriation exchange relations shift from direct to indirect. In the context of this reticule of complementary indirect interdependencies (from trade and the later prominence of money and the financial system), formal economic, political and legal institutions emerge and differentiate themselves from the original informal institutions. Service activities, apparently non-productive, form part of this complex web and constitute a fabric that sustains and articulate it. From this web of formal and informal institutions, with asymmetrical intersections of exchange, power, and sanction relations, the hegemony of the dominant classes is gradually imposed through the ideological practices that constitute each social formation. Ideological practices (and concepts with their justifications) emerge based on the notions of class, caste, race, god, homeland, nation or state. All ideological practices are regulated by formal institutions and, within them, as governance and institutional or esprit de corps. The various religious ministries are included, based on the individualization of responsibilities, duties, and rights, which distinguish between members of the dominant classes and of the dominated classes, sometimes sharply, sometimes subtly (as in the recognition of private property). The social individual is the artifice or device that allows to articulate ideological practices, thereby transforming the transversal power relations that characterize societies without State or hierarchies, into vertical, asymmetrical and indirect political power relations (including the representation or delegation of functions). This process of usurpation and supplanting of collective interests by the interests of particular groups masks the direct dependence of political (and legal) power on economic power (the factors of production, and the unequal appropriation of products). Substantive (economic) power is masked in formal and delegated power (political power).

Power is based on domination: making something one's own, in this case, making one's own what constitutes a collective good and result of a social formation. Power consists in making possible the appropriation of goods and the performance of acts or actions of some with respect to others, of what one has and what one does, of what one can have and what one can do, of what others can or cannot have and what they can or cannot do. Power doesn't manifest itself as an abstract dimension, but in the differentiated realization of these forms of possibility in the different individuals of a social formation, based on their belonging to a class or segment thereof. Power is exercised, not "held" as a formal attribute, and is always directly or indirectly exercised through the appropriation of resources, goods and the availability of services provided by others, in a broad sense. Appropriation usually occurs through one or another form of coercion, through the force of wealth or by means of the direct or indirect exercise of violence, origins and sources of power alongside knowledge in the form of various kinds of practical expertise. Power is not always directly or immediately exercised, especially in differentiated social formations. Power is usually exercised through subordinate and vertical authorization. Hegemony, as a consensual (though not rational and voluntary) form of recognition of power, also requires persuasion processes that precisely configure the intervention of politics (and of religion on a convergent plane), as an ideological practice. Power practices of a minority over a majority are maintained and reproduced through persuasion, namely practices referring to the power to have and the power to do of a few, and to the power that many others may or may not have and may or may not be able to do.

Power relations permeate the entire social formation in different ways, explicit on some occasions, implicit on others. Power radiates vertically and horizontally, in the form of subordination relations at different levels and spheres of the social formation. In formal institutions, the functions to be exercised are vertically organized, and constitute differential and differentiated delegations of the authority of a superordinate power. In informal institutions, power relations are transmitted as and through customs. In formal institutional relations, their impersonal character doesn't prevent power functions from being allocated in specific individuals based on dominant class interests. Interpersonal power relations in informal institutions are also based on the axis of having and doing with respect to others seen as "given" privileges, historically developed on the basis of strength, available wealth, and expertise, so that, although more flexible and less predictable, the informally constituted power relations are modulated by the same criteria that prevail in formal institutions. In this sense, it can be said that all interindividual relations have an implicit political background or underpinning, just as they have a legal framework explicitly delimiting them. The institutional delegation of power as authority also entails the distribution of privileges in the appropriation and enjoyment of social satisfiers, whether goods or services. The distribution of privileges, resulting from the totality of work and social production of wealth and relative services, constitutes a simultaneous process to that of ideological practice, which contributes to maintaining the domination over wealth and its appropriation by a segment of the social formation.

Hegemony, as a political result of ideological practice, generally occurs on two axes: a horizontal axis between individuals belonging to the same class or subclass, and a vertical axis between individuals belonging to different classes in the exercise of power, the dominant and the dominated. In the first case, ideological practice as a realization of political management consolidates subordination relations in the form of necessary dependence relations between individuals of different classes: workers need the entrepreneurs and they recognize and appreciate this. In the second case, individuals belonging to the dominant and dominated classes behave differently. Whereas members of the dominant classes recognize each other impersonally regardless of interpersonal differences, in the dominated classes interpersonal differences interfere with and prevent the impersonal recognition of class interests, as the political history of humanity unfortunately shows. Whereas impersonal interindividual relations prevail over interpersonal relations in the dominant classes, the opposite is the case in the dominated classes. Interindividual relations between the dominant and dominated classes are always configured in the form of what we might call the language-game of persuasion, always unidirectionally from the perspective of the dominant class towards the dominated. In contrast, in intraclass interindividual relations, whether dominant or dominated class, what we might describe as the language-game of acceptance stands out, although obviously different circumstances are accepted in each class.

The hegemony of the dominant classes not only occurs through the dispositions and acts framed by formal institutions, but is complemented by the ideological practices that occur informally in the areas of work, education, health care, communication, recreation, and family relations as the basic nucleus. These ideological practices constitute a complement and extension of religion and the official "customs" of the State. Politics is not reduced to the prescription, administration, regulation, and supervision of social power, but subtly or overtly permeates all interindividual relations of the social formation. In fact, political discourse itself is more than a statement, it is actually an act of justification (or questioning at times) of the domination practices at its various levels. In this sense, the articulation between the formal institutions representing the dominant classes, and hegemony as tacit acceptance by all individuals of the social relations existing in the various informal institutions, occurs through political practice as ideological practice. Politics as ideological practice always occurs in language, even when force and violence are used. In formal institutions, politics adopts the form of power management, and the formulation of laws and sanctioning procedures that favor or ensure the maintenance of the *status quo.*

The ideological nature of political practice in informal institutions is more elusive. Political practice consists of promoting and encouraging the dominated to accept their living conditions (and those of the dominant classes) as inevitable and necessary circumstances. Customs (traditions), as well as educational, religious, health, recreational, and communication practices, constitute the support that reproduces the power and sanction relations (and, less visibly, the exchange relations that sustains them) among individuals, always as interpersonal relations in the different segments of the social formation. The ideological practice of the dominant classes corresponds to and is congruent with their effective practice of life, while the ideological practice of the dominated classes is a simple "representation" of that of the dominant classes. In this case, the term representation doesn't refer to a mental representation or a social imaginary, as it is customary to propose, but rather to a simulated performance, such as that which occurs in the theater. Individuals, through their behavior, perform, represent a life form that doesn't belong to them, but one that has been imposed on them. Individuals behave "as if" what they do and what they have were the only thing they could do or have. The hegemony of the dominant classes is achieved through the ideological practice in which the dominated classes make their own (even if they are alien to them) the values and criteria imposed on them as natural forms of life. These include, most notably, the myths of freedom and will or free will, as well as those of resignation and hope. Values have to do with what is considered good or bad, natural or strange, attainable or unaffordable and what is considered immutable or mutable, among many others. Ideological practice, including in the sphere of formal institutions, is not a declarative matter, but occurs as acts and outcomes, with their corresponding justifications. Acting as if is established by example, recognition, instructions, habits and routines, and the sanction and administration of power as cooptation, complicity, and submission.

Ideology is not a system of mental representations, but consists of practical representations (or perhaps practices of representation) that support and justify beliefs and values, that is, that induce and encourage the acceptance of doing and having what is possible and what is due. Through politics and religion, with their corresponding legal and moral-ethical criteria, social practices that threaten the continuity of the system of state of affairs are discouraged, while at the same time promoting the practices that maintain it. To the extent that the dominated classes participate in and accept this tacitly imposed form of life, they believe in the justifications that sustain it, despite the fact that it subjugates them. In turn, the dominant classes are congruent in their ideological practices with respect to their effective social practice, their everyday form of life: they don't live any representation.

The interrelation of ideological practices as formal and informal practices, and the importance of interpersonal (and embedded personal) relations in the production of customs, culture, and social institutions will now be examined. A corollary of this analysis will be to show how all behavior between individuals is always embedded in a political dimension, and that it is therefore not possible to understand individual psychological behavior apart from the circumstances that insert it as a component of social behavior.

Interindividual behavior and psychological behavior

Interindividual relations are not relations between subjectivities. They are the expression of objective practices characterizing the functioning of a social formation. To speak of intersubjectivity is a psychological reductionism, in which social relations and practices are restricted to the views and opinions of each individual. It assumes a psychological individual who operates as a rational cognizant mind, whose behavior with respect to other(s) results from a process of prior decision-making, and who associates with others for selfish reasons. Sometimes this profile is complemented by the pressure to satisfy needs, rooted in its biological nature, and which require collective, coercive regulation to attenuate or prevent their destructiveness.

Interindividual relations are of two types: interpersonal or impersonal, depending on the institutional context in which they occur. Horizontal interindividual relations —characteristic of archaic segmentary or tribal, chiefdom social formations (Semo, 2018), developed in a framework regulated by mutuality and reciprocity, in which labor and products were collective, although their use was individualized according to circumstances. Relations in these societies or collectivities were interpersonal. Impersonal interindividual relations, regulated by class interest, arose in hierarchical social formations in the course of State formation or thus organized, and were vertically structured. Both production and appropriation were differentiated, and property emerged as indicative of social power. The individual in archaic society, who continued to maintain interpersonal relations on a horizontal level —now subordinated to impersonal relations—, always had a social "marker" that identified him as a member of a social class: king, nobleperson, priest, warrior, merchant, farmer, potter, slave, and others. In impersonal interindividual relations, mutuality and reciprocity were subordinated to service and the production of goods. From contributive exchange in the archaic and chiefdom formations, there was a shift to tributary and retributive exchange of various kinds. At present, in the capitalist world-system (Wallerstein, 2005), social life is organized around financial capital and the continuous obtaining of profits and greater wealth. Social wealth, not only in each nation, but in the entire planet, is found in a reduced percentage of the population, a social segment that, as a rule, doesn't directly exercise power, but delegates it to another segment, that of politicians and professional experts, who, in turn, rely on the judiciary strata to socially endorse their practices and operations. The rest of the population constitutes the sustenance of the system: those who produce, offer services, and consume what is produced so that profits can continue to be made. There are obviously differences in welfare among different segments of the population, depending on the different allocations in the global division of labor, and on the restrictions that this allocation represents in different continents, nations, and sectors of the population.

The complexity and globalization of the capitalist world-system as universal social formation makes it difficult to trace interrelation lines between the various institutions embedded in the economic, political, and ethical/juridical axes. Paraphrasing La Boétie, it could be stated that the indirect nature and multiple intermediations between wealth, power, and sanction blur the horizon in which the voluntary servitude of individuals who are part of the dominated classes is perceived, especially when some of them have significant levels of comfort in their material life. In a previous paper (Ribes, 2012), the utility of considering individual behaviors always as components always related to what Wittgenstein (1953) calls language games was examined. It was suggested "…to consider psychological phenomena as various forms of acting as if. This notion underscores the functional relativity of all behavior and its belonging always to one of multiple institutionally identified criterion-practices" (p. 117). Following this logic, political practice is expressed in an acting as if, whether at the macro-institutional or micro-institutional level. Political practice, as an ideological practice, occurs in both spheres in the context of formal (impersonal) or informal (interpersonal) relations. In the sphere of formal institutions and impersonal relations, political practice is governed by ethical/juridical criteria, generally taken from the very social practices and customs that one wishes to preserve and reproduce. In the sphere of informal institutions and interpersonal practices, political practice, usually tacit or implicit, is governed by the moral criteria of individuals. These criteria are usually, but not necessarily, also framed by the customs and traditions of the class or social segment to which individuals belong. In any case, political practice aims and fosters the adjustment of individuals to socially accepted practices.

The main function of ideological practice, as the hegemonic political practice of the dominant classes or groups, is to articulate and preserve social cohesion, but this practice is instrumental in generating changes and transformations of different magnitudes in the social formation at times of transition to new forms of organization. Such changes are not intrinsic to the different segments, strata, groups or classes and, at the most general level of organization, neither to the particular social formation. At a global level, changes in history have been the result of the dynamics of the economic apparatus based, beginning with feudalism, on the industry-trade-finance triad. Politics and justice have lagged behind economic changes and have never preceded them. Changes are usually induced and/or imposed from the outside, either from the group or class, or from another dominant social formation. No social formation or grouping changes its organization and system of exchange, power, or sanction relations by itself. Changes occur as a result of commercial, financial, and cultural exchanges (including knowledge), or by the conquests and imposition of social institutions and their corresponding ideological practices. For this reason, political practice, as the management of power and hegemony, can also operate in the sense of changing the predominant ideological practices at a given moment, usually as influences or inductions between classes, between groups or between strata of the same social formation. Such changes can, given particular historical circumstances, reconfigure in a restricted way the exchange and power-sanction relations of the social formation at certain moments, without altering its structure and foundations.

The social articulation of ideological practices occurs in different ways and directions. The relations that are established between impersonal practices on the basis of impersonal relations between two or more individuals correspond to what is usually considered the sphere of politics as a formal institution. However, there are also three additional types of relations: one, as interpersonal practices between two or more individuals based on interpersonal relations; another, as interpersonal practices between two or more individuals based on impersonal relations; and finally, as impersonal practices between two or more individuals based on interpersonal relations. Therefore, ideological practices as diverse forms of political practice, can transit from the interpersonal to the interpersonal, from the interpersonal to the impersonal, from the impersonal to the interpersonal, and from the impersonal to the impersonal. Corruption, as an institutional phenomenon, is likely to occur when impersonal practices based on impersonal relations are replaced by interpersonal relations. In the same way, the personal element in such relations can qualify their characteristics and directionality, and in this aspect lies the individual's contribution to the reproduction or change of practice, especially in the micro-institutional sphere, whether formal or informal. The individual can affect other individuals in the context of their practices related to the management and administration of existing relations and, to that extent, have a "cascading" effect on the set of institutionally stratified practices given their membership to a social class and to one or more formal and informal micro-institutions (such as the family, the school, the company or work, the hospital, and others). Any micro-institutional change consists of a change in practices between individuals through the influence of one individual on another. From this point of view, the psychological episode is embedded in the ideological practice as a social episode from the first person's perspective (Ribes, 2018), acting with respect to a second and/or third person, identified as members of a class and an institution. The ideology of the isolated individual as a rational individual and/or as an individual in need of wealth (Polanyi, 1989) doesn't cancel the concept of the individual as a differential unit of social formation, in any of its segmentations or groupings. Individual practice, as a catalyst for the change of beliefs, that is, of accepting the criteria and justifications for the participation in social practices allows their modification within some of the micro-institutional strata of the social formation, breaking their uniform ideological articulation.

The main argument of this essay is that every interindividual relation has a political dimension, insofar as it is embedded in the ideological practices, such as customs, traditions, beliefs, and laws, proper to a given social formation. As such, all constituent behavior of an interindividual relation is always self-interested behavior, in one sense or another. The ideological practices of

260

reference constitute indicators of the characteristics and limits of possible change in the different spheres of a social formation.

Thus every relation between individuals always has a political background insofar as it is an acting as if, representing, consciously or inadvertently, an ideological practice as an acceptance (or rejection, in some cases) of the forms of domination between classes or class segments proper to a micro-institution. In any case, every relation between individuals can be located on an axis of conservatism-reformism. This axis is never linked to an authentic social transformation, at least at the moment when such a relation occurs. It is important to consider that, since the 20th century, hegemony is no longer maintained only through the use of force, political or religious promises of a better life or well-being in the future, the personal example of figures of power, or the practices highlighted by some texts, but also through the significant influence of the audiovisual (cinema and television) and electronic (the Internet) media, which represent and continuously bombard with representations of acting as if they were the dominant class. The media replace real life with virtual life as a form of impersonal hegemonic culture. Their impersonal nature is an additional obstacle to any possibility of micro-institutional change through interpersonal relations between individuals, the only ones that can bring about lasting changes and not simply transitory and momentary ones. It is important to stress that, although it is on the basis of the criteria of formal institutions that ideological practices are characterized and generalized within and between social formations (e.g., European universalism, Eastern essentialism, and scientific universalism, as pointed out by Wallerstein, 2007), it is ultimately in interpersonal relations at the micro-institutional level that these practices are reproduced or modified and, as a consequence, these criteria of domination. This is not a sudden process, but a gradual one, which, however, can progressively transform domination practices in specific segments of the social formation.

Final Remarks

It was proposed that the relations between individuals (and, consequently, individual behavior) are always embedded in the political axis that regulates the ideological practices of the social formation, be they impersonal or interpersonal in nature. It has been examined how politics (and the corresponding ideological practices) appear with the differentiation and complexification of the social formation as it organizes itself in the form of the State.

The State emerges with the polis as population nucleus differentiated into classes of very diverse types, which reflect the differences in production and in the appropriation/distribution of social wealth. The conformation of society into classes reflects the inequality between the constituent groups of individuals, inequality in obligations and in rights to differential forms of social life. In stateless societies there were also differences, but they were (or are as isolated populations today) the result of the surplus of resources or products, or of the public availability of instruments and tools for collective use, but which can also be used individually. The appropriation of goods is collective and may even be unequal in favor of some of its members, who require certain satisfiers in special circumstances (the elderly, children, the sick). Thus, power relations always occur at an interpersonal level and reflect the capacities and needs of individuals. Moreover, in tribal societies, constituting formations in transition to the polis, the existing hierarchies do not constitute manifestations of class, but are transitory functions, exercised by some individuals on the basis of their capacity and experience. The collectivity recognizes them, installs them, and removes them from their function. In this sense, power relations are horizontal and transversal. With the emergence of the State, social classes, privileges, lack thereof and, consequently, inequality are consolidated. This historical process is a consequence of the increasingly complex organization of social formations, of their different activities, fundamentally linked to agricultural and livestock production, to the manufacture of utensils, textiles and weapons, to the defense of the territory, and as an inevitable corollary to trade and warfare as a way of expanding the complementation of goods and services. The creation of currency and the market will be the following factors that will make social formations increasingly differentiated and complex, their organization, their rise, fall and decline, and the dynamic transformation of human societies in history.

Underscoring the inequality between individuals as members of distinct social classes on the basis of the organization in the form of the State doesn't constitute an evaluation of this form of social organization (which can be done anyway). It is only merely pointing to a de facto historical situation, which is there in front of us, as part of the very nature of social life. Social inequality is and has been historically consubstantial with the existence of the State. In each type of social formation the forms of inequality are different. There is not a single dominant class and a single dominated class. More than one dominant class can coexist and there is always more than one dominated class. Some dominated classes may enjoy some privileges and benefits with respect to the others, but they never have those of the dominant classes. Such benefits are nothing more than concessions granted by the dominant classes, given their momentary weakness or given the organic articulation of some of the dominated classes, in order to maintain hegemony, whether in economic or political terms. Fried (1967) has examined the political change and transformation of social formations in terms of the progressive inequalities that take place. Egalitarian societies were characterized by the fact that all their members, usually related by direct kinship and common lineage, could perform, in principle (except for biological reasons of age, strength, or disability), collectively valued activities and had access to the resources and satisfiers of the group. Demographic growth, associated with the sedentary nature of agricultural and livestock raising practices, promoted the transformation of egalitarian formations into hierarchical or rank formations, in which resources and satisfiers began to be internally redistributed. In these societies, having a rank represented a sign of prestige and collective recognition, which could be disregarded at any time, so that individuals with rank had no additional privileges in the use and consumption of resources. On the contrary, they had to exert more effort in the tasks corresponding to the assigned division of labor, in order to maintain their rank and their hierarchical differentiality. There is an intermediate stage between hierarchical societies and societies with a State: stratified societies contain the germ of classes in the State, but still lack an institutional organization. In stratified societies, kinship relations are lost as a system of control of collective activities, functions, and privileges. Their members, of same age and sex, do not have the same access to the basic resources for subsistence, considered as "capital" rather than consumption resources, that is, direct goods. Thus, stratified societies needed to maintain the new order through the use of power and sanctions that transcended the possibilities of kinship relations. The breakdown of these relations allowed the emergence of societies with a state, organized into delimited classes or strata. The function of the State as a stratified organizations was to maintain hierarchies, differential degrees of access to basic resources, obedience to the authorities, and the defense of the territory. Fried points out that "[...] The state must maintain itself externally and internally, and it does so by physical and ideological means, sustaining military forces and establishing an identity among other similar units" (p. 234).

Ideological practices and politics, as the management of power unequally distributed among the various social classes, are another unquestionable fact.

History also shows us that politics, in its various practical forms at the formal level, can contribute to temporary adjustments that reduce or mitigate inequalities, but never transform the essential existing power relations. Formal institutions may change and yet there may be only a mere apparent replacement of individuals or social classes in power (the famous *gatopardismo*[4]). Major social transformations are not the result of the voluntary practices of individuals, classes or even nations. They are the result of complex dynamic processes, still difficult to observe, anticipate or regulate, including wars, catastrophes, new technologies, new resources, and the interdependence of multiple factors within and between different social formations. Contributive, segmentary societies without class inequality are not utopias to return to. State-structured societies with classes are not generalized dystopias either, but they are niches of inequalities, sometimes brutal. Where to go from here? It is difficult to even hazard a guess. At present, as with other types of world-systems, the current world-system seems to have reached its limits of functionality. Formal economic and political institutions will not bring about its transformation. Rather, they tend to mitigate its crisis in order to alleviate the negative effects on the whole encompassing social formation. At the level of the capitalist world-system, it is illusory to suppose that a system governed by the criterion of constant and continuous profit can be modulated so that wealth is redistributed among the entire population and thus foster a collective system of well-being (Kitching, 2020; Picketty, 2019). There remains only the possibility of trying out at the microsocial level other types of economic and political relations, considering the current complexity of life in society. We cannot go back to the past, but neither can the future be a remodeling of the present. Revealing the functions of the different ideological practices at their interindividual level is a first step in this direction, not the only one, but the fundamental one for rethinking how we human beings should share wealth, knowledge, resources, and available goods, without subjugating one another, even if only subtly. However, in order to achieve this, we cannot overlook the fact that ideological practice is always regulated by the political criteria of the ruling power in its various manifestations. The function of ideological practice is to "mediate", more often than not in a subtle and inconspicuous manner, the complex web of interindividual relations in the

---

4 Changing something so that everything stays the same, see "The Leopard" by G. di Lampedusa (1960) *(Translator's note)*.

form of formal and informal institutional contingencies. The possibility of social change, even at the micro-institutional level, lies in making these practices and their social function manifest and evident.

References

Anderson, P. (1979). Transiciones de la antigüedad al feudalismo. [Passages from antiquity to feudalism]. CDMX: Siglo XXI Editores.

Anderson, P. (1979). El estado absolutista [Lineages of the absolutist state]. DMX: Siglo XXI Editores.

Aristotle (1985). The complete works, Vols. I & II (revised Oxford trans.; J. Barnes, Ed.). Princeton University Press.

Braudel, F. (1986). La dinámica del capitalismo [The dynamics of capitalism]. CDMX: Fondo deCultura Económica.

Braudel, F. (1989). El Mediterráneo: el espacio y la historia [The Mediterranean: The space and the history]. CDMX: Fondo de Cultura Económica.

Clastres, P. (1987). Society against the state. New York: Zone Books.

Clausewitz, K.V. (2006). De la guerra [On war]. CDMX: Colofón.

Erasmus of Rotterdam (2007). Educación del príncipe cristiano [The education of a Christian prince]. Madrid: Tecnos.

Frankfort, H., H.A., Wilson, J.A., & Jacobsen, T. (1967). El pensamiento prefilosófico I. Egipto y Mesopotamia [Before philosophy: The intellectual adventure of ancient man: An essay on speculative thought in the ancient Near East] CDMX: Fondo de Cultura Económica.

Fried, M.H. (1967). The evolution of political society: An essay in political anthropology. New York, NY: Random House

Hobbes, T. (2011). Leviatán [Leviathan]. CDMX: Fondo de Cultura Económica.

Kitching, G. (2020). Capitalism and democracy in the twenty-first century. A global future beyond nationalism. New York/London: Routledge.

La Boétie, E. de (2016). Discurso de la servidumbre voluntaria [Discourse on voluntary servitude]. Barcelona: Vaus Editorial.

Maquiavelli, N. (2012). El príncipe [The prince]. Madrid: Espasa Calpe.

Montesquieu (2003). Del espíritu de las leyes [The spirit of the laws]. Madrid: Alianza Editorial.

Müller, M. (1889). Natural religion. London: Longmans, Gree, andCo.

Piketty, T. (2019). Capital e ideología [Capital and ideology]. Barcelona: Deusto.

Polanyi. K. (1989). La gran transformación: Crítica del liberalismo económico [The great transformation]. Madrid: La Piqueta.

Polanyi, K., Arensberg, C.M., & Pearson, H.W. (1957). Trade and market in the early empires: economies in history and theory. Glencoe,Ill: The Free Press of Glencoe.

Ribes, E. (2001). Functional dimensions of social behavior: Theoretical considerations and some preliminary data. Revista Mexicana de Análisis de la Conducta, 27, 285-306.

Ribes, E. (2012). Funciones heurísticas para la psicología de algunasnociones wittgensteinianas [Heuristic functions of certain Wittgensteinian notions for psychology]. In A. Tomasini (Ed.): Wittgenstein en español III (pp. 99-123). Xalapa: Universidad Veracruzana.

Ribes, E. (2018). El estudio científico de la conducta individual: una introducción a la teoría de la psicología [The scientific study of individual behavior: An introduction to the theory of psychology]. CMDX: El Manual Moderno.

Ribes, E., Pulido, L. Rangel, N. & Sánchez-Gatell, E. (2016). Sociopsicología: instituciones y relaciones interindividuales [Sociopsychology: institutions and interindividual relations]. Madrid: La Cascada.

Sahlins, M.D. (1972). Las sociedades tribales [Tribal societies]. Barcelona: Labor.

Sahlins, M.D. (1974). Stone age economics. Piscatanay, NJ: Aldine Transaction.

Scott, J.C. (2010). The art of not being governed: An anarchist history of upland southeast Asia. New Haven/London: Yale University Press.

Semo, E. (2019). La conquista: catástrofe de los pueblos originarios,vol. 1 [The conquest: Catasprohe of the original peoples, Vol. I]. CDMX: Siglo XXI.

Wallerstein, I. (2005). Análisis de sistemas-mundo: una introducción [World-systems analysis: An introduction] CDMX: Siglo XXI.

Wallerstein, I. (2007). Universalismo europeo: el discurso del poder [European universalism: The rethoric of power]. CDMX: Siglo XXI.

Wittgenstein, L (1953). Philosophical investigations. Oxford: Basil Blackwell

Co-presencias aims to be a critical publisher of Psychology and Philosophy of Psychology, with the commitment to build approaches to these areas with nuances of honesty and truth.

...And not only co-presences participate in the psychological game, but also absences, because everything co-present inescapably refers us to everything absent and vice versa.

Behavior and knowledge function inseparably within the textures co-present at a distance. You only know what you do and how you do it and you only do what you know and how you know it.

OTROS TÍTULOS DE LA EDITORIAL